maran illustrated™

Guitar

maranGraphics™

&

THOMSON
™
COURSE TECHNOLOGY
Professional ■ Trade ■ Reference

BOOK BONUS!

Visit www.maran.com/guitar
to download MP3 files you
can listen to and play along
with for all the chords, scales,
exercises and practice
pieces in the book.

MARAN ILLUSTRATED™ Guitar

Distributed in the U.S. and Canada by Thomson Course Technology PTR. For enquiries about Maran Illustrated™ books outside the U.S. and Canada, please contact maranGraphics at international@maran.com

For U.S. orders and customer service, please contact Thomson Course Technology at 1-800-354-9706. For Canadian orders, please contact Thomson Course Technology at 1-800-268-2222 or 416-752-9448.

ISBN: 1-59200-860-7

Library of Congress Catalog Card Number: 2005921012

Printed in the United States of America

05 06 07 08 09 BU 10 9 8 7 6 5

Trademarks

Important

maranGraphics and Thomson Course Technology PTR cannot provide software support. Please contact the appropriate software manufacturer's technical support line or Web site for assistance.

maranGraphics and Thomson Course Technology PTR have attempted throughout this book to distinguish proprietary trademarks by following the capitalization style used by the source. However, we cannot attest to the accuracy of the style, and the use of a word or term in this book is not intended to affect the validity of any trademark.

Copies

Educational facilities, companies, and organizations located in the U.S. and Canada that are interested in multiple copies of this book should contact Thomson Course Technology PTR for quantity discount information. Training manuals, CD-ROMs, and portions of this book are also available individually or can be tailored for specific needs.

maranGraphics™

maranGraphics Inc.
5755 Coopers Avenue
Mississauga, Ontario
L4Z 1R9
www.maran.com

THOMSON
COURSE TECHNOLOGY
Professional ■ Trade ■ Reference

Thomson Course Technology PTR, a division of Thomson Course Technology
25 Thomson Place ■ Boston, MA 02210 ■ http://www.courseptr.com

maranGraphics is a family-run business

At maranGraphics, we believe in producing great consumer books—one book at a time.

Each maranGraphics book uses the award-winning communication process that we have been developing over the last 28 years. Using this process, we organize photographs and text in a way that makes it easy for you to learn new concepts and tasks.

We spend hours deciding the best way to perform each task, so you don't have to! Our clear, easy-to-follow photographs and instructions walk you through each task from beginning to end.

We want to thank you for purchasing what we feel are the best books money can buy. We hope you enjoy using this book as much as we enjoyed creating it!

Sincerely,

The Maran Family

We would love to hear from you! Send your comments and feedback about our books to family@maran.com

Please visit us on the Web at:
www.maran.com

CREDITS

Author:
maranGraphics
Development Group

Content Architects:
Ruth Maran
Kelleigh Johnson

**Technical and
Photographic Consultant:**
Tim Martin

Project Manager:
Judy Maran

Copy Development Director:
Jill Maran-Dutfield

Copy Development and Editing:
Roxanne Van Damme
Raquel Scott
Roderick Anatalio
Megan Robinson

Layout Designers:
Sarah Jang
Steven Schaerer

**Front Cover, Backgrounds
and Overviews:**
Designed by Russ Marini

Digital Editing and Illustration:
Russ Marini
Steven Schaerer
Paolo Rizzo

**Home Recording
Chapter Consultants:**
Dennis Patterson
Kevin Little

Indexer:
Raquel Scott

Models:
Jill Maran-Dutfield
Kade Dutfield
Shawn Lavery
Christian Kennerney
Judy Maran
Robert Maran
Tim Martin
Paolo Rizzo

**Photography and
Post Production:**
Robert Maran

**President,
Thomson Course Technology:**
David R. West

**Senior Vice President of
Business Development,
Thomson Course Technology:**
Andy Shafran

**Publisher and General Manager,
Thomson Course Technology PTR:**
Stacy L. Hiquet

**Associate Director
of Marketing,
Thomson Course Technology PTR:**
Sarah O'Donnell

**National Sales Manager,
Thomson Course Technology PTR:**
Amy Merrill

**Manager of Editorial Services,
Thomson Course Technology PTR:**
Heather Talbot

ACKNOWLEDGMENTS

Thanks to the dedicated staff of maranGraphics, including Roderick Anatalio,
Sarah Jang, Kelleigh Johnson, Wanda Lawrie, Jill Maran Dutfield,
Judy Maran, Robert Maran, Ruth Maran, Russ Marini, Paolo Rizzo,
Megan Robinson, Steven Schaerer, Raquel Scott and Roxanne Van Damme.

Finally, to Richard Maran who originated the easy-to-use graphic format
of this guide. Thank you for your inspiration and guidance.

Tim Martin

Tim Martin is head of the Guitar Department at the Merriam School of Music. With over 2,000 students, Merriam is an internationally recognized center for music education. In 1997, Tim achieved an Honors Degree in music from the University of Waterloo studying classical guitar. Tim plays in Nadjiwan—an exciting original rock quartet and in an R & B quintet. He is also part of a classical chamber trio and has played in numerous musical pit bands (*Grease*, *Tommy*, *Hair*, *Jesus Christ Superstar* and *Little Shop of Horrors*). Tim also serves as an adjudicator at music festivals and is an active session musician, specializing in live performance and studio recording.

A few words from Tim...

I would like to thank maranGraphics for this opportunity to create a helpful resource for budding guitar players everywhere. I would also like to thank my wife, Christine, for all of her support and the Merriam School of Music for giving me the opportunity to do what I do, day in and day out. Working on this book has been an excellent experience and I am confident that you will find this book an invaluable tool.

Special thanks to...

Christian Kennerney

Christian Kennerney is a song writer, composer and music shop owner. As early as he can remember, Christian has been surrounded by music. Christian and his father, Kevin, co-own a music shop called "Strings Attached" *(www.stringsattachedmusic.com).* The shop opened in 1995 and has grown tremendously, carrying the world's top guitar brand names, as well as other popular instruments and amplifiers. Christian is also the bass player and backup vocalist for an up-and-coming new metal band called The Livid *(www.thelivid.com).*

Thanks to the following companies for allowing us to show photographs of their equipment in our book:

- Cakewalk
- Dunlop Manufacturing, Inc.
- Ernie Ball, Inc.
- Evets Corporation
- Fender Musical Instruments Corporation
- GHS Corporation
- Gibson Guitar Corp.
- Godin Guitar Company
- Harman Music Group
- Hoshino (USA), Inc.
- J. D'Addario & Co. Inc.
- Kaman Music Corporation
- Korg USA, Inc.
- Kyser Musical Products
- Line 6, Inc.
- Mackie Designs, Inc.
- The Martin Guitar Co.
- Marshall Amplification
- Maxell Corporation of America
- Roland Corporation, U.S.
- Sony of Canada Ltd.
- Steinberg Media Technologies AG
- St. Louis Music, Inc.
- VTG Corporation
- Washburn International Inc.

Table of Contents

Table of Contents

Table of Contents

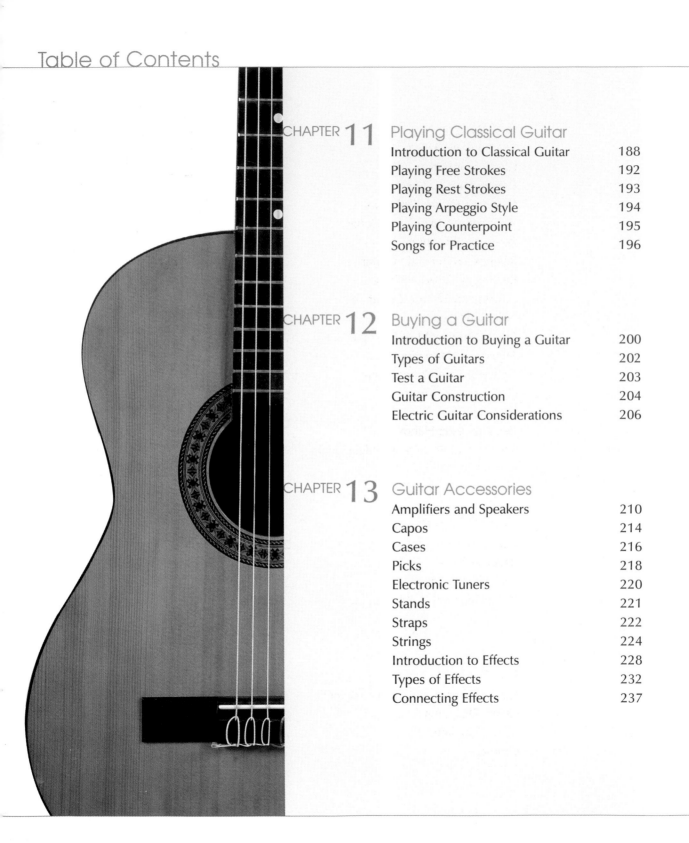

Chapter 1

The guitar is one of the most popular instruments used to play music. This chapter introduces you to the guitar and to some of the most influential guitarists. Here you will find an outline of the history of the guitar, a summary of the parts of acoustic and electric guitars, as well as an introduction to some basic concepts you need to understand when learning to play the guitar.

Guitar Basics

In this Chapter...

history of the guitar

In the Beginning

The history of the guitar spans over a few thousand years. Illustrations found on clay artifacts show instruments that generally resemble guitars.

Guitars are thought to have directly evolved from the Ud, a stringed instrument dating back to 800 AD. The Moors brought the Ud to Europe during their invasion and capture of Spain.

The first real guitars emerged by the late 15th century. These early guitars had four or five pairs of strings, called courses, to help produce a more powerful sound. Each course, or pair of strings, was tuned to the same note. The frets were not permanently set into the fingerboard but were wrapped around the neck of the guitar.

17th Century

During the early history of the guitar, it was seen as a relatively simple instrument compared to the vihuela. The vihuela was a 12-stringed instrument that musicians once preferred over the guitar. However, by the start of the 17th century, the vihuela's popularity significantly declined and the guitar became the new preferred instrument.

18th Century

The contemporary design of the guitar came about by the middle of the 18th century. The double strings of earlier guitars were replaced by single strings, and the number of strings was increased to six. The frets of 18th century guitars were permanently set into the fingerboard and the strings were tuned to the now familiar E-A-D-G-B-E tuning.

19th Century

Between 1850 and 1860, Antonio de Torres Jurado of Spain built a guitar that closely resembled the modern classical guitar. In addition to creating a template for the modern classical guitar, Torres radically changed the way guitars were built. He used a larger body than other guitars of the time and improved the way the braces were attached to the inside of the guitar, resulting in louder sounds.

Musician Francesco Tarrega (1852-1909) raised public interest in the guitar by creating musical pieces that demonstrated the guitar's ability to deliver unique, ear-catching sounds. Tarrega's efforts contributed to the guitar's increasing popularity and helped establish the development of modern guitar techniques.

20th Century

Starting in the late 19th century, important developments in guitar design began when C. F. Martin and Orville Gibson created two distinct guitar designs—the flat-top and archtop guitars. Guitar design also took a step forward in this century with the introduction of nylon strings, while the guitar's popularity was largely influenced by the musical works of Andrés Segovia.

Flat-top Guitars

In 1916, Christian Frederick Martin introduced a guitar called the Dreadnought, which featured a wider lower part of the body and a stronger assembly to handle the use of steel strings. Martin's guitars were called flat-tops since they featured a flat soundboard design. To this day, Martin's flat-top guitars are still known around the world.

Archtop Guitars

Orville Gibson created a new type of acoustic guitar by using building methods more typically used in the construction of violins. Gibson's guitars were known as archtops because of their rounded top design. In 1922, Lloyd Loar, an engineer at Gibson's company, developed one of many famous guitars—the Gibson L5.

Nylon Strings

In 1946, guitar manufacturers began using nylon strings instead of gut strings. Nylon strings generate a clearer, louder sound and make guitars simpler to play. They are also more dependable than gut strings, which have a tendency to go out of tune when the humidity rises.

Andrés Segovia

During the first half of the 20th century, guitarist Andrés Segovia (1893-1987) greatly increased the popularity of the guitar by demonstrating to the world that a solo guitarist could successfully play to large audiences in music halls. Segovia's musical skills gave the guitar the recognition it now holds.

Today and Beyond

Today, some of the best and most widely-known acoustic guitars are still made by C. F. Martin and Orville Gibson's companies. Flat-top guitars have become the most common type of acoustic guitars, but archtop guitars are still used today for more specialized music, such as jazz.

In the past few years, there has not been a significant change with regard to the design of acoustic guitars, but guitar manufacturers continue to experiment with better building techniques and new materials to come up with better-sounding instruments.

history of the electric guitar

The first electric guitar was developed in the 1930s to increase the guitar's volume so it can be heard when playing with other instruments. Back then, no one could have imagined how the creation of the electric guitar would significantly affect the course of 20th century music.

In the beginning, the electric guitar had its share of critics, but it quickly won people over because of its ability to let musicians play more creatively than ever before. Many decades after its birth, the electric guitar is widely used in various types of music and is played by people all over the world.

The First Pickup

In 1924, Lloyd Loar, an engineer working for the Gibson guitar company, designed the first magnetic pickup. Loar used a magnet to convert the vibrations of the guitar strings into electrical signals, which were then amplified and channeled through a speaker system.

The First Electric Guitar

In 1931, Paul Barth, George Beauchamp and Adolph Rickenbacker founded the Electro String Company and developed the first electric guitars made available to the public. These cast-aluminum guitars, called "Frying Pans," were played on a person's lap using a steel slide.

In 1935, the achievements of the Electro String Company pushed the Gibson guitar company to create their first electric guitar, the legendary ES-150 model.

The First Solid-Bodied Electric Guitar

Although electric guitars were gaining popularity, there was a significant problem with their construction. Amplified sounds coming from the speakers caused the guitar body to vibrate, which produced a loud wailing noise called feedback. The solution was to create a solid-bodied electric guitar that did not easily vibrate.

There are two stories on who developed the first solid-bodied electric guitar in the 1940s. Guitarist Les Paul is said to have developed a solid-bodied electric guitar, known as "The Log," by affixing a Gibson neck to a piece of solid wood. At about the same time, engineer Paul Bigsby and guitarist Merle Travis developed a solid-bodied electric guitar that looked very much like the solid-bodied electric guitars we see today.

The First Mass-Produced Solid-Bodied Electric Guitar

In 1950, Leo Fender developed the first mass-produced, solid-bodied electric guitar, which was originally called the Fender Broadcaster. Unfortunately, the name Broadcaster was already used by another guitar company, so Leo Fender renamed his guitar the Fender Telecaster. Later in 1954, Fender produced one of the most renowned guitars of all time, the Stratocaster.

The success of Leo Fender prompted other guitar manufacturing companies to develop their own mass-produced, solid-bodied electric guitars. In 1952, the Gibson guitar company teamed up with guitarist Les Paul to create the famous Gibson Les Paul electric guitar.

More Affordable Electric Guitars

In the 1960s and 1970s, famous name electric guitars were too expensive for the average person to afford. There were some less expensive imitations available, but they sounded sub-standard and were difficult to play. Then in the 1980s, a Japanese company started to manufacture inexpensive electric guitars that were of similar quality to their more expensive counterparts. Fender and other guitar manufacturing companies reacted by producing similar, less expensive versions of their classic electric guitar designs. This made electric guitars more accessible, as people could own an original, top quality electric guitar at an affordable price.

Today and Beyond

The Gibson and Fender guitar companies still produce some of the most well-known and finely crafted electric guitars today. Gibson and Fender, along with other manufacturers, have continued to try out new shapes and materials and also incorporate new technologies to produce better-sounding electric guitars.

You can find modern electric guitars that have built-in software, allowing them to mimic the sound of different types of guitars, such as the Stratocaster, Les Paul and Telecaster. Other electric guitars are fitted with special pickups that sense the notes you are playing. The notes are then sent to a MIDI synthesizer, which can be programmed to do a number of things, such as play the notes using different instrument sounds or record the notes you are playing in standard musical notation.

parts of an acoustic guitar

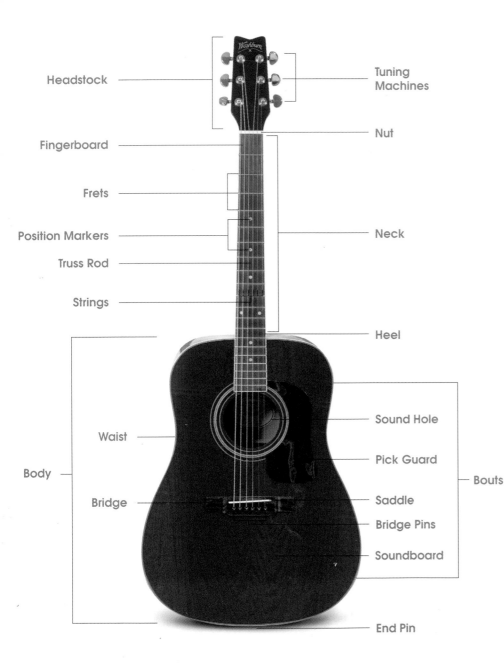

Headstock

Fingerboard

Frets

Position Markers

Truss Rod

Strings

Waist

Body

Bridge

Tuning Machines

Nut

Neck

Heel

Sound Hole

Pick Guard

Bouts

Saddle

Bridge Pins

Soundboard

End Pin

Body
The body is the largest section of the guitar and is usually hollow.

Bouts
The upper and lower bouts are the wider areas of the body.

Bridge
The bridge is the wooden piece that connects the strings to the body of the guitar.

Bridge Pins
Bridge pins fasten the strings to the body of the guitar.

End Pin
The end pin is the plastic post at the bottom of the guitar used for attaching a guitar strap. On acoustic guitars that have a pickup, which electronically picks up and sends sounds to an amplifier, the end pin also serves as an output jack you can use to plug the guitar into an amplifier.

Fingerboard
The fingerboard is the flat piece of wood on the neck, where you press your fingers down on strings to form notes and chords. The fingerboard is also referred to as the fretboard, since frets are located on the fingerboard.

Frets

Frets are the thin metal wires situated along the fingerboard, perpendicular to the strings. When you press a string down against a fret, you shorten the part of the string that will vibrate in order to change the pitch the string produces.

Headstock

The headstock, also known as the head, is the section at the very top of the guitar. Tuning machines are attached to the headstock.

Heel

The heel is the wooden section behind the neck where the neck meets the body.

Neck

The neck is the long, narrow, wooden section between the body and the headstock of the guitar.

Nut

The nut is the bar at the top end of the fingerboard. The nut spaces the strings out evenly and keeps the strings at the correct height over the fingerboard.

Pick Guard

The pick guard protects the top of the guitar from getting scratched when you strum and pick the strings.

Position Markers

Position markers, also called position dots, are dots or decorative markings that help you determine the number of each fret. They are usually found on the top and/or side of the fingerboard so you can easily see them as you play the guitar. Some guitars do not have position markers.

Saddle

The saddle is attached to the bridge and keeps the strings at the correct height.

Sound Hole

The sound hole releases the sound from the body of the guitar. Some guitars have a decorative design, known as a rosette, around the sound hole.

Soundboard

The soundboard is the top, or face, of the guitar. When you strum the strings, the soundboard vibrates, producing the guitar's sound.

Strings

Strings are the metal or nylon wires, numbered 1 through 6, which create notes when strummed or picked. The thinnest and highest-sounding string is the 1st string. The thickest and lowest-sounding string is the 6th string.

Truss Rod

The truss rod is a steel rod found inside the neck of a guitar. This rod ensures that the neck will not bend or warp from the tension of the strings.

Tuning Machines

Tuning machines allow you to increase and decrease the tension of each string to tune, or change the pitch of, each string. Tuning machines are also referred to as machine heads, tuning pegs, tuning keys and tuners.

Waist

The waist is the curved area in the middle of the body. If you are playing the guitar while seated, you rest the waist on your leg.

parts of an electric guitar

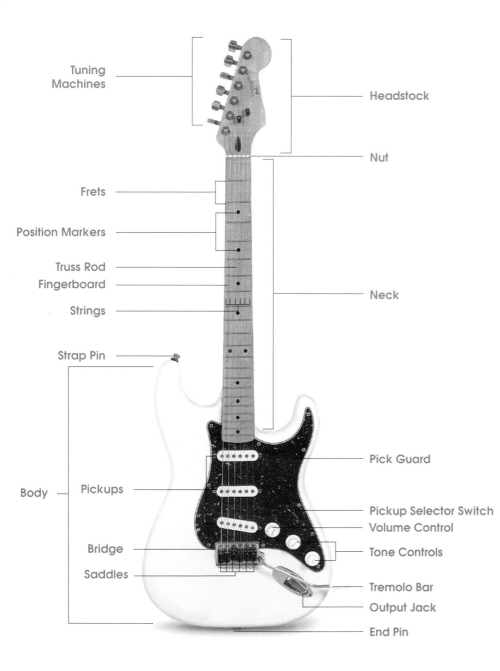

Tuning Machines

Headstock

Frets

Nut

Position Markers

Truss Rod

Fingerboard

Strings

Neck

Strap Pin

Pick Guard

Body

Pickups

Pickup Selector Switch

Volume Control

Bridge

Tone Controls

Saddles

Tremolo Bar

Output Jack

End Pin

Body

The body is the largest section of the guitar and is usually made of solid wood.

Bridge

The bridge is the metal plate that connects the strings to the body of the guitar.

End Pin

The end pin, also known as a strap pin, is the metal post at the bottom of the guitar used for attaching one end of a guitar strap.

Fingerboard

The fingerboard is the flat piece of wood on the neck, where you press your fingers down on strings to form notes and chords. The fingerboard is also referred to as the fretboard.

Frets

Frets are the thin metal wires situated along the fingerboard, perpendicular to the strings. When you press a string down against a fret, you shorten the part of the string that will vibrate to change the pitch of the string.

Headstock

The headstock is the section at the top of the guitar. Tuning machines are attached to the headstock.

Neck

The neck is the long, narrow section between the body and the headstock of the guitar.

Nut

The nut is the bar at the top end of the fingerboard, between the headstock and neck. The nut spaces the strings out evenly and keeps the strings at the correct height over the fingerboard.

Output Jack

You can plug a cord into the output jack to connect the guitar to an amplifier.

Pick Guard

The pick guard, also known as a scratchplate, protects the top of the guitar from getting scratched when you strum and pick the strings.

Pickup

A pickup is a magnet that converts the strings' vibrations into electrical currents that an amplifier can use to produce sound. Most guitars have two or more pickups.

Pickup Selector Switch

The pickup selector switch allows you to select which pickups you want to use. Using different pickups affects the guitar's sound.

Position Markers

Position markers, also called position dots, are dots or decorative markings that help you determine the number of each fret. They are usually found on the top and/or side of the fingerboard so you can easily see them as you play the guitar. Some guitars do not have position markers.

Saddles

Saddles are attached to the bridge and keep each string at the correct height.

Strap Pin

A strap pin is a metal post used for attaching one end of a guitar strap.

Strings

Strings are the metal wires, numbered 1 through 6, which create notes when strummed or picked. The thinnest and highest-sounding string is the 1st string. The thickest and lowest-sounding string is the 6th string.

Tone Control

The tone control is a knob you can turn to alter the treble (high) frequencies in the guitar's sound. Guitars can have more than one tone control.

Tremolo Bar

The tremolo bar is a metal bar that connects to the bridge. You can use the tremolo bar to change the angle of the bridge, which adjusts the tension, and thereby the pitch, of the strings. The tremolo bar is also referred to as the whammy bar, vibrato bar and tremolo arm.

Truss Rod

The truss rod is a steel rod found inside the neck of a guitar. This rod ensures that the neck will not bend or warp from the tension of the strings.

Tuning Machines

Tuning machines allow you to increase and decrease the tension of each string to tune, or change the pitch of, each string. Tuning machines are also referred to as machine heads, tuning pegs, tuning keys and tuners.

Volume Control

The volume control is a knob you can use to adjust the volume of the guitar's sound.

basic guitar concepts

There are some basic concepts you should understand when learning to play the guitar.

Types of Guitars

There are three main types of guitars: acoustic, classical and electric.

Acoustic guitars are portable and can be played anywhere, which makes them ideal for people who simply want to strum their favorite tunes.

Classical guitars are specialized instruments used primarily to play classical or flamenco music.

Electric guitars are smaller than acoustic and classical guitars. You will need additional equipment to play an electric guitar, such as an amplifier and speakers.

Strings

Strings are the metal or nylon wires, numbered 1 through 6, which create notes when strummed or picked. The thinnest and highest-sounding string, which is closest to the floor when you are holding a guitar, is the 1st string. The thickest and lowest-sounding string, which is closest to the ceiling, is the 6th string. The three thinnest strings are treble strings and the three thickest strings are bass strings.

How Sound is Produced

When you strike strings on a guitar, the strings and the guitar top vibrate. The hollow body, or acoustic chamber, on an acoustic or classical guitar amplifies these vibrations and produces the sound. An electric guitar has magnetic pickups that sense the strings' vibrations and convert them into electrical signals that an amplifier can use to produce sound.

Names of Notes

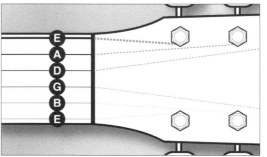

It is a good idea to learn the name of the note each string plays when you strike the string without holding it down. Starting from the 1st string, the notes are E, B, G, D, A and E. Although strings 1 and 6 both play an E note, the notes are two octaves apart. To help remember the names of the notes, try making up a phrase starting with each letter.

Strumming

Strumming refers to striking two or more strings. You can use a pick, your thumb or the back of your fingernails to strum. You strum when playing chords, accompanying a voice or playing with other instruments.

Picking

Picking refers to striking only one string. You can use a pick, your fingers or thumb, or a combination of all of these to pick strings. You pick when playing single notes or when playing a melody or solo.

Half steps

As you move from one fret to the next, each note you play on the same string will be a half step higher or lower in pitch. A half step, or semi-tone, is the smallest interval between two notes. To lower the pitch, move to a lower fret, toward the tuning machines. To increase the pitch, move to a higher fret, toward the body of the guitar.

Frets

Frets are thin metal wires situated along the fingerboard, perpendicular to the strings. When you press a string down against a fret, you shorten the part of the string that will vibrate in order to change the pitch the string produces. This is called fretting a note or string.

Fret Numbers

Frets are numbered starting from the nut, with the number increasing as you move up the neck toward the body. Position markers, also called position dots, are markings that help you quickly determine the number of each fret. They are usually found on the top and side of the fingerboard so you can easily see them as you play the guitar.

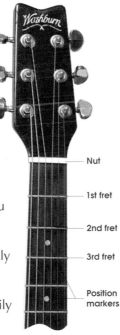

Nut

1st fret

2nd fret

3rd fret

Position markers

Fretting and Picking Hands

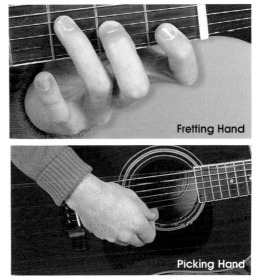

Fretting Hand

Picking Hand

Your fretting hand is the hand you use to fret, or press strings down on the fingerboard. Your picking hand is the hand you use to pick or strum the strings. Right-handed guitarists fret with their left hand and pick with their right hand. Left-handed guitarists fret with their right hand and pick with their left hand.

Open Strings

An open string is a string you play without holding down, or fretting, the string. For example, when you play the open 6th string, you play the 6th string without holding down the string.

Open-Position Chords

Open-position chords, also called first-position chords, are chords that are played near the nut and require you to strum open strings. A chord consists of two or more different notes played at the same time.

famous guitarists

Famous Blues Guitarists

Buddy Guy (1936 -)

One of the most popular Chicago-style blues players, Buddy Guy is known not only for his vigorous guitar playing, which makes frequent use of the over-bending technique, but for his excellent singing. Some of the most famous rock and roll musicians were influenced by this Louisiana-born guitarist. Guy's most popular songs include "First Time I Met the Blues."

Elmore James (1918 - 1963)

This amazing guitar player is famous for his masterful slide technique, which involves using a slide instead of fretting the strings with the fingers. James spearheaded the transformation of the Mississippi Delta Blues of his home state into what would eventually become rock 'n' roll. James also wrote many great blues songs, such as "Dust My Broom," during his career.

Robert Johnson (1911 - 1938)

This Mississippi-born legend wowed the blues circuit with his skillful fingerstyle blues playing during his short life. Johnson's incredible talent prompted rumors that his musical gift was the result of a deal he had made with the devil. "Cross Road Blues" is a well-known Robert Johnson song.

Albert King (1923 - 1992)

Albert King is among the most influential blues guitarists of all time. Though left-handed, King played using a right-handed guitar he held upside down. King's unique style, which focused on technique rather than showmanship, has influenced many modern blues players. The songs of this Mississippi native include "Born Under a Bad Sign."

B.B. King (1925 -)

B.B. King is undoubtedly the most recognizable electric blues guitarist today. King, along with his famous guitar, Lucille, is best known for his wide vibrato technique, for which he frequently uses his index finger instead of the more typical ring finger. King's best-known songs include "The Thrill Is Gone."

Stevie Ray Vaughan (1954 - 1990)

Texas-born Stevie Ray Vaughan's great talent, incredible stage presence and showmanship helped bring new popularity to the blues guitar genre in the 1980s and inspired a new generation to play the blues. Vaughan's status as a blues guitar icon was enhanced after he died in a helicopter accident. His popular songs include "Pride and Joy."

Famous Classical and Flamenco Guitarists

Ramón Montoya (1880 - 1949)

This master guitarist helped expand the range of techniques available to flamenco players. Montoya was the first to showcase the flamenco guitar as a solo instrument. His sophisticated style and creative improvisations have inspired generations of flamenco guitarists.

Paco Peña (1942 -)

Paco Peña is a favorite among modern flamenco enthusiasts. Peña is known for his subtle, yet powerful playing technique as well as for his smooth, skillful presentation. Peña's many recordings and concert performances have earned him worldwide recognition and numerous awards.

David Russell (1953 -)

This Scottish-born modern classical guitar virtuoso has captivated concert audiences with his confident and inspired performances. Russell has won many competitions and enjoys overwhelming acclaim from both audiences and critics all over the world.

Sabicas (1912 - 1990)

A self-taught guitarist, Sabicas is considered a genius of the flamenco guitar. His inventiveness, amazing speed and flawless technique helped shape modern flamenco music. Sabicas' unique melodic and harmonic style helped enrich the repertoire of the flamenco guitarist.

Andrés Segovia (1893 - 1987)

Andrés Segovia helped popularize classical guitar in the 20th century and is considered the originator of modern classical guitar. By demonstrating to the world that a solo guitarist could successfully play to large audiences in music halls, Segovia's work inspired musicians to play traditional classical compositions on the guitar and encouraged composers to write music for classical guitarists.

John Williams (1941 -)

John Williams is one of the most popular classical guitarists today and is widely sought after for his brilliant recordings. This Australian-born musician, who received his first guitar at age four, garnered worldwide admiration for his excellent technique at an early age. Williams has also been highly praised by the master guitarist, Andrés Segovia, with whom he studied for a time.

CONTINUED...

famous guitarists

Famous Country and Folk Guitarists

Chet Atkins (1924 - 2001)

This Tennessee-born guitarist inspired many musicians from a number of genres, but had an especially great impact on country music. His masterful fingerpicking style and his ability to play two independent melodies simultaneously earned him the title "Mr. Guitar." Atkins also helped develop the style of country music known as the "Nashville sound."

Bob Dylan (1941 -)

Bob Dylan has had an immense impact on folk and rock music. Dylan's confrontational, political lyrics, rasped out to a simple chord accompaniment on his guitar, fueled his rise to stardom in the 1960s. As a musician, vocalist and songwriter, Dylan was a pioneer of different styles, inspiring generations of musicians. Dylan's popular songs include "Like a Rolling Stone."

Joni Mitchell (1943 -)

Joni Mitchell is among the world's most celebrated and influential female guitarists. Her innovative approach to the guitar helped her create a distinctive guitar style that involves liberal use of alternate tunings. This Canadian guitarist is also acclaimed for her excellent songs, which include "Both Sides Now" and "The Circle Game."

Carl Perkins (1932 - 1998)

Although best known as an originator of the country-blues blend of music referred to as rockabilly, Carl Perkins was also a talented songwriter and singer. His music has influenced many prominent musicians, including the Beatles. Perkins' repertoire includes the hit "Blue Suede Shoes."

Pete Seeger (1919 -)

Pete Seeger instigated the folk music revival in the late 50s and 60s, helping to bring folk music to mainstream audiences. This New York native is known, not only for his contributions as a musician and songwriter, but also for his social activism. Seeger's most popular songs include "Where Have All the Flowers Gone?"

Merle Travis (1917 - 1983)

This innovative country songwriter and guitarist popularized the style of playing that bears his name—Travis picking. Travis was much more than a guitarist. In the 1940s, he teamed up with engineer Paul Bigsby to develop one of the first solid-body electric guitars, and also performed in films, such as *From Here To Eternity*, in which he sang "Re-enlistment Blues."

Famous Jazz Guitarists

Lenny Breau (1941 - 1984)

An innovative guitarist who often mixed country, flamenco and classical styles into his jazz playing, Lenny Breau is considered one of the most underrated jazz players. Known for his excellent technical guitar skills, which included his trademark bell-like harmonics, Breau died under mysterious circumstances in 1984.

Charlie Christian (1916 - 1942)

Charlie Christian was one of the first jazz guitar players to play an electric guitar. His superb playing helped popularize the electric guitar by showcasing it as a serious musical instrument for the first time. Christian was also among the first jazz guitarists to play solos. Christian played with Benny Goodman for a number of years before his death in 1942.

Jim Hall (1930 -)

This New York state native is widely respected as an excellent jazz player and is a favorite among other jazz guitarists. Also known for his ability to play in different guitar genres, Hall's subtle, warm style and consummate professionalism continues to inspire jazz players worldwide.

Pat Metheny (1954 -)

Pat Metheny is a very influential modern jazz player. His innovative compositions, which frequently incorporate elements of other musical genres, such as rock, are of a style usually referred to as jazz fusion. In addition to his contributions to jazz, Metheny has also helped develop several new types of guitars.

Wes Montgomery (1925 - 1968)

Wes Montgomery has been generally acknowledged as a superstar of jazz guitar. This inspirational jazz player is famous for playing notes with his thumb instead of the traditional pick, as well as for his interesting method of playing two notes one octave apart.

Joe Pass (1929 - 1994)

Joe Pass' outstanding unaccompanied performances and his technical prowess earned him a place among the jazz greats. Very few solo guitarists have been able to match Pass' masterful fingerstyle playing and technique.

Django Reinhardt (1910 - 1953)

This Belgian-born soloist was the first famous non-American jazz player and one of the first swing players. Despite having limited use of only the thumb and first two fingers of his fretting hand as a result of burns he received in a fire, Reinhardt was able to play fast-paced solos with unmatched skill and dexterity.

CONTINUED...

famous guitarists

Famous Rock and Pop Guitarists

Duane Allman (1946 - 1971)

Duane Allman was a member of The Allman Brothers Band and was well known for his amazing slide guitar skills. Before his tragic death in a motorcycle accident, this highly inventive guitarist made recordings with many musicians, such as Aretha Franklin and Eric Clapton. "Statesboro Blues" is one of Allman's most famous recordings.

Jeff Beck (1944 -)

Jeff Beck is regarded as one of the best rock guitarists of his time and was one in a string of famous guitarists from the band The Yardbirds. Known for his distinct playing style, which often featured smooth note bending techniques, he performed with numerous bands in addition to his own solo work. One of Beck's most famous songs is "Freeway Jam."

Chuck Berry (1926 -)

Considered one of the first rock 'n' roll players, Chuck Berry's signature style of guitar playing includes the use of high-speed double-stops. In addition to his widespread influence on other players, Berry also created many well-known rock riffs. One of Berry's most famous songs is "Johnny B. Goode."

Eric Clapton (1945 -)

Eric Clapton's bluesy, virtuoso style of guitar playing made him a pioneer of classic rock. He belonged to a number of famous bands, including The Yardbirds, Cream and Derek and the Dominoes, before going solo and becoming one of the most popular recording artists of recent time. Some of Clapton's well-known songs include "Layla" and "After Midnight."

Jimi Hendrix (1942 - 1970)

Jimi Hendrix's innovative use of the whammy bar and feedback in his guitar playing took rock guitar to a new level by reinventing the sound and concept of playing the electric guitar. A spectacular showman, Hendrix was known for playing the guitar behind his back, with his teeth and even above his head. "Purple Haze" is one of his most famous songs.

Mark Knopfler (1949 -)

Mark Knopfler was the leader of Dire Straits and is well known for his fingerstyle technique, which is unique in rock music. His ability to improvise and create distinct melodies helped to make him and his band an international success. Two of Knopfler's well-known songs include "Sultans of Swing" and "Money for Nothing."

Jimmy Page (1944 -)

Jimmy Page was a member of Led Zeppelin and is one of the leading composers of rock riffs for the guitar. He is a prolific songwriter and is known for his use of unique guitar tunings. "Stairway to Heaven" is one of Page's most famous songs.

Keith Richards (1943 -)

Keith Richards of the Rolling Stones is regarded as the ultimate rhythm guitarist. Richards' distinctive guitar sound is created by his frequent use of the Open-G tuning. Some of his best-known songs include "Start Me Up" and "Satisfaction."

Carlos Santana (1947 -)

Mexican-born Carlos Santana fused rock and blues with Latin-influenced melodies and rhythms to create distinct and original sounds. He is a great improvisational player, who likes to perform long guitar solos. Santana has expanded pop music with his blend of Latin, blues and rock 'n' roll sounds. He is well known for his recordings of famous songs, such as "Oye Como Va" and "Black Magic Woman."

Pete Townshend (1945 -)

Pete Townshend is the theatrical guitar player and songwriter from The Who. He is famous for using the windmill technique, which involves hitting the guitar strings as the entire arm circles 360 degrees. Townshend also helped popularize the Marshall stack—an amplifier with speakers stacked on top of each other to increase the sound level. "Pinball Wizard" is one of Townshend's most well-known songs

Steve Vai (1960 -)

Steve Vai is a prominent, modern guitar hero and is recognized as one of the most highly skilled guitarists in rock. In terms of sound, technique and speed, Vai has pushed the boundaries of what can be done on the guitar. Steve Vai began his career playing with Frank Zappa.

Eddie Van Halen (1957 -)

Eddie Van Halen of Van Halen is well known for his use of the two-handed fingertapping technique, which involves sounding notes by tapping the strings on the fingerboard using the fingers of both hands. He is also known for his extremely fast guitar playing and use of the whammy bar. Some of his famous songs include "Eruption" and "Jump."

Chapter 2

This chapter helps you prepare to play the guitar by showing you the proper way to hold a guitar, how to position your hands for pressing down and striking the strings and how to get your guitar in tune. In addition to providing tips on how to practice to develop good technique, this chapter also explains how to read chord diagrams and tablature, which are important skills, especially if you cannot read standard musical notation.

Getting Ready to Play

In this Chapter...

how to hold a guitar

The decision to sit or stand when playing the guitar is a personal choice. In most cases, whether you sit or stand will not affect the sound of the guitar or your ability to play properly. Many guitarists prefer to sit when practicing and to stand when performing in public.

You should hold the guitar properly to avoid injuring yourself. For example, you can develop back problems if you hunch over while playing. Holding the guitar correctly also gives you more control over your fingers and allows you to fully access all parts of the guitar.

General Considerations

It is important to focus on maintaining good posture while playing the guitar. Always remember to sit up straight when seated and remain tall with your back straight when standing. When you first start playing, you may have a tendency to face the body of the guitar toward you to look at the strings. Instead, keep the guitar close to your body with the body of the guitar facing forward.

The clothing you wear can affect your playing. For example, bulky clothing may limit your movement, while loose sleeves can mute the sound of the strings. Keep in mind that jewelry, metal buttons or belt buckles may scratch your guitar.

Standing Position

To play a guitar while standing, you will need to securely fasten a guitar strap to your guitar. A guitar strap holds the guitar in front of your body and allows you to move your hands freely. When using a strap, your shoulder supports most of the weight of the guitar.

To ensure the strap is at the proper height, sit down wearing the strap and then stand back up. When you stand up, the guitar should be in the same position as it was when you were sitting down. If this option is uncomfortable for you, try positioning the bridge at about waist height and tilt the neck of the guitar slightly up.

If you play a guitar for long periods of time, you can develop shoulder problems. This is especially a problem when playing a heavy guitar. Make sure you take frequent breaks to avoid this problem.

Sitting Position

As a beginner, you will probably play the guitar while seated, since this position is less likely to tire you and will not place pressure on your shoulders. The seated position is good for playing either the acoustic or electric guitar.

There are two main sitting positions for guitarists—casual and classical. The casual position is the most common and is the one you will most likely use to practice. The classical position is primarily used when playing classical music.

Casual

To hold the guitar in the casual position, rest the curve of the guitar on your right leg if you are right-handed. If you are left-handed, place the curve on your left leg. Sit in a solid, upright, armless chair that allows you to place your feet flat on the floor. A seat that is too soft, such as a bed or couch, can make it difficult to hold the guitar correctly. Also, make sure your feet are about shoulder width apart.

The front of the guitar should be vertical and the neck of the guitar should be tilted up slightly. You should not have to use your hand to hold the neck up.

Classical

The classical position is a formal seated position that is usually only used when performing classical music. This position helps you better play the complex fingerings classical guitar requires.

In the classical position, you hold the guitar over your left leg if you are right-handed and over your right leg if you are left-handed. The guitar neck should be angled so that the head of the guitar is at eye level. To keep the guitar neck at the proper angle, you need to rest your foot on a small stool that is 4 to 6 inches high. Place the stool under your left foot if you are right-handed and under your right foot if you are left-handed. Tilt the guitar slightly away from your body so the guitar can vibrate freely.

fretting hand position

Your fretting hand is the hand you use to fret, or press strings down on the fingerboard as you play the guitar. Becoming comfortable with the fretting hand position is essential when learning to play the guitar.

To get into position to fret the strings, curl your fingers toward the fingerboard so that only the very tips of your fingers touch the strings. With your thumb at the back of the neck, press your fingertips firmly against the strings, directly behind the appropriate frets. It is important to keep your fingernails short so they are not

in the way when you press down the strings. Your thumb should remain vertical on the back of the neck of the guitar. Placing your thumb on the back gives you a more secure grip and helps you press the strings more firmly to the fingerboard.

Some guitarists prefer to place the thumb on top of the neck instead of at the back. This allows them to use the thumb to fret strings and makes some techniques, such as bending, easier.

1 Arch your fingers so your fingertips will touch the strings at 90-degree angles. There should be a space between the neck of the guitar and your palm.

- Make sure all your fingers stay close to the strings.

2 Place your thumb in the middle of the back of the neck, roughly behind the fret played by your middle finger. Keep your thumb straight and pointing toward the ceiling.

- Many rock and blues players rest their thumb on the top of the neck. When playing classical guitar, the thumb should never rest on the top of the neck.

Tip

The strings do not play clearly. What is wrong?

You may not be pressing your finger at the correct position behind a fret. Pressing too far behind a fret can cause the string to buzz and pressing too close to the fret will partially mute the string. You should position your finger directly behind the fret to produce the best quality sound.

How is fretting strings on an acoustic guitar different from an electric guitar?

An electric guitar has a thinner, narrower neck than an acoustic guitar. Since the fingerboard of the electric guitar is narrower, the strings are closer together, making it more difficult to fret a string without touching adjacent strings. However, a smaller neck makes gripping the electric guitar easier. Electric guitar strings are also easier to play, since they are positioned closer to the fingerboard and are usually lighter than acoustic guitar strings.

Move Along the Fingerboard

3 To fret a string, press the string firmly to the fingerboard with the tip of your finger just behind the fret.

- To maximize the pressure on the string and to avoid touching other strings, press your fingertip down vertically on the string.

- Keep the fingers you are not using slightly away from the fingerboard to avoid hitting other strings.

1 As you move your hand along the fingerboard, you should maintain your hand position.

- Move your arm and hand at the same time so all your fingers stay close to the strings.

- When you play the lower frets, position your elbow away from your body. When you play the higher frets, position your elbow closer to your body.

picking hand position

The picking hand is the hand you use to pick or strum the strings when playing the guitar. You can pick or strum the strings in different ways, depending on your preference and the style of music you are playing.

To use a pick, hold the pick firmly between your thumb and index finger and strike the string(s) by flicking your wrist and forearm. You normally play an electric guitar with a pick. In addition to using a pick, many guitarists sometimes strike the strings with their fingers to achieve specific effects.

You can strike the strings using downstrokes or upstrokes. Downstrokes are useful when playing long notes or when you want to produce a strong sound. Combining downstrokes and upstrokes is a popular technique that helps produce a smoother sound when playing melodies.

Classical and flamenco guitarists usually use the fingerstyle technique, which involves using their thumbs and fingers to pluck or strum the strings instead of using a pick.

Using a Pick	Downstrokes and Upstrokes

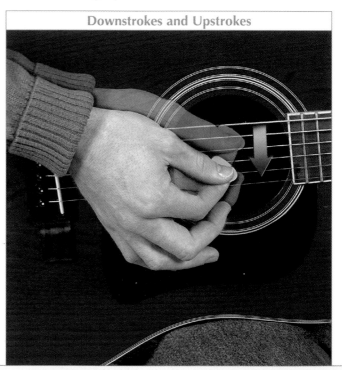

1 Hold the pick firmly between your thumb and index finger. Angle the pick slightly across the strings.

2 Strike all or one of the strings with the pick by flicking your wrist and forearm.

- You can also strike strings with your thumb or the back of your fingernails.

- You can strike strings using a downstroke, upstroke or both. Using both downstrokes and upstrokes increases playing speed and is a popular technique.

1 To perform a downstroke, strike all or one of the strings toward the floor.

2 To perform an upstroke, strike all or one of the strings toward the ceiling. To get a better sound when performing an upstroke, strike only strings 1 to 4.

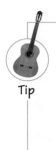

Tip

How can I use my picking hand to change the tone of a note?

The area where you strike a string affects the way the string sounds. Striking the string directly above the guitar's sound hole or the pickup closest to the neck produces a strong, deep sound. Striking the string closer to the bridge produces a thinner, brighter sound, while playing the string closer to the fingerboard generates a smoother, mellower sound. You can vary where you strike a string to add variety to your playing.

How are downstrokes and upstrokes shown in music notation?

In music notation, the ⊓ symbol indicates a downstroke. The ∨ symbol indicates an upstroke.

Fingerstyle

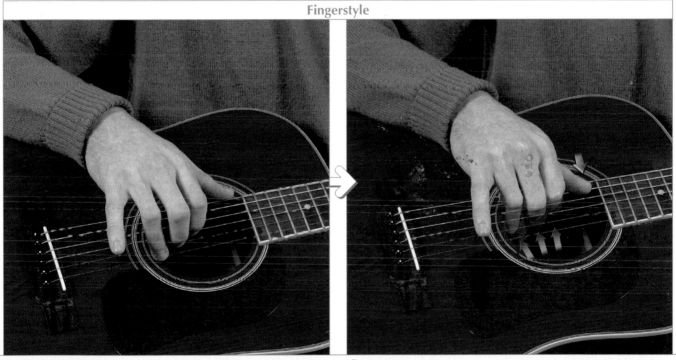

1 Arch your fingers so your fingers will strike the strings at a 90-degree angle. Your knuckles should be parallel to the strings.

- Your thumb plays the three lowest-pitched strings. Your index finger plays the 3rd string, your middle finger plays the 2nd string and your ring finger plays the 1st string. You usually do not use your pinky finger.

2 To play the strings, pluck upward with the tips of your fingers and pluck downward with your thumb.

- Make sure you keep your wrist stationary.

reading a
chord diagram

Reading a chord diagram, also called a chord chart, is a quick and easy way to learn how to play a chord on the guitar.

A chord diagram is a visual representation of the strings and frets on a guitar. The horizontal lines represent the frets and the vertical lines represent the strings. The markings on the diagram show you how to position your fingers on the guitar to play the chord.

Vertical Lines

The vertical lines on a chord diagram represent the six strings on the guitar. The line on the far right represents the 1st string, which is the string closest to the floor when you are holding the guitar. The line on the far left represents the 6th string.

Horizontal Lines

The horizontal lines on a chord diagram represent the frets on a guitar, which are the metal strips on the fingerboard. The thick horizontal line at the top of the diagram represents the nut of the guitar, where the fingerboard ends.

If you need to play a chord that requires you to place your fingers closer to the bridge on the fingerboard, a numeral is shown beside the top fret to the right of the chord diagram. This number specifies the fret where the chord begins. For example, if the chord begins at the seventh fret, VII or 7fr will appear beside the top fret.

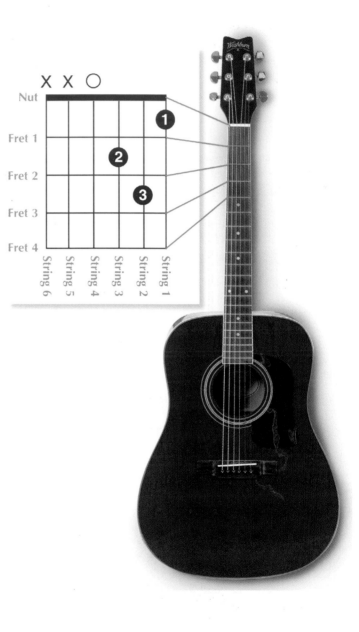

Dots

The position of the dots (●) on the lines indicates which strings you place your fingers on and which frets you place your fingers behind.

Curved Line

A curved line above a chord diagram indicates that you press down multiple strings with a single finger. This is known as a barre. For information on barre chords, see page 82.

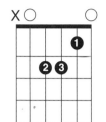

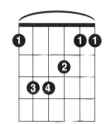

X or O

On a chord diagram, the symbols X and ○ appear above strings that are not held down by any fingers to indicate if you have to play the strings. An ○ indicates that you play the string. An X indicates that you do not play the string. A string that you play, but do not hold down on the fingerboard, is called an open string.

Numbers

The numbers on a chord diagram indicate which finger you use to hold down, or fret, each string. Each number represents a particular finger:

❶ index finger
❷ middle finger
❸ ring finger
❹ pinky finger

The thumb is rarely used to fret. However, a ❤ appears on the chord diagram when you need to use your thumb to fret.

On some chord diagrams, the numbers appear in the middle of the dots, as shown on the chord diagrams above. You also may find these numbers above or below the chord diagram. Keep in mind that these numbers usually only appear on chord diagrams designed for those who are just learning to play chords. A piece of sheet music that also provides chord diagrams does not usually include these numbers.

reading tablature

Tablature is a notation system that visually depicts the strings on the guitar. This system, often called guitar tab, indicates the strings you need to press down on and which frets you need to position your fingers behind.

Tablature is especially useful if you cannot read the traditional music notation staff. As with a music staff, you read tablature from left to right.

Tablature does not indicate if you need to use your index, middle, ring or pinky finger to press down each string. You are more likely to find this information on a chord diagram. For information on chord diagrams, see page 28.

Example of Tablature

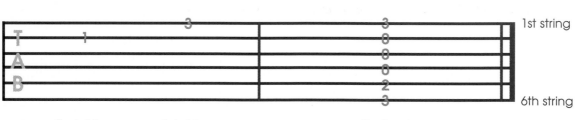

1st string

6th string

2nd string,
first fret

1st string,
third fret

G chord

TAB

The word "TAB" appears at the beginning of tablature to indicate that you are looking at tablature and not a music staff.

Horizontal Lines

The horizontal lines represent the six strings on the guitar. The top line represents the 1st string, which is the string closest to the floor when you are holding the guitar. The bottom line represents the 6th string.

Numbers

The numbers on the lines indicate at which frets you position your fingers. For example, the number 3 indicates you should position your finger just behind the third fret. A zero (0) indicates that you play the string without positioning a finger on it. When a chord is written in tablature, the numbers are written on different strings but in a vertical line.

Bar Lines

The vertical lines on tablature, called bar lines, help to break down tablature into units of time that are smaller and easier to manage. These units of time are called bars or measures.

Tablature With Music Staff

Tablature is often shown below the traditional music notation staff in guitar books and magazines. Since traditional tablature does not tell you how long to play each note, you can look at the music staff above tablature to determine how long to play each note. You play a whole note (o) for 4 beats, a half note (♩) for 2 beats, a quarter note (♩) for 1 beat, an eighth note (♪) for a 1/2 of a beat, and a sixteenth note (♬) for a 1/4 of a beat. For more information on note values, see page 45.

Example of Tablature With Music Staff

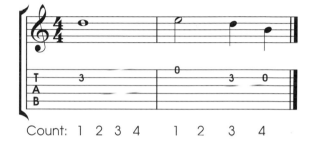

Count: 1 2 3 4   1 2 3 4

Tablature With Rhythm

Although traditional tablature does not tell you how long to play each note, some books and magazines are beginning to include tablature that indicates the rhythm of the song. Tablature with rhythm works the same as regular tablature, except that each note includes a stem to indicate how long you should play each note. Use the following chart to determine how long to play the notes.

Stem	Note	Hold Note For
No stem	whole note	4 beats
|	half note	2 beats
|	quarter note	1 beat
♪	eighth note	1/2 of a beat
♬	sixteenth note	1/4 of a beat

In most cases, the half note looks the same as a quarter note, but the distance to the next note is larger for a half note. Sometimes a circle appears around the number for a half note to differentiate the half note from the quarter note.

Example of Tablature With Rhythm

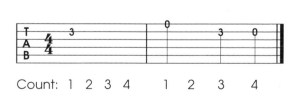

Count: 1 2 3 4   1 2 3 4

tune a guitar (using relative tuning)

Guitars constantly go out of tune, so learning to tune your guitar is important. It is a good idea to always check your guitar's tuning before each session.

There are different ways to tune a guitar. Relative tuning, also called the fifth-fret method, is the most convenient method. Relative tuning involves tuning the guitar to itself, which means you do not need to use an outside source for reference.

To tune the guitar to itself, you select a string that is in tune and then tune each of the other strings relative to that string. In the example below, we use the 6th string as the starting point. If you want to be more accurate, you can use a reference source, such as a piano, to tune the 6th string before you begin.

When tuning, if you are uncertain about the pitch of a note, you can deliberately tune the string too sharp (high) or too flat (low) and then review the pitch later. It is usually best to tune the string too flat and then retune to increase the pitch.

1 Place your index finger on the 6th string, just behind the fifth fret. Pick the string.

2 Pick the 5th string without holding down the string.

• Allow both strings to play at the same time. The pitches should match.

3 If the pitches do not match, use the tuning machine for the 5th string to adjust the pitch.

4 Place your index finger on the 5th string, just behind the fifth fret. Pick the string.

5 Pick the 4th string without holding down the string.

• Allow both strings to play at the same time. The pitches should match.

6 If the pitches do not match, use the tuning machine for the 4th string to adjust the pitch.

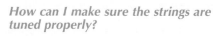

How can I make sure the strings are tuned properly?

When tuning the guitar to itself, it is very easy to make a mistake with one string and keep compounding the error as you tune each of the other strings. To check the tuning, you can play a chord slowly, deliberately striking one string at a time so you can listen to the strings playing together to determine if a string is out of tune.

Is there a quick reference I can use to learn relative tuning?

You can use this diagram as a guide for using relative tuning.

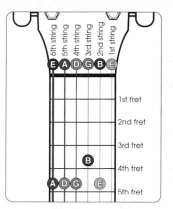

7 Place your index finger on the 4th string, just behind the fifth fret. Pick the string.

8 Pick the 3rd string without holding down the string.

• Allow both strings to play at the same time. The pitches should match.

9 If the pitches do not match, use the tuning machine for the 3rd string to adjust the pitch.

10 Place your index finger on the 3rd string, just behind the fourth fret and pick the string. Pick the 2nd string without holding down the string.

11 Adjust the pitch of the 2nd string to match the 3rd string.

12 Place your index finger on the 2nd string, just behind the fifth fret and pick the string. Pick the 1st string without holding down the string.

13 Adjust the pitch of the 1st string to match the 2nd string.

tune a guitar (to a reference source)

When you are playing with other musicians or accompanying a vocalist, it is important to tune your guitar to a reference source to ensure that you are in tune with everyone you are playing with. A reference source is an external fixed source that allows you to determine whether your strings are tuned to a standardized pitch, known as concert pitch.

An electronic tuner is the easiest and most accurate

reference source, making it ideal for beginners. You can accurately tune a string on your guitar without relying solely on your ears by using an electronic tuner. For more information on electronic tuners, see page 220.

You can also use a piano or an electronic keyboard as a reference source. Alternatively, you can use the companion Web site for this book as a reference source. This Web site includes recordings of all six open strings played in concert pitch.

Using an Electronic Tuner

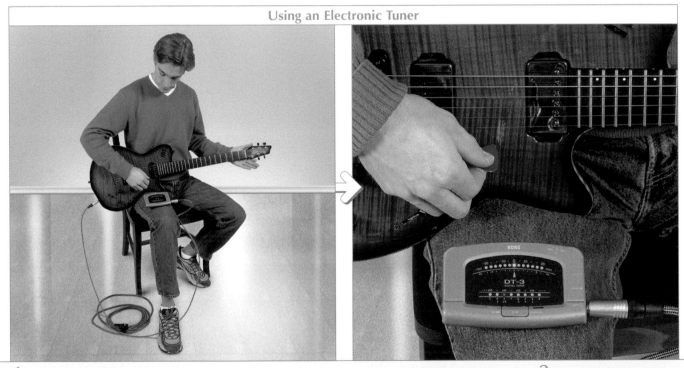

1 If you are tuning an electric guitar, plug the guitar into the tuner using the cord you use to plug the guitar into an amplifier.

- If you are tuning an acoustic or classical guitar, position the guitar near the microphone built into the tuner.

2 Pick a string on your guitar without holding down the string.

- The tuner indicates the note you are closest to and whether the note you played is flat (too low) or sharp (too high) in relation to the closest note.

- For some tuners, you need to select the note for the string you are tuning.

3 Turn the tuning machine for the string until the tuner indicates that the string is in tune.

4 Repeat steps 2 and 3 for each string on your guitar.

Tip

What note should each open string on my guitar be tuned to?

The diagram below shows which note each open string on your guitar should be tuned to.

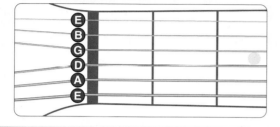

What should I do if the note displayed on the electronic tuner does not match the note I am picking?

If the letter name of the note displayed on the electronic tuner does not match the note you are trying to play, you should tune the string until the letter names match. You can then fine-tune the string to match the note precisely.

Using a Piano

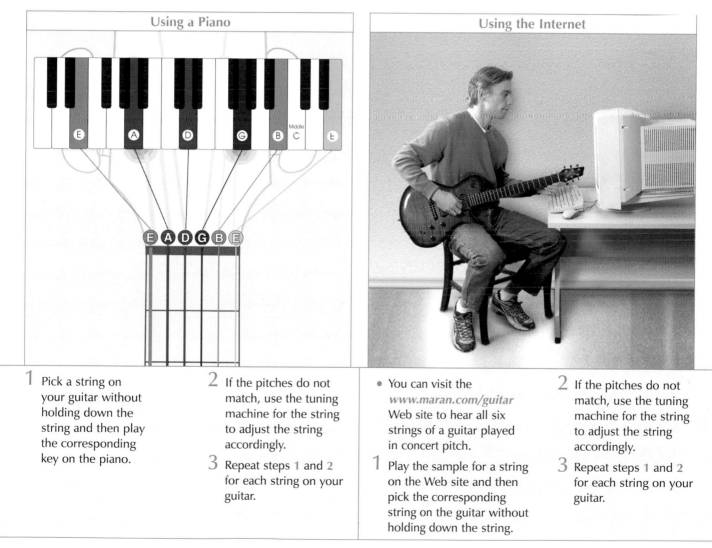

Using the Internet

1 Pick a string on your guitar without holding down the string and then play the corresponding key on the piano.

2 If the pitches do not match, use the tuning machine for the string to adjust the string accordingly.

3 Repeat steps 1 and 2 for each string on your guitar.

● You can visit the *www.maran.com/guitar* Web site to hear all six strings of a guitar played in concert pitch.

1 Play the sample for a string on the Web site and then pick the corresponding string on the guitar without holding down the string.

2 If the pitches do not match, use the tuning machine for the string to adjust the string accordingly.

3 Repeat steps 1 and 2 for each string on your guitar.

how to practice

You should practice regularly to develop your guitar playing skills. Practicing for only 15 minutes every day is better than practicing for an hour one day and then not practicing for the next three days. To help you practice regularly, create a realistic practice schedule and then do your best to stick to that schedule.

When practicing, you should take breaks to help rest your muscles and help you avoid mistakes that can occur when you rush through your practice sessions. You should also rest when your fingertips start to feel very sore. However, until you develop calluses, you may want to continue playing despite mild discomfort in your fingertips.

Your guitar playing skills can improve more rapidly if you let your fingers and hands progress at their own pace. Your fingers need to gradually get used to how to form chords and play scales. With regular practice, your hands and fingers will become more accustomed to what to do and where to go when playing the guitar.

Types of Exercises to Perform

Performing the following exercises can help improve your guitar skills and warm up your fingers before playing.

- Perform finger exercises *(page 37)*.
- Play chords *(pages 58 to 101)*.
- Practice strumming patterns *(page 76)*.
- Play single notes *(pages 104 to 115)*.
- Play scales *(page 122)*.
- Play songs.

Tips for Practicing

- When fretting, or holding down, a string, press the string firmly to the fingerboard with your fingertip just behind the fret. Make sure you arch your fingers so your fingertips touch the strings at a 90-degree angle.

- When playing an exercise, play slowly and methodically at first and increase the pace only after you are able to play all the notes cleanly. Playing too fast too soon can lead to bad habits.

- You should identify the parts of each exercise that you are having trouble with so you can spend extra time on those parts.

- Set goals for yourself. For example, you could aim to play an exercise 10 times in a row without making any mistakes.

Finger Exercise 1

1 Place your index finger on the 1st string, just behind the first fret. Pick the 1st string toward the floor. Keep your index finger on the string.

2 Place your middle finger on the 1st string, just behind the second fret. Pick the 1st string toward the ceiling. Keep your index and middle fingers on the string.

3 Place your ring finger on the 1st string, just behind the third fret. Pick the 1st string toward the floor. Keep your index, middle and ring fingers on the string.

4 Place your pinky finger on the 1st string, just behind the fourth fret. Pick the 1st string toward the ceiling and then toward the floor. Take your pinky finger off the string.

5 Pick the 1st string toward the ceiling and then take your ring finger off the string.

6 Pick the 1st string toward the floor and then take your middle finger off the string.

7 Pick the 1st string toward the ceiling and then take your index finger off the string.

8 Repeat steps 1 to 7, moving each finger one fret closer to the body of the guitar until you have played the 1st string at every fret.

9 Repeat steps 1 to 8 on every string on the guitar.

Finger Exercise 2

1 On the 1st string, place your index finger just behind the ninth fret, your middle finger just behind the tenth fret, your ring finger just behind the eleventh fret and your pinky finger just behind the twelfth fret.

2 Pick the 1st string toward the floor and then take your pinky finger off the string.

3 Pick the 1st string toward the ceiling and then take your ring finger off the string.

4 Pick the 1st string toward the floor and then take your middle finger off the string.

5 Pick the 1st string toward the ceiling and then take your index finger off the string.

6 Repeat steps 1 to 5, except place your fingers on the next string. Then repeat the steps for the remaining strings.

7 Repeat steps 1 to 6, except place your fingers one fret closer to the nut and start by performing all the steps on the 6th string.

8 Repeat steps 1 to 7, moving one fret closer to the nut each time you finish performing the steps for all the strings.

Chapter 3

While you do not need to know how to read music to play the guitar, understanding the basic elements of music theory can be very useful. In this chapter, you will be introduced to the notes on the musical staff, sharps and flats, rests and other common musical symbols. You will also learn to read rhythm slashes and lead sheets to help you play songs on your guitar.

Reading Music

In this Chapter...

the staff

Music is written on a grid called a staff. Written music indicates many important aspects of your playing simultaneously. For example, you can determine what notes to play, how long to play the notes and exactly how the notes should be played, such as loud or soft.

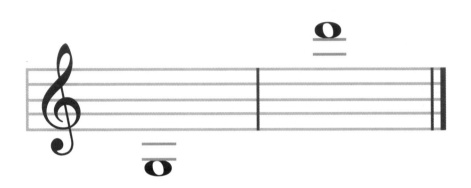

Staff

A staff (plural:staves) consists of five lines and four spaces between the lines. Each line and space corresponds to a letter name so that when a note is drawn on the line or space, you know which note to play. The position of the note on a staff tells you whether the pitch of the note is high or low. The higher a note is on the staff, the higher the sound of the note.

Clef

The beginning of a staff is always marked with a symbol called a clef. The letter names of the lines and spaces on the staff will change depending on the clef of the staff. The treble clef (𝄞) is the only clef used for guitar music.

Bar Lines

The vertical lines on the staff, called bar lines, help to break down the staff into units of time that are smaller and easier to manage. These units of time are called bars or measures. To indicate the end of a song, you will see a double bar written at the end of a staff.

Ledger Lines

Notes that are higher or lower than the five lines on the staff are written on ledger lines. The letter names of ledger lines progress alphabetically just as the letter names on the staff do. For example, since the lowest line of the staff is E in the treble clef, the first space below the lowest line is D and the ledger line below the space is C. For information on the note names, see page 41.

notes on
the staff

Note Names

The letter names of the lines and spaces on the staff are listed from A to G. Once you reach G, the names start over again at A in a never-ending loop. To read music, you need to memorize the letter names of the lines and spaces on the staff. In the treble clef (𝄞), the letter names of the lines from bottom to top are E, G, B, D and F. To help you remember the letter names of the lines, you can use a saying in which each word begins with the letters you need to remember, such as "Every Good Boy Deserves Fudge" or "Every Guitarist Begins Doing Fine." The notes of the spaces in the treble clef from bottom to top are F, A, C and E. To remember the letter names of the spaces, notice how the letters spell the word "face."

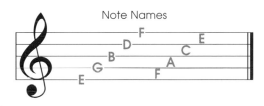

Note Names

Notes on the Staff and your Guitar

A note you play on your guitar without pressing down on a string is called an open-string note. The six open-string notes you can play on the guitar appear on the neck of the guitar below.

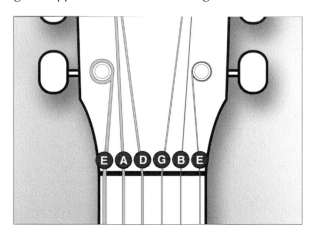

You can use the following diagram to see how the notes on the music staff correspond to the notes you play when you play each open-string note on your guitar. The chord diagrams below the staff indicate which string you will pick. For more information on reading chord diagrams, see page 28.

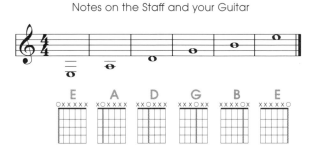

Notes on the Staff and your Guitar

sharps
and flats

The notes on the lines and spaces of the staff are referred to as "natural notes." You can play other notes that occur between the natural notes. These other notes are called sharps and flats.

Sharps and Flats

The following chart indicates the sharps and flats you can play.

Between	Note is Called
F and G	F-sharp or G-flat
G and A	G-sharp or A-flat
A and B	A-sharp or B-flat
C and D	C-sharp or D-flat
D and E	D-sharp or E-flat

There is no sharp or flat note between E and F or between B and C.

What is the difference between a sharp and a flat?

If you move one half step higher than a natural note, you play a sharp. For example, A-sharp is one half step higher than A. If you move one half step lower than a natural note, you play a flat. For example, B-flat is one half step lower than B. If you move from A to B, this is known as a full step.

Sharps and Flats Before a Note

You may see a symbol in front of a note on the staff, indicating that a note is sharp or flat. The ♯ symbol represents a sharp and the ♭ symbol represents a flat. When you see the sharp or flat symbol in front of a note in a bar, all the other notes on the same line or space in that bar will also be sharp or flat. When a sharp or flat affects one bar of a song, the sharp or flat is referred to as a local accidental. A bar is a section of music between two vertical lines on the staff.

A piece of music does not usually combine sharps and flats. You typically see either sharps or flats used throughout a song.

Example of a Sharp
Before a Note

Note: F♯   E   D   F♯   E

key signatures

For some songs, sharps or flats appear on a specific line or space just after the treble clef (𝄞) on a staff. These sharps or flats are called a key signature and indicate the notes in the song that you must play as sharp or flat. For example, if there is an F-sharp in the key signature, you must play all the F notes in the song as F♯ notes.

The number of sharps or flats in a key signature indicates what key a song is played in. For example, a key signature with one sharp indicates that the song is played in the key of G major or E minor. Every major key has a corresponding minor key.

When you know what key a song is in, you will know which chords and scales you can play on your guitar for the song.

Common Key Signatures

See below for common key signatures and the major and minor keys each key signature represents.

Natural Symbols

A **natural symbol** (♮) appears in a song to specify you do not need to play a sharp or flat as indicated in the key signature. For example, you may have an F-sharp in the key signature, but there may be an F in the song that should be played as an F instead of an F-sharp. In this case, the natural symbol appears in front of the note.

When the natural symbol appears in front of a note in a specific bar, you should play all the notes on the same line or space in that bar as natural notes as well. When a natural symbol affects one bar of a song, the natural symbol is referred to as a local accidental. For information on bars, see page 40.

time signatures
and note values

Time Signatures

Time signatures are written near the clef symbol (𝄞) at the beginning of a staff. Time signatures are made up of two numbers, one on top of the other, that describe the beats in every bar. The top number indicates the number of beats in each bar and is usually 4, 3 or 2. The bottom number indicates the type of note that counts as one beat, such as a half note (𝅗𝅥), quarter note (𝅘𝅥) or eighth note (𝅘𝅥𝅮). The bottom number is usually 2, 4 or 8.

4/4 Time Signature

The most common time signature is 4/4, which specifies that each bar has four beats and each quarter note (𝅘𝅥) counts as one beat. Because the 4/4 time signature is considered "common time," you may also see the 4/4 time signature indicated by **C** , instead of 4/4.

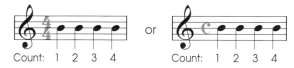

Examples of 4/4 Time Signatures

Count: 1   2   3   4   Count: 1   2   3   4

3/4 Time Signature

The 3/4 time signature is also quite common. In the 3/4 time signature, each bar has three beats and each quarter note (𝅘𝅥) counts as one beat. Traditionally, waltzes are written in 3/4 time, so you may find that songs written in 3/4 have a waltz-like feel to them.

Example of a 3/4 Time Signature

Count: 1   2   3

2/4 and 2/2 Time Signatures

Some less common time signatures that you may come across are 2/4 and 2/2 time. The 2/4 time signature, which is the traditional polka time signature, has two beats in a bar and each quarter note (𝅘𝅥) counts as one beat.

Example of a 2/4 Time Signature

Count: 1   2

The 2/2 time signature is commonly referred to as cut time and is often indicated by **¢** on the staff. In cut time, each bar has two beats and each half note (𝅗𝅥) counts as one beat.

Examples of 2/2 Time Signatures

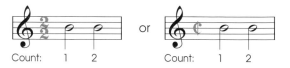

Count: 1   2   Count: 1   2

Note Values

The shape of a note indicates the note value, which is the amount of time you should hold the note. The chart below indicates the values for specific types of notes in a 4/4 time signature.

Note	Symbol	Number of Beats in 4/4 Time
whole note	o	4
half note	♩	2
quarter note	♩	1
eighth note *When two or more eighth notes appear in a row, they are joined with a beam.*	♪ or ♫	1/2 (2 eighth notes = 1 beat)
sixteenth note *When two or more sixteenth notes appear in a row, they are joined with a double beam.*	♪ or ♬	1/4 (4 sixteenth notes = 1 beat)

You will see any number of combinations of note values together in a bar. The note values in each bar must add up to the correct number of beats according to the time signature. For example, in a 4/4 time signature, you can have one whole note or two half notes in a bar since both sets of note values add up to four beats.

Example of Note Values

Pickup Notes

Some songs do not start on the first beat of a bar. In this case, the first bar of the song does not have the complete number of beats that is required by the time signature. The notes that occur in this bar are called pickup notes. If a song begins with pickup notes, the last bar of the song will also usually have an incomplete number of beats. When you add up the number of beats in the first and last bar, they should equal the correct number of beats in a complete bar. When you play a song with pickup notes, make sure you count out the missing beats in the first bar before you play the pickup notes to start the song—otherwise you may be off beat for the rest of the song.

Example of Pickup Notes

Londonderry Air
(O Danny Boy)

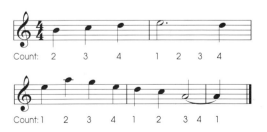

CONTINUED...

time signatures and note values

Tempo

Tempo refers to the pace of a song. More specifically, the tempo refers to how much time elapses between each beat in a song. Specific tempos are often indicated above the staff by a quarter note next to a number, such as ♩ = 76. This equation signifies the number of beats per minute (bpm) in the piece of music. The quarter note is used as a frame of reference because the value of a quarter note is usually one beat. For example, ♩ = 120 means you play 120 quarter notes (or beats) per minute, which is relatively fast paced. A higher number indicates a faster tempo and a lower number indicates a slower tempo.

Tempo can also be marked in words above the staff. Although you may sometimes find tempo written in English, such as "lively" or "moderately," tempo is usually written in Italian, such as *"allegro"* or *"moderato."* The following chart lists common Italian terms for tempos and each term's corresponding bpm.

Italian Term	Definition	Beats per Minute (bpm)
largo	very slow	40-66
adagio	slow	66-76
andante	somewhat slow	76-108
moderato	at a moderate pace	108-120
allegro	quick and cheerful	120-168
presto	very fast	168-200

Example of Tempo

Silent Night

Joseph Mohr
F. X. Gruber

Andante (♩ = 76)

Keep in mind that even when a fast tempo is specified for a song, you should begin practicing the song at a slow and steady pace and then work up to the desired tempo. Practicing a song at a slow tempo will eventually allow you to play the song much faster than if you began practicing the song fast from the start.

Keeping the Beat

You should always keep the beat when you are playing music. To count the beat in a 4/4 time signature, you count "1, 2, 3, 4" repeatedly for each bar in the song. To count the beat in a 3/4 time signature, you count "1, 2, 3" repeatedly for each bar. If you are playing eighth notes and you need to count half beats, you can add "and" between every full beat. For example, instead of counting "1, 2, 3, 4," count "1 and 2 and 3 and 4 and."

Example of Keeping the Beat

When you are counting the beat, you need to count in a steady rhythm to keep a consistent tempo throughout a song. You should also strum chords with a steady, fluid motion to help you keep the beat. You can use special devices to help you maintain a steady beat. For example, a metronome can help you keep the beat by making a tapping or clicking noise for every beat. You can also use a drum machine or MIDI sequencer to help you maintain a steady beat. You can adjust these devices to indicate how many beats you want to play per minute.

With practice, you may find that keeping the beat becomes natural and you do not have to count the beats anymore. Once you develop a good internal sense of rhythm, you will rarely get off beat and when you do, you will be able to get back on beat without much difficulty.

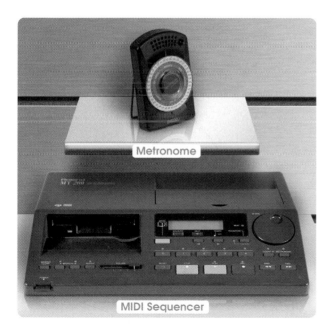

Metronome

MIDI Sequencer

dots, ties and rests

Dots

A note with a dot beside it is known as a dotted note. When you see a dotted note, you need to add half of the value of the note to the note. For example, if you see a dotted quarter note (♩.), add the value of one eighth note to the quarter note. In the most common time signatures, such as 4/4 time, you can think of this as adding half a beat to the quarter note, so you should hold the dotted quarter note for one and a half beats. The following chart shows the values of different types of dotted notes in common time signatures. For information on note values, see page 44. For information on time signatures, see page 45.

Note	Description	Number of Beats
♩.	dotted half note	3
♩.	dotted quarter note	1 ½
♪.	dotted eighth note	³/₄

If two dots follow a note, the second dot increases the length of the note again by half the amount of the first dot. For example, a half note followed by two dots (♩..) is equal to three and a half beats because you count two beats for the half note, one beat for the first dot and half a beat for the second dot.

You may also see one or two dots beside a rest symbol. Dotted rests work exactly the same way as dotted notes.

Example of Dotted Notes

Count: 1 & 2 &   3 & 4 &   1 & 2 & 3 & 4 &

Ties

A tie is another way to increase the amount of time you hold a note. A tie is a curved line that joins two notes that have the same pitch, which means they are on the same line or space on the staff. A tie indicates that you should add the value of the second note to the first note and not play the second note. In other words, the first note should be held for the combined value of the two notes. Ties are a useful method of joining notes that are in separate bars, as they indicate that you should keep holding the note into the next bar.

Example of Ties

Count: 1 & 2 & 3 & 4 &   1 & 2 & 3 & 4 &

Rests

In written music, rest symbols indicate moments of silence. Like notes, each type of rest signifies a number of beats, except rests signify that you should not play during those beats. The value of all the notes and rests in a bar must add up to the total number of beats specified by the time signature.

To play a rest on a guitar, you need to stop the strings from vibrating to silence your guitar. To stop the strings from vibrating, you should mute, or damp, the strings. To mute strings, lay your fingers across all six strings on the neck of your guitar.

Moments of silence, as well as sound, are an important part of music. In fact, many people consider the combination of notes and silences to be what makes music interesting. Silences, in the form of rests, can be a vital part of the rhythm and structure of a song. For example, in reggae songs, you often see a bar starting with an eighth rest, followed by an eighth note, followed by an eighth rest, followed by an eighth note and so on. Since you are not playing a note on the first beat of the bar, you end up shifting the beat off of where it would normally fall. This use of rests gives reggae its distinctive pulse and rhythm.

Types of Rests

Each type of rest corresponds to a type of note that has the same value. For example, in 4/4 time, you will hold a quarter note for one beat and remain silent for one beat when you see a quarter rest.

You can also have a multimeasure rest, which means you rest for a certain number of bars, or measures. A multimeasure rest looks like a long whole rest with a vertical line on each end. The number above the thick line tells you how many bars to rest for.

Example of a Multimeasure Rest

The chart below shows the amount of time you should remain silent for each type of rest.

Rest Symbol	Description	Number of Beats
	whole rest	4
	half rest	2
	quarter rest	1
	eighth rest	1/2
	sixteenth rest	1/4

common musical symbols

Volume Symbols

The change of volume, known as dynamics, in a piece of music can greatly affect the character of a song. For example, when a song becomes gradually louder, it can have an extremely powerful effect. A change in volume is usually indicated by symbols that appear beneath the staff. When you see a volume symbol, play the music at the specified volume. Continue playing at that volume until you see a new symbol indicating you should play at a different volume. Volume symbols are usually written as abbreviations of Italian words.

Example of Volume Symbols

This chart shows common volume symbols.

Symbol	Italian term	Definition
pp	pianissimo	very soft
p	piano	soft
mp	mezzo-piano	moderately soft
mf	mezzo-forte	moderately loud
f	forte	loud
ff	fortissimo	very loud
cresc. or <	crescendo	gradually get louder
decresc. or >	decrescendo	gradually get softer
dim.	diminuendo	gradually get softer

Speed Symbols

The change in speed, or tempo, of a song can also affect the character of the music. Songs do not necessarily have to be played at the same pace throughout. Composers will sometimes change the speed of a song part way through to produce a certain effect. For example, a song can gradually speed up to suggest anticipation, or a song can gradually slow down to suggest sorrow.

Example of a Speed Symbol

This chart shows some common symbols that indicate a change in speed.

Symbol	Italian term	Definition
accel.	accelerando	gradually speed up
rall.	rallentando	gradually slow down
rit.	ritardando	gradually slow down

Phrasing Symbols

Phrasing symbols indicate how you should articulate notes. For example, phrasing symbols can specify that the notes are to be played smoothly one after the other, or that the notes should be played short and detached.

Staccato Dot

Example of a Staccato Dot

A dot above or below a note indicates that the note should be played staccato, which means short, sharp and detached from the adjacent notes. When playing a staccato note, the note that follows should not come more quickly—the music should keep the same rhythm. For example, if you see a staccato quarter note (♩), the distance between the staccato quarter note and the note that follows is still the value of one quarter note. However, you play the staccato quarter note for a shorter amount of time than you normally would. To play a staccato note, you need to quickly stop the string from ringing after you play the note, which is called muting the string. To mute a string, rest your finger on the string or release the pressure of your finger from the string to prevent the string from making a sound.

Slur

Example of a Slur

You may see an arch, or curved line, connecting two or more different notes on the staff. This arch is known as a slur and it indicates that the transition between the notes connected by the slur should be smooth. You should not hear a pause in sound between any of the notes connected by the slur. You can use techniques such as hammer-ons, pull-offs and slides to achieve this effect on the guitar. For information on these techniques, see pages 134 to 136.

Accent

Example of an Accent

You may also see an accent (>) above or below a note. Accents indicate that you should play the note louder and with more force than you usually would. Accents are commonly used to emphasize individual notes.

CONTINUED...

common musical symbols

Repetition Symbols

Songs are often structured around repetition. Just think of any popular song on the radio—the chorus is usually repeated after every verse. For this reason, you will often find symbols in music telling you to repeat certain sections of the music. At first, these symbols may seem confusing when you see them in written music, but once you learn what they mean, you will be able to navigate easily through the music.

Repeat Markers

Repeat markers appear in written music to indicate that you should repeat the bars that fall between the starting repeat marker and the ending repeat marker once. The starting repeat marker is a thick vertical bar followed by two dots, one on top of the other. The ending repeat marker is a thick vertical bar preceded by two dots.

 starting repeat marker

ending repeat marker

You should ignore the starting repeat marker the first time it appears in a song. When you come to an ending repeat marker, go back to the starting repeat marker and play the passage again.

Repeat Between Bars Example

If there is no starting repeat marker, go back to the beginning of the song and play from there. The second time you play through the song, ignore the ending repeat marker and continue playing the rest of the song.

Repeat to Beginning Example

A song or repeated passage may have multiple endings. If music has multiple endings, play the first ending the first time you play through the song or passage, and then play the second ending when you play the song or passage again. The first and second endings will be marked with the numbers 1 and 2 with a horizontal bracket above the staff over each ending, as shown below.

Multiple Endings Example

Repetition Symbols (continued)

D.S.

D.S. is short for the Italian term *Dal Segno*, which means "from the sign." When you see *D.S.* in written music, you should go back to the D.S. sign (𝄋) and repeat the section between 𝄋 and *D.S.* Ignore *D.S.* the second time through the song and play to the end of the song.

D.S. Example

When you see *D.S. al Coda*, you should go back to 𝄋 and then play until you reach *To Coda* ⊕. You should then skip to the section marked ⊕ *Coda* and play to the end of this section to end the song. The Coda section is usually a separate passage of music at the end of a song.

D.S. al Coda Example

D.C.

D.C. is short for the Italian term *Da Capo*, which means "from the beginning." When you see *D.C.* in written music, you should go back to the beginning of the song and play to the end of the song, ignoring *D.C.* the second time through.

D.C. Example

When you see *D.C. al Fine*, you should go back to the beginning of the song, then play until you see *Fine* written above the staff and end the song there. Since *Fine* usually appears before you see *D.C. al Fine*, make sure you ignore *Fine* the first time you play through the song.

D.C. al Fine Example

You may also see *D.C. al Coda* written in music. *D.C. al Coda* is very similar to *D.S. al Coda*, except you should go back to the beginning of the song and then play until you reach the *To Coda* ⊕. Then skip to the section marked ⊕ *Coda* and play to the end of this section to end the song.

reading rhythm slashes

What are Rhythm Slashes?

Rhythm slashes are a kind of musical shorthand that indicates how to play, without using standard musical notation. Since standard notation can be difficult to learn, rhythm slashes provide a simple and straightforward way to tell the musician how to play.

All the chord diagrams needed for a piece of music are usually provided at the beginning of the

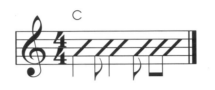

music. Although these chord diagrams are helpful, you should memorize how to play each chord because only the chord names are shown above the rhythm slashes throughout the rest of the music.

There are two different types of rhythm slashes—one type shows exact strumming patterns and the other type allows you to improvise the rhythm.

Rhythm Slashes with Strumming Patterns

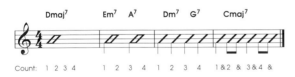

Rhythm slashes with strumming patterns clearly indicate the rhythm that you should be playing. The rhythm slashes are written on a staff as different note values, including whole notes ( ), half notes ( ), quarter notes ( ) and eighth notes ( ). These note values indicate how long you should hold each note, which together make up the rhythm of the song. For more information on note values, see page 44. The chord names are written above the staff to indicate which chord to play and when you need to change the chord. You will find guitar music written as rhythm slashes with strumming patterns in many guitar magazines.

Rhythm Slashes for Improvisation

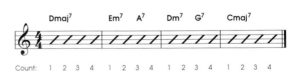

Rhythm slashes for improvisation simply tell you the number of beats that each chord should receive—they do not tell you the exact rhythm that you should play. Slash marks (/) are shown to indicate each beat. For example, in 4/4 time, every bar will have four slash marks, signifying four beats. For information on time signatures, such as 4/4 time, see page 45. The chord names are written above the staff to indicate which chord to play and when you need to change the chord. With this type of rhythm slash, you should make the rhythm up as you go along, which is known as improvising the rhythm. Professional musicians usually use this type of rhythm slash.

reading lead sheets

What is a Lead Sheet?

A lead sheet is a piece of written music that provides an outline for the melody and harmony of a song. Melody is the main line of music that you hear in a song; for example, the lead vocalist usually sings the melody of a song. Harmony is all the music that supports the melody, making it sound richer and more interesting. By providing just an outline of the essential elements of a song, the lead sheet allows room for a musician to improvise.

A lead sheet includes a melody written in

standard notation on a music staff and the accompanying harmony written as chord names above the staff. You can either play the melody by reading the notes on the staff, or just play the chords where indicated. If you are more advanced, you can play the melody and the chords at the same time. You can also improvise around this outline provided by the lead sheet. Improvising can involve making up rhythms, embellishing on the melody or playing a solo. Lead sheets are often organized into collections called fake books.

Parts of a Lead Sheet

Staff

Treble Clef

Time Signature

Melody

Chord Symbol

Who Uses Lead Sheets?

Musicians that play popular styles of music, such as jazz and rock, often use lead sheets. Jazz musicians find lead sheets especially useful since a lot of jazz music is improvised and lead sheets provide jazz musicians with a basic structure to guide their improvisation.

Chapter 4

Many new guitar players like to start by strumming chords. Starting with basic chords is a great way to make learning the guitar exciting, since you can use these chords right away to play many songs. This chapter introduces you to chords and shows you how to play some simple chords. You will also learn strumming patterns you can use to enhance your technique.

Playing Basic Chords

In this Chapter...

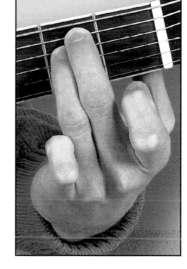

how to play a chord

Learning basic chords is a great way to start playing the guitar. If you can play basic chords, you should be able to play many popular songs. A chord consists of two or more different notes that you play at the same time. Each note in a chord has a different pitch and letter name.

Most basic chords are open-position chords. An open-position chord is a chord that you play by strumming strings without fretting, or pressing down, some of the strings. Open-position chords are played near the nut.

Major Chords and Minor Chords

The two most basic types of chords are major and minor chords. These types of chords each have their own distinct sound. Major chords produce uplifting, happy sounds, whereas minor chords are characterized by dark, sad sounds.

Chords are named after the root note of the chord, which is usually the lowest-pitched note in the chord. For example, in the E major chord, the root note is E. Major chords are referred to by only their letter name, such as C. Minor chords are written with an "m" beside their letter name, such as Dm.

The easiest major chords to play include C, D, E, F, G and A. The easiest minor chords to play include Em, Am and Dm.

Major and minor chords consist of three different notes. Whether a chord is a major or minor chord is determined by the interval, or distance, between the notes in the chord. When you compare a major chord and a minor chord with the same letter name, such as the C major and C minor chords, only one note is different between the chords. In a minor chord, this note is a half step lower than the note in the corresponding major chord. For example, in the C major chord, the note is E, while in the C minor chord, the note is E-flat (E♭).

A major

A minor

Chord Families

A chord family is a group of related chords. The chords in a family are related because all the notes in each chord come from the same scale. For example, all the chords in the C family only use notes that come from the C major scale. For more information on scales, see page 122.

Songs are usually written in a certain key. When you play a song in a specific key, you generally play only chords in that key, or chord family. For example, a song in the key of C will contain mostly chords in the C family.

The chart below indicates the most commonly used chord families. You will notice that many of the families share chords. For example, the C and G families both contain the C, G, Em and Am chords. Some of the chords in this chart are not included in this chapter because they require you to use a barre to play the chord. Chords that use a barre, known as barre chords, involve holding down multiple strings with a single finger. For more information on barre chords, see pages 82 to 95.

Chord Family	Chords in the Family
C family	C, F, G, Dm, Em, Am
D family	D, G, A, Em, F#m, Bm
E family	E, A, B, F#m, G#m, C#m
F family	F, B♭, C, Gm, Am, Dm
G family	G, C, D, Am, Bm, Em
A family	A, D, E, Bm, C#m, F#m
B family	B, E, F#, C#m, D#m, G#m

CONTINUED...

how to
play a chord

Fingering Chords

When fingering chords, you should curl your fingers so that you only use your fingertips to press down on the strings. Your fingertips should be pressed firmly against the strings and positioned directly behind the appropriate frets. You should keep your fingernails short so they are not in the way when you press down the strings. Also, keep your thumb on the back of the neck of the guitar, usually opposite your middle or ring finger.

Strumming Chords

You can use a pick, your thumb, your fingers or the back of your fingernails to strum chords. When strumming, you usually start with the string closest to the ceiling and then strum along the strings toward the floor. When playing songs, you can also strum toward the ceiling. Strumming chords should always produce a clear tone, not a buzzing or muted sound.

Avoid Buzzing or Muted Sounds

If you hear a buzzing sound when you strum, you may not be pressing down hard enough on a string or your fingertip may not be close enough to the fret. A buzzing sound can also occur when one of your fingers accidentally touches another string on the fingerboard.

If you hear a buzzing sound, try rolling your fingertips from side to side and back and forth, while keeping your fingers on the strings. If you are sure your fingers are positioned properly, there could be a problem with the guitar, such as the strings being too close to the neck.

If you hear a muted sound, your finger might be touching the fret.

Develop Calluses

When you first start playing the guitar, your fingertips may hurt when you press down on the strings. If you ever feel pain in your fingertips when playing, make sure you take a break. With practice, your fingertips should start to develop calluses to protect you from this soreness. It may take several weeks or months to develop calluses, depending on how much you practice. A good way to develop calluses is to play the basic chords repeatedly. Be aware that if you stop practicing for an extended period of time, you may lose these calluses.

Changing Chords

Learning how to move seamlessly between chords requires a lot of practice. Once you memorize where your fingers need to be positioned for each chord, you will be able to position all your fingers for the chord at the same time. You should then be able to move from one chord to the next easily. You may find it helpful to practice moving your fingers between chords without strumming.

When changing chords, make sure your hand and fingers have to move as little as possible. When moving from one chord to another chord that uses some of the same notes, keep your fingers pressing down on the strings for the notes that do not change from one chord to the next. This allows you to avoid moving your fingers unnecessarily and helps keep your hand stable. For example, when you are switching from the D chord to the Dm chord, you can leave your ring finger pressing down on the 2nd string, because the note played at that position is shared by both chords.

playing major chords

A major chord consists of three notes you play at the same time. In comparison to minor chords, major chords are uplifting, happy sounds. You can easily recognize a major chord because it is referred to by its letter name, such as C. The most commonly used major chords include G, C, D, E, A and F.

Chords are organized into groups called families, or keys. When you play a song, you usually use chords from the same family. For example, the G chord belongs to the G, C and D families, the C chord belongs to the C, F and G families and the D chord belongs to the D, A and G families.

When playing the C chord, your index finger may accidentally touch the 1st string, causing a muffled sound. To ensure your index finger does not touch the 1st string and is positioned correctly, make sure your fingers are arched over the strings.

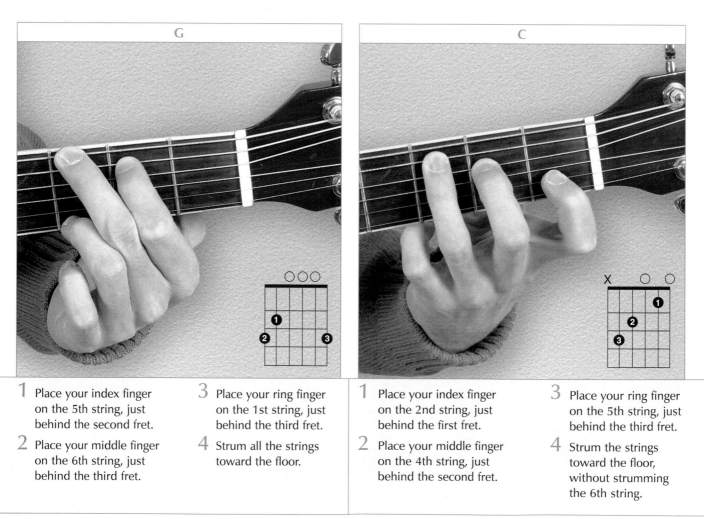

G

1 Place your index finger on the 5th string, just behind the second fret.

2 Place your middle finger on the 6th string, just behind the third fret.

3 Place your ring finger on the 1st string, just behind the third fret.

4 Strum all the strings toward the floor.

C

1 Place your index finger on the 2nd string, just behind the first fret.

2 Place your middle finger on the 4th string, just behind the second fret.

3 Place your ring finger on the 5th string, just behind the third fret.

4 Strum the strings toward the floor, without strumming the 6th string.

Tip

Is there an alternate fingering for the G chord?

Yes. Although beginners often find the fingering in the steps below easier, you can play the G chord by placing your middle finger on the 5th string, just behind the second fret, your ring finger on the 6th string, just behind the third fret and your pinky finger on the 1st string, just behind the third fret. Learning the alternate fingering makes it easier to move to some other chords, such as the C chord.

How can I improve the sound of the G chord?

You can use four fingers to play the G chord to make the chord sound more vibrant. Place your index and middle fingers on the 5th and 6th strings as shown below, but place your ring finger on the 2nd string, just behind the third fret and your pinky finger on the 1st string, just behind the third fret. This fingering can also make the transition to the D chord easier.

D

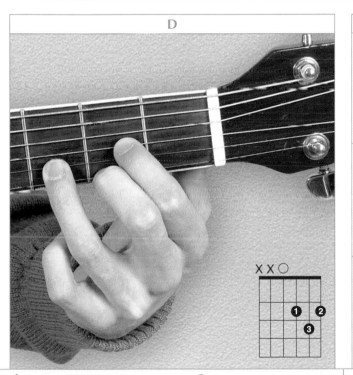

1 Place your index finger on the 3rd string, just behind the second fret.

2 Place your middle finger on the 1st string, just behind the second fret.

3 Place your ring finger on the 2nd string, just behind the third fret.

4 Strum the strings toward the floor, without strumming the 5th and 6th strings.

PRACTICE

- These exercises show a simple chord progression that you can play by using major chords. Perform these exercises to practice switching between the chords.

- Strum each chord toward the floor each time you see the ⊓ symbol. The shape of the note indicates how long you should hold each chord: ⫽ (4 counts), ⌐ (2 counts), ⌐ (1 count).

CONTINUED...

playing major chords

Popular major chords include the E, A and F chords. Make sure all the strings ring clearly when you strum the guitar to play these chords.

Beginners often find the F chord is a difficult major chord to play. Playing the F chord is more difficult since it uses no open strings, which means every string in the chord has a finger on it. In addition, your index finger has to hold down two strings at once. Holding down more than one string at a time using a single finger is known as a barre. The ⌒ symbol in the F chord diagram indicates the need for a barre.

To make the F chord easier to play, you can try rolling your finger onto its side to play the barre. You may also need to readjust the position of your thumb on the neck of the guitar. Also, keep in mind that playing a barre also requires you to press harder on the strings.

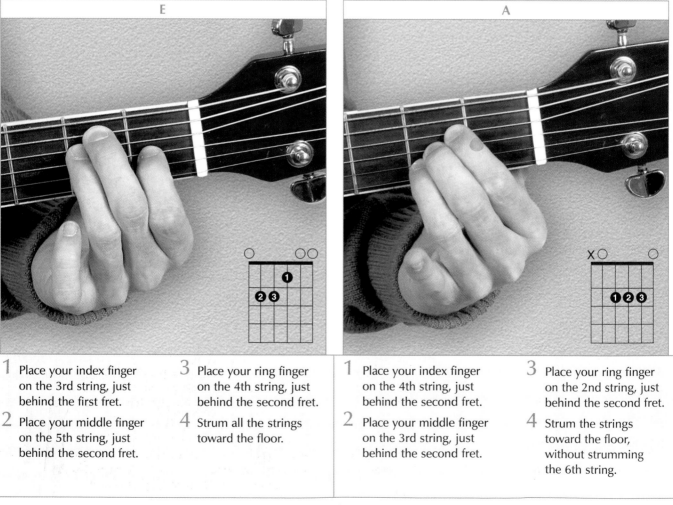

E

1 Place your index finger on the 3rd string, just behind the first fret.

2 Place your middle finger on the 5th string, just behind the second fret.

3 Place your ring finger on the 4th string, just behind the second fret.

4 Strum all the strings toward the floor.

A

1 Place your index finger on the 4th string, just behind the second fret.

2 Place your middle finger on the 3rd string, just behind the second fret.

3 Place your ring finger on the 2nd string, just behind the second fret.

4 Strum the strings toward the floor, without strumming the 6th string.

Tip

Is there an alternate fingering for the A chord?

If you have big fingers, you may want to use an alternate fingering for the A chord. Instead of using the fingering in the steps below, place your middle finger on the 4th string, your ring finger on the 3rd string and your pinky finger on the 2nd string, all just behind the second fret. With this fingering, you may find it easier to switch to some other chords, such the E chord.

When playing the A chord, can I use a barre instead of using separate fingers?

Yes. Place your index finger across the 4th, 3rd and 2nd strings, just behind the second fret. When you first try using the barre, you may find it difficult to not press down on the 1st string. However, with practice, this fingering can make it easier for you to switch to the A chord and to some other barre chords.

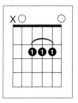

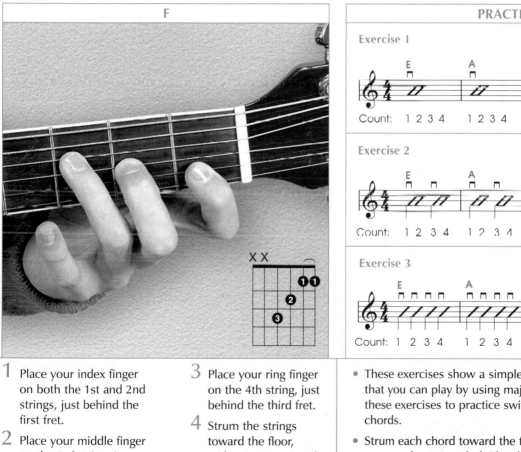

F

1 Place your index finger on both the 1st and 2nd strings, just behind the first fret.

2 Place your middle finger on the 3rd string, just behind the second fret.

3 Place your ring finger on the 4th string, just behind the third fret.

4 Strum the strings toward the floor, without strumming the 5th and 6th strings.

PRACTICE

Exercise 1

E   A   F   E

Count: 1 2 3 4   1 2 3 4   1 2 3 4   1 2 3 4

Exercise 2

E   A   F   E

Count: 1 2 3 4   1 2 3 4   1 2 3 4   1 2 3 4

Exercise 3

E   A   F   E

Count: 1 2 3 4   1 2 3 4   1 2 3 4   1 2 3 4

- These exercises show a simple chord progression that you can play by using major chords. Perform these exercises to practice switching between the chords.

- Strum each chord toward the floor each time you see the ⊓ symbol. The shape of the note indicates how long you should hold each chord: ⧸⧸ (4 counts), ⌐ (2 counts), ⌐ (1 count).

playing minor chords

Minor chords are characterized by the gloomy, sad sounds they produce. An "m" beside the letter for a minor chord allows you to differentiate a minor chord from a major chord. For example, Dm indicates a D minor chord. The minor chords that are easiest to play are Am, Em and Dm.

Chords are organized into groups called families, or keys. When you play a song, you usually use chords from the same family. Minor chords can belong to more than one chord family. For example, the Am chord belongs to the C, G and F families, the Em chord belongs to the C, G and D families and the Dm chord belongs to the C and F families.

When playing minor chords, remember that you should not strike strings that display an X or place your finger on strings that display an 0.

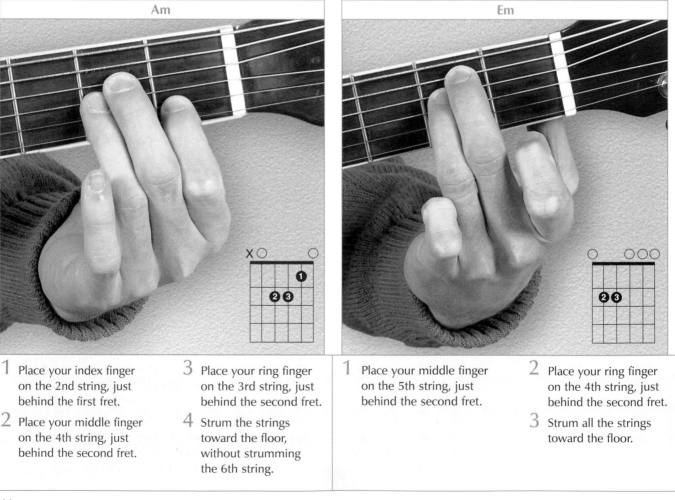

| Am | Em |

Am

1 Place your index finger on the 2nd string, just behind the first fret.

2 Place your middle finger on the 4th string, just behind the second fret.

3 Place your ring finger on the 3rd string, just behind the second fret.

4 Strum the strings toward the floor, without strumming the 6th string.

Em

1 Place your middle finger on the 5th string, just behind the second fret.

2 Place your ring finger on the 4th string, just behind the second fret.

3 Strum all the strings toward the floor.

Tip

How can I tell the difference between a minor and major chord sound?

To hear the difference between a minor chord, such as Em, and a major chord, such as E, you can play the chords back to back. After playing the Em chord as described in the steps below, keep your middle and ring fingers in position and place your index finger on the 3rd string, just behind the first fret. Then strum all the strings toward the floor to play the E chord.

Is there an easier way to play the Dm chord?

If you find that your fingers are too close together when playing the Dm chord, you can use your pinky finger to play the 2nd string instead of your ring finger.

How can I quickly switch from the Am chord to the Em chord?

When your fingers are in position to play the Am chord, you can quickly change to the Em chord by moving up your middle and ring fingers together so that each finger is one string above its original position.

Dm

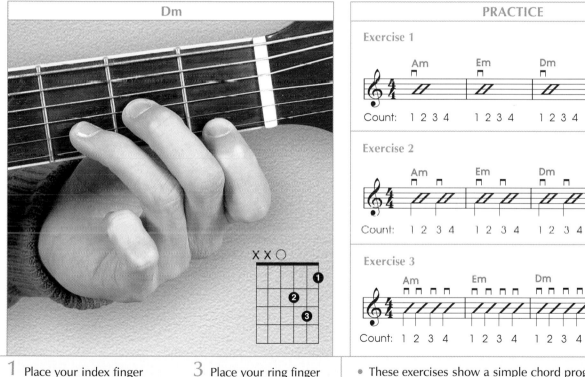

PRACTICE

Exercise 1

Am   Em   Dm   Am

Count: 1 2 3 4   1 2 3 4   1 2 3 4   1 2 3 4

Exercise 2

Am   Em   Dm   Am

Count: 1 2 3 4   1 2 3 4   1 2 3 4   1 2 3 4

Exercise 3

Am   Em   Dm   Am

Count: 1 2 3 4   1 2 3 4   1 2 3 4   1 2 3 4

1 Place your index finger on the 1st string, just behind the first fret.

2 Place your middle finger on the 3rd string, just behind the second fret.

3 Place your ring finger on the 2nd string, just behind the third fret.

4 Strum the strings toward the floor, without strumming the 5th and 6th strings.

- These exercises show a simple chord progression that you can play by using minor chords. Perform these exercises to practice switching between the chords.

- Strum each chord toward the floor each time you see the ⊓ symbol. The shape of the note indicates how long you should hold each chord: ⧧ (4 counts), ⌐ (2 counts), ⌐ (1 count).

playing dominant 7th chords

Dominant 7th chords, which are also known simply as sevenths, are typically used in blues, jazz and funk songs. These 7th chords are termed dominant because they are based on the 5th note of a major scale, which is a strong sounding note.

Dominant 7th chords are created by adding a minor 7th sound to a major chord. Although not more difficult to play than major or minor chords, dominant 7th chords have a more complex sound than major or minor chords.

The easiest dominant 7th chords to play are D7, G7, A7, E7, C7 and B7. The D7 and G7 chords are the most common open-position dominant 7th chords. The term open position refers to chords that are played near the nut and have strings you strum without pressing your fingers down on them.

| D7 | G7 |

1 Place your index finger on the 2nd string, just behind the first fret.

2 Place your middle finger on the 3rd string, just behind the second fret.

3 Place your ring finger on the 1st string, just behind the second fret.

4 Strum the strings toward the floor, without strumming the 5th and 6th strings.

1 Place your index finger on the 1st string, just behind the first fret.

2 Place your middle finger on the 5th string, just behind the second fret.

3 Place your ring finger on the 6th string, just behind the third fret.

4 Strum all the strings toward the floor.

Tip

Is there an alternate fingering for the A7 chord?

Yes. Place your middle finger on the 4th string and your ring finger on the 2nd string with both fingers just behind the second fret. Strum all the strings toward the floor, without strumming the 6th string. This alternate fingering for the A7 chord allows you to easily change to some chords, such as D7 and E.

How can I make the A7 chord sound more pronounced?

You can play an alternate voicing for the A7 chord to make the chord sound more pronounced. A voicing is a different arrangement of notes to achieve a slightly different sound. Place your index finger on the 2nd, 3rd and 4th strings, just behind the second fret, and your middle finger on the 1st string, just behind the 3rd fret. Strum all the strings toward the floor, without strumming the 6th string. This alternate voicing is useful when playing blues songs that need the A7 chord emphasized.

A7

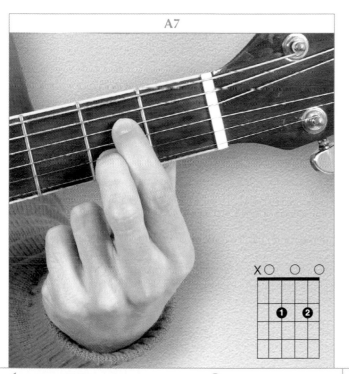

1 Place your index finger on the 4th string, just behind the second fret.

2 Place your middle finger on the 2nd string, just behind the second fret.

3 Strum the strings toward the floor, without strumming the 6th string.

PRACTICE

Exercise 1

Exercise 2

Exercise 3

- These exercises show a simple chord progression that you can play by using dominant 7th chords. Perform these exercises to practice switching between the chords.

- Strum each chord toward the floor each time you see the ⊓ symbol. The shape of the note indicates how long you should hold each chord: ⧸⧸ (4 counts), ⧸ (2 counts), ⌠ (1 count).

CONTINUED...

playing dominant 7th chords

The A7, E7 and B7 chords are used to play most blues songs. Mastering the dominant 7th chords will allow you to play almost all blues songs.

Of all the dominant 7th chords, the C7 and B7 chords are more difficult to play since you need to use all four fingers. If you have learned to play the C chord, you can form the C7 chord by simply adding your pinky finger on the 3rd string, just behind the third fret.

When playing the B7 chord, make sure each of your fingers is only touching the one string to avoid muting the other strings. You can practice playing each string to ensure your fingers are positioned properly. When you play each string, the sound should be clear. You may also want to move your thumb on the back of the neck to help you get a better position for your fingers.

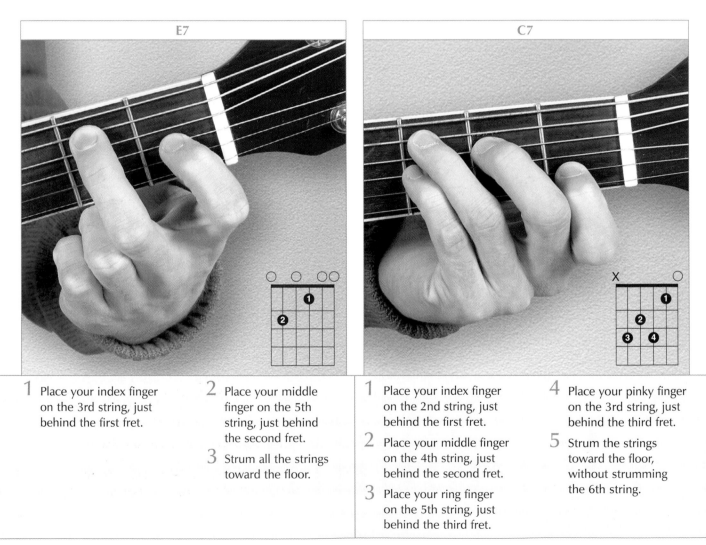

E7

1 Place your index finger on the 3rd string, just behind the first fret.

2 Place your middle finger on the 5th string, just behind the second fret.

3 Strum all the strings toward the floor.

C7

1 Place your index finger on the 2nd string, just behind the first fret.

2 Place your middle finger on the 4th string, just behind the second fret.

3 Place your ring finger on the 5th string, just behind the third fret.

4 Place your pinky finger on the 3rd string, just behind the third fret.

5 Strum the strings toward the floor, without strumming the 6th string.

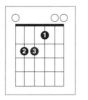

Tip

How can I quickly switch from the E chord to the E7 chord?

With your fingers in position to play the E chord, raise your ring finger from the 4th string to form the E7 chord.

How can I make the E7 chord sound stronger?

You can play an alternate voicing for the E7 chord using all four fingers to make the chord sound stronger. A voicing is a different arrangement of notes to achieve a slightly different sound. Place your index finger on the 3rd string, just behind the first fret. Then put your middle finger on the 5th string and your ring finger on the 4th string with both fingers just behind the second fret. Lastly, place your pinky finger on the 2nd string, just behind the third fret.

B7

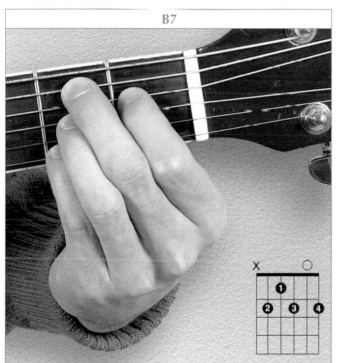

1 Place your index finger on the 4th string, just behind the first fret.

2 Place your middle finger on the 5th string, just behind the second fret.

3 Place your ring finger on the 3rd string, just behind the second fret.

4 Place your pinky finger on the 1st string, just behind the second fret.

5 Strum the strings toward the floor, without strumming the 6th string.

PRACTICE

Exercise 1

E7   C7   B7   E7

Count: 1 2 3 4   1 2 3 4   1 2 3 4   1 2 3 4

Exercise 2

E7   C7   B7   E7

Count: 1 2 3 4   1 2 3 4   1 2 3 4   1 2 3 4

Exercise 3

E7   C7   B7   E7

Count: 1 2 3 4   1 2 3 4   1 2 3 4   1 2 3 4

- These exercises show a simple chord progression that you can play by using dominant 7th chords. Perform these exercises to practice switching between the chords.

- Strum each chord toward the floor each time you see the ⊓ symbol. The shape of the note indicates how long you should hold each chord: ♫ (4 counts), ♪ (2 counts), ♩ (1 count).

playing major 7th chords

Major 7th (maj7) chords have a cheerful, jazzy sound. When you play a major 7th chord, you are simply adding a major 7th sound to a major chord. In many cases, you can play a major 7th chord instead of a major chord to jazz up the sound.

The easiest major 7th chords to play are Cmaj7, Fmaj7, Amaj7 and Dmaj7. All of these chords are open-position chords, which means they involve playing strings that do not have fingers pressing down on them.

The Dmaj7 chord requires a three-string barre, indicated by ⌢ in the chord diagram. To play a barre, you press down on multiple strings with a single finger. In most cases, you will use your index finger to barre the strings in the Dmaj7 chord, but you can also use any other finger. To make the Dmaj7 chord easier to play, roll your finger onto its side toward the nut to play the barre.

You can practice playing these major 7th chords individually and then practice switching between the chords.

Cmaj7

1 Place your middle finger on the 4th string, just behind the second fret.

2 Place your ring finger on the 5th string, just behind the third fret.

3 Strum the strings toward the floor, without strumming the 6th string.

Fmaj7

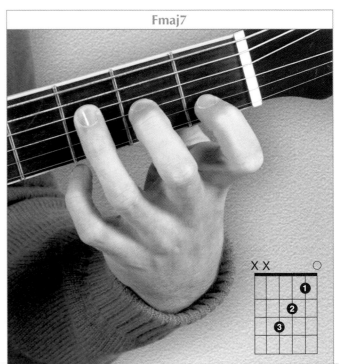

1 Place your index finger on the 2nd string, just behind the first fret.

2 Place your middle finger on the 3rd string, just behind the second fret.

3 Place your ring finger on the 4th string, just behind the third fret.

4 Strum the strings toward the floor, without strumming the 5th and 6th strings.

Why does the Fmaj7 chord sound the same as the F chord?

You may accidentally be touching the 1st string with your index finger. This mutes the 1st string, making the chord sound like the F chord.

Is there an alternate fingering for the Amaj7 chord?

Yes. You can place your middle finger on the 3rd string, behind the first fret, your ring finger on the 4th string, behind the second fret, and your pinky finger on the 2nd string, behind the second fret.

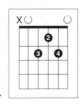

How should I move between the Cmaj7 and Fmaj7 chords?

To switch between the Cmaj7 and Fmaj7 chords, try to keep your middle and ring fingers in the same shape as they move across the strings. Even though you do not use your index finger in the Cmaj7 chord, keep this finger above the 2nd string and first fret, so it is ready to play this note for the Fmaj7 chord.

Amaj7

1 Place your index finger on the 3rd string, just behind the first fret.

2 Place your middle finger on the 4th string, just behind the second fret.

3 Place your ring finger on the 2nd string, just behind the second fret.

4 Strum the strings toward the floor, without strumming the 6th string.

Dmaj7

1 Place your index finger on the 1st, 2nd and 3rd strings, just behind the second fret.

2 Strum the strings toward the floor, without strumming the 5th and 6th strings.

playing minor 7th chords

You can play a minor 7th chord whenever a minor chord, such as Am, Em or Dm, is needed to jazz up a song. Minor 7th chords are created by adding a minor 7th sound to a minor chord. These chords are also referred to as open-position minor 7th chords. The term open-position refers to chords played near the nut and have strings that are strummed but do not have fingers pressing down on them. The easiest minor 7th chords to play are Am7, Em7 and Dm7.

The ⌒ symbol on the Dm7 chord diagram indicates that you need to barre or press down on two strings with a single finger. In this case, your index finger is placed on the 1st and 2nd strings, just behind the first fret. An easy way to play the barre in the Dm7 chord is to roll your finger onto its side toward the nut. You can also reposition your thumb on the back of the guitar to make it easier to play the barre in the Dm7 chord.

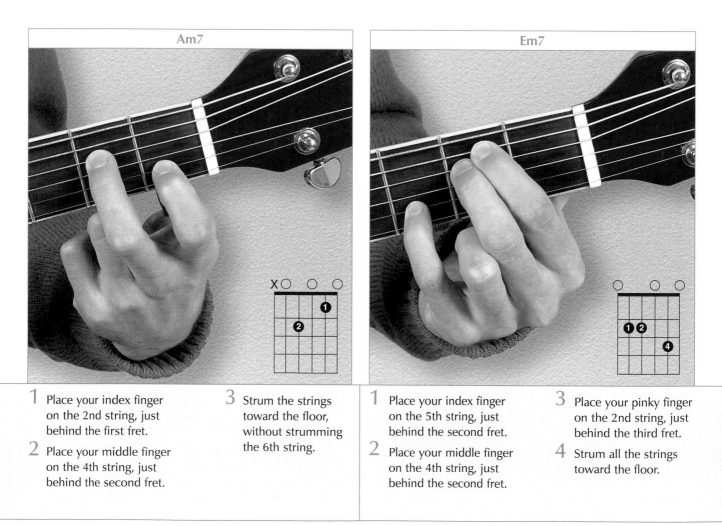

Am7	Em7

1 Place your index finger on the 2nd string, just behind the first fret.

2 Place your middle finger on the 4th string, just behind the second fret.

3 Strum the strings toward the floor, without strumming the 6th string.

1 Place your index finger on the 5th string, just behind the second fret.

2 Place your middle finger on the 4th string, just behind the second fret.

3 Place your pinky finger on the 2nd string, just behind the third fret.

4 Strum all the strings toward the floor.

Tip

Is there a way to create a more subtle sound when playing the Em7 chord?

Yes. You can use an alternate fingering for the Em7 chord to create a more subtle sound. Place your index finger on the 5th string, just behind the second fret, and strum the strings toward the floor. You may also find this alternate fingering easier since it only requires the use of one finger.

How can I quickly switch from the C chord to the Am7 chord?

With your fingers in position to play the C chord, raise your ring finger from the 5th string to form the Am7 chord.

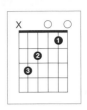

How can I quickly switch from the F chord to the Dm7 chord?

With your fingers in position to play the F chord, raise your ring finger from the 4th string to form the Dm7 chord.

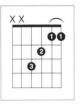

Dm7

1 Place your index finger on both the 1st and 2nd strings, just behind the first fret.

2 Place your middle finger on the 3rd string, just behind the second fret.

3 Strum the strings toward the floor, without strumming the 5th and 6th strings.

PRACTICE

Exercise 1

Am⁷   Em⁷   Dm⁷   Am⁷

Count: 1 2 3 4   1 2 3 4   1 2 3 4   1 2 3 4

Exercise 2

Am⁷   Em⁷   Dm⁷   Am⁷

Count: 1 2 3 4   1 2 3 4   1 2 3 4   1 2 3 4

Exercise 3

Am⁷   Em⁷   Dm⁷   Am⁷

Count: 1 2 3 4   1 2 3 4   1 2 3 4   1 2 3 4

- These exercises show a simple chord progression that you can play by using minor 7th chords. Perform these exercises to practice switching between the chords.

- Strum each chord toward the floor each time you see the ⊓ symbol. The shape of the note indicates how long you should hold each chord: ⫽ (4 counts), ⌒ (2 counts), ⌒ (1 count).

strumming patterns

There are many different strumming patterns that you can use when playing the guitar. Sometimes, written music will indicate which strumming pattern to use. You can also listen to a recording of a song to determine an appropriate strumming pattern or you can make up your own strumming pattern.

When choosing a strumming pattern for a song, you should consider the time signature of the song. For example, if the song you are playing is in 4/4 time, you would need to use a strumming pattern in 4/4 time. For information on time signatures, see page 44.

You should also consider the feel you are trying to create for the song, keeping in mind that more strums over a period of time produces an energetic feel and less strums over a period of time produces a more relaxed feel.

You can strum the strings using a combination of downstrokes and upstrokes to increase your playing speed. To perform a downstroke, strike all the strings toward the floor. To perform an upstroke, strike all the strings toward the ceiling.

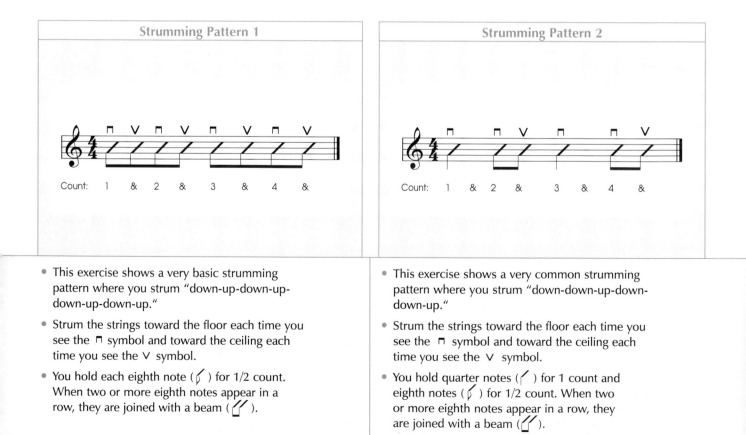

Strumming Pattern 1	Strumming Pattern 2

- This exercise shows a very basic strumming pattern where you strum "down-up-down-up-down-up-down-up."

- Strum the strings toward the floor each time you see the ⊓ symbol and toward the ceiling each time you see the ∨ symbol.

- You hold each eighth note (♪) for 1/2 count. When two or more eighth notes appear in a row, they are joined with a beam (♫).

- This exercise shows a very common strumming pattern where you strum "down-down-up-down-down-up."

- Strum the strings toward the floor each time you see the ⊓ symbol and toward the ceiling each time you see the ∨ symbol.

- You hold quarter notes (♩) for 1 count and eighth notes (♪) for 1/2 count. When two or more eighth notes appear in a row, they are joined with a beam (♫).

Tip

Are there other strumming patterns I can use?

Yes. Here are some more examples of strumming patterns you may want to use in your playing.

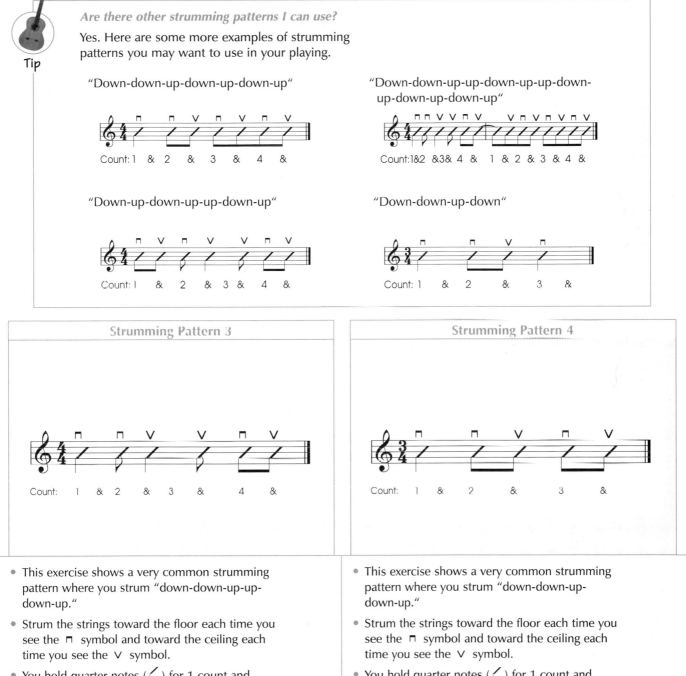

"Down-down-up-down-up-down-up"

Count: 1 & 2 & 3 & 4 &

"Down-down-up-up-down-up-up-down-up-down-up"

Count: 1&2 &3& 4 & 1 & 2 & 3 & 4 &

"Down-up-down-up-up-down-up"

Count: 1 & 2 & 3 & 4 &

"Down-down-up-down"

Count: 1 & 2 & 3 &

Strumming Pattern 3

Count: 1 & 2 & 3 & 4 &

Strumming Pattern 4

Count: 1 & 2 & 3 &

- This exercise shows a very common strumming pattern where you strum "down-down-up-up-down-up."

- Strum the strings toward the floor each time you see the ⊓ symbol and toward the ceiling each time you see the ∨ symbol.

- You hold quarter notes ( ) for 1 count and eighth notes ( ) for 1/2 count. When two or more eighth notes appear in a row, they are joined with a beam ( ).

- This exercise shows a very common strumming pattern where you strum "down-down-up-down-up."

- Strum the strings toward the floor each time you see the ⊓ symbol and toward the ceiling each time you see the ∨ symbol.

- You hold quarter notes ( ) for 1 count and eighth notes ( ) for 1/2 count. When two or more eighth notes appear in a row, they are joined with a beam ( ).

songs for practice

Amazing Grace

Man of Constant Sorrow

Scarborough Fair

Chapter 5

After learning basic chords, you can play barre chords and power chords to add flair to your music. This chapter discusses E-based and A-based barre chords, which are the most popular types of barre chords, as well as open-position and movable power chords. Some sample songs are also included to help you practice.

Playing Barre Chords and Power Chords

In this Chapter...

introduction to
barre chords

Barre (pronounced "bar") chords are chords that require you to use a barre. To form a barre, you press down on multiple strings with a single finger, usually your index finger. You also position the rest of your fingers on specific strings to form a chord. You can then move this finger shape to any location on the fingerboard to allow you to play many different chords. The finger shape you use to form a chord and the fret your index finger is positioned at determine which chord you will play.

Barre chords that use the same finger shape as the open-position E chord and the open-position A chord are the most common types of barre chords. Open-position chords are chords you play near the

nut that use strings that do not have a finger pressing down on them.

Since barre chords allow you to play chords at different locations on the fingerboard, these chords are often referred to as movable chords. Using movable chords allows you to play chords away from the nut of the guitar and gives you more versatility in your playing.

Learning to play barre chords can be difficult. You may find playing barre chords painful at first because you need to hold your fingers in an awkward position and exert enough pressure to get all the strings to ring properly. This discomfort will subside with practice.

What do barre chord diagrams look like?

Chord diagrams for barre chords look slightly different from regular chord diagrams. The following chord diagram is color coded to show the three main parts of a barre chord diagram.

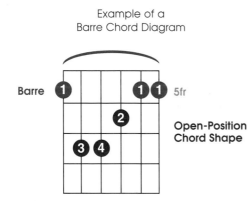

Example of a
Barre Chord Diagram

Barre

This part of the barre chord diagram represents the barre. The ❶, which represents your index finger, only appears on the strings that do not have another finger pressing down on them. Your index finger should be pressing down on all the strings under the ⌒ symbol.

Open-Position Chord Shape

While your index finger forms the barre, you use your middle, ring and pinky fingers to form the chord shape for the chord.

Fret Indicator

Most barre chord diagrams indicate at which fret to position your index finger by displaying the fret number followed by the letters "fr". If a barre chord is to be played close to the nut, the fret indicator is not included.

What are the benefits of playing barre chords?

More Versatility

Learning barre chords can give you more options when playing the guitar. For example, barre chords allow you to play in all of the twelve keys, whereas you can only play in five or six keys when you are just using open-position chords. A key determines the notes and chords you play in a song. Moreover, certain chords cannot even be played as open-position chords, and therefore you need to play them as barre chords.

Less Memory Work

Another advantage to using barre chords instead of open-position chords is that you only have to learn one finger shape to play twelve different chords. The finger shape you use and the location of your fingers on the fingerboard determine the chord you will play. If you played every chord as an open-position chord, you would need to learn a different finger shape for each chord. The reason why barre chords allow you to play so many chords with one finger shape is that your index finger acts as a new nut, allowing you to play chords at any fret on the fingerboard.

Easier to Switch Between Chords

Barre chords can make playing the guitar easier. The location of a barre chord on the fingerboard can sometimes be closer to other chords you want to play than if you were playing open-position chords. This way you do not have to move your hand as much to switch between chords.

More Control

Barre chords give you more control over the sounds your guitar makes. For example, when you play a barre chord and you want a string to stop ringing, you simply release the pressure of your finger from the string slightly. When you play an open-position chord, which contains strings that do not have a finger pressing down on them, you cannot easily stop a string from ringing. The ability to control how long strings ring when playing barre chords can give your playing a cleaner sound.

CONTINUED...

introduction to
barre chords

How can I improve my sound when playing a barre chord?

Position Your Fingers Correctly

When you form a barre chord, try to apply equal pressure with your index finger across all the strings. You should also bend your index finger very slightly and roll this finger slightly onto its side toward the nut. Using the side of your finger rather than the flat surface of your finger will help you achieve the best tone.

When you position your other fingers to form the chord, make sure you are using the tips of your fingers to press down on the strings. You should also ensure that each finger is just behind the fret and not accidentally touching other strings. Be careful that you do not pull your index finger out of place when you position your other fingers.

You may want to try picking each string individually to make sure they ring clearly. If you hear buzzing or muted sounds, check your fingers to make sure they are positioned correctly.

Position Your Hand Correctly

If you find that any of the notes in the chord are not sounding when you play a barre chord, try moving your palm more in front of the fingerboard. You may also want to try moving your elbow closer to your body to change the angle that your hand approaches the strings on the fingerboard.

Position Your Thumb Correctly

The placement of your thumb is also important. Make sure you position your thumb between your index and middle finger on the back of the neck, which will allow you to add pressure to the strings. Even though the pressure should be firm, try to keep your wrist and hand as relaxed as possible.

What can I do to make playing barre chords easier?

- To become more comfortable forming a barre with your index finger, you may want to try the following exercise. Hold down the 1st and 2nd strings with your index finger. When this feels comfortable, try holding down the 1st, 2nd and 3rd strings. Keep increasing the number of strings until you are holding down all six strings.

- Try to determine whether it is easier for you to form the barre first and then form the chord with your other fingers, or to form the chord first and then form the barre.

- Try practicing barre chords on the frets closer to the body of the guitar. Since the frets are closer together in this area, your fingers do not have to stretch as far.

- If possible, practice on an electric guitar because the strings on an electric guitar are easier to press down than on an acoustic guitar.

- Try to keep your hand relaxed, making sure your fingers are not stiff.

- You can perform finger exercises, such as the exercises shown on page 37, before you practice barre chords.

Is there a different strumming technique I can use to make barre chords more interesting?

Once you are comfortable playing barre chords, you may want to play arpeggios, instead of strumming all the strings for chords. To play an arpeggio, you simply pick individual strings rather than strumming them all at once. For more information on playing arpeggios, see page 194.

the E-based major barre chord

E-based barre chords are the most common types of barre chords. The E-based major barre chord is based on the finger positioning of the E major chord. For information on the E major chord, see page 64.

To form the E-based major barre chord, you use your middle, ring and pinky fingers to form an E major chord. Keeping the E major chord formation, you then slide your fingers along the fingerboard toward the bridge by one fret and form a barre by using your index finger to press down all the strings one

fret behind. You can keep your fingers in the same formation and slide your fingers along the fingerboard to another fret to play a different chord.

The name of each chord you play using the E-based major barre formation is determined by the note your index finger plays on the 6th string. For example, when your index finger is behind the first fret, you play an F major chord because the note played by the 6th string at the first fret is F.

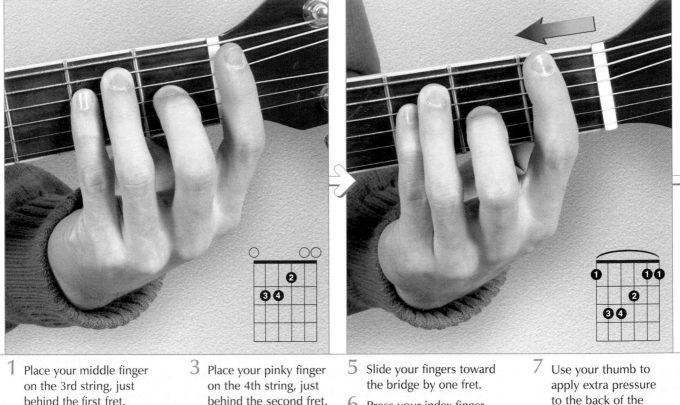

1 Place your middle finger on the 3rd string, just behind the first fret.

2 Place your ring finger on the 5th string, just behind the second fret.

3 Place your pinky finger on the 4th string, just behind the second fret.

4 Position your index finger above the nut, but not touching the strings.

5 Slide your fingers toward the bridge by one fret.

6 Press your index finger firmly across the strings just behind the first fret, pressing down all the strings.

7 Use your thumb to apply extra pressure to the back of the neck of the guitar.

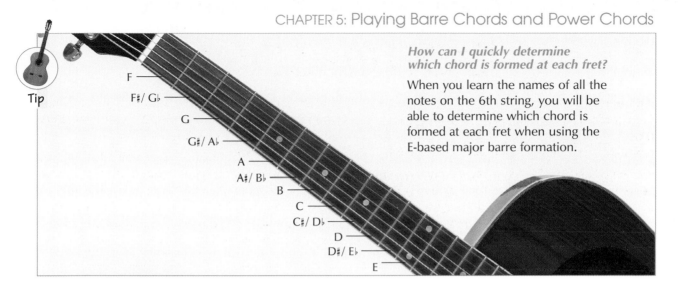

Tip

F
F♯/ G♭
G
G♯/ A♭
A
A♯/ B♭
B
C
C♯/ D♭
D
D♯/ E♭
E

How can I quickly determine which chord is formed at each fret?

When you learn the names of all the notes on the 6th string, you will be able to determine which chord is formed at each fret when using the E-based major barre formation.

PRACTICE

Exercise 1

G   A   C   A

Count: 1 2 3 4   1 2 3 4   1 2 3 4   1 2 3 4

Exercise 2

B   E   D   E

Count: 1 2 3 4   1 2 3 4   1 2 3 4   1 2 3 4

Exercise 3

D   A   C   A

Count: 1 2 3 4   1 2 3 4   1 2 3 4   1 2 3 4

8 Strum all the strings toward the floor.

9 Repeat steps **5** to **8** on each fret to play all possible major chords.

• These exercises show simple chord progressions that you can play by using E-based major barre chords. Perform these exercises to practice switching between the chords.

• Strum each chord toward the floor each time you see the ⊓ symbol. The shape of the note indicates how long you should hold each chord: ♩ (4 counts), ♩ (2 counts), ♩ (1 count).

other E-based barre chords

Once you are familiar with the E-based major barre chord, you can learn the E-based minor, minor 7th and dominant 7th chords using the same method of barring strings with your index finger. Minor 7th chords have a mellower, jazzier sound than minor chords and dominant 7th chords produce a more complex sound than major chords.

To form one of these E-based barre chords, you use different combinations of your middle, ring and pinky fingers to form the chord. You then form the barre by placing your index finger across all six strings.

The name of each chord you play using these E-based barre chord formations is determined by the note your index finger plays on the 6th string. For example, when your index finger is behind the tenth fret and you are using the minor fingering, you play a D minor chord because the note played by the 6th string at the tenth fret is D. For more information on the names of the notes on the 6th string, see the top of page 87.

E-Based Minor Barre Chord

E-Based Minor 7th Barre Chord

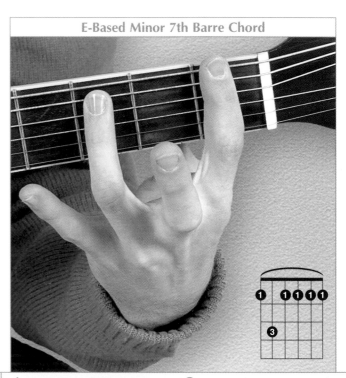

1 Place your ring finger on the 5th string, just behind the third fret.

2 Place your pinky finger on the 4th string, just behind the third fret.

3 Press your index finger across all the strings, just behind the first fret.

4 Strum the strings toward the floor.

5 Slide your fingers toward the bridge by one fret at a time, repeating step 4 to play all the minor chords.

1 Place your ring finger on the 5th string, just behind the third fret.

2 Press your index finger across all the strings, just behind the first fret.

3 Strum the strings toward the floor.

4 Slide your fingers toward the bridge by one fret at a time, repeating step 3 to play all the minor 7th chords.

Can I use my thumb to help me form an E-based minor, minor 7th or dominant 7th barre chord?

Yes. You can wrap your thumb around the fingerboard to hold down the 6th string for the barre. Your index finger only needs to hold down the 1st, 2nd, 3rd and 4th strings, since your ring finger always plays the 5th string. If you have large hands, you may want to try this modification. Otherwise, this technique is best left to more advanced guitarists.

I am having trouble playing the E minor (Em) barre chord at the twelfth fret. What can I do?

On an acoustic guitar, playing the Em barre chord at the twelfth fret is almost impossible. Instead, you should play the Em open-position chord. An open-position chord is a chord you play with some strings not held down. For information on the Em open-position chord, see page 66.

E-Based Dominant 7th Barre Chord

1 Place your middle finger on the 3rd string, just behind the second fret.

2 Place your ring finger on the 5th string, just behind the third fret.

3 Press your index finger across all the strings, just behind the first fret.

4 Strum the strings toward the floor.

5 Slide your fingers toward the bridge by one fret at a time, repeating step 4 to play all the dominant 7th chords.

PRACTICE

Exercise 1

Fm   Am   Cm   Fm

Count: 1 2 3 4   1 2 3 4   1 2 3 4   1 2 3 4

Exercise 2

F^7 D$\flat^7$ G^7 C^7

Count: 1 2 3 4   1 2 3 4   1 2 3 4   1 2 3 4

Exercise 3

Bm^7 Am^7 Dm^7 Gm^7

Count: 1 2 3 4   1 2 3 4   1 2 3 4   1 2 3 4

• These exercises show simple chord progressions that you can play by using E-based barre chords. Perform these exercises to practice switching between the chords.

• Strum each chord toward the floor each time you see the ⊓ symbol. The shape of the note indicates how long you should hold each chord: ⫿⫿ (4 counts), ⫽ (2 counts), ⟋ (1 count).

the A-based major barre chord

The A-based major barre chord is one of the most common types of barre chords. You can use the finger position for the A-based major barre chord on any fret on the fingerboard to play many different major chords.

An easy way to learn the A-based major barre chord is to first form the A major chord using your middle, ring and pinky fingers. For information on the A major chord, see page 64. Then slide your fingers down one fret, keeping the same position of your fingers. You then need to form a barre by pressing down on the first five strings with your index finger just behind the first fret. Even though you do not need to barre the 6th string, you can barre the 6th string if it feels more comfortable.

To practice A-based major barre chords, you can practice the exercises on pages 63 and 65, substituting the A-based major barre chords for the major chords.

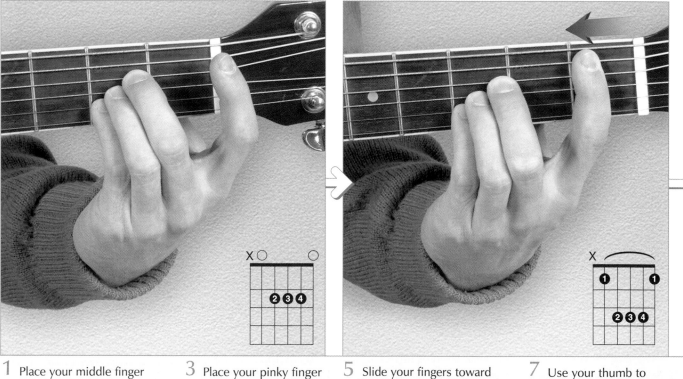

1 Place your middle finger on the 4th string, just behind the second fret.

2 Place your ring finger on the 3rd string, just behind the second fret.

3 Place your pinky finger on the 2nd string, just behind the second fret.

4 Position your index finger above the nut, but not touching the strings.

5 Slide your fingers toward the bridge by one fret.

6 Press your index finger firmly across the strings just behind the first fret, pressing down the first five strings.

7 Use your thumb to apply extra pressure to the back of the neck of the guitar.

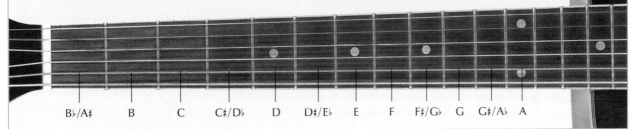

Tip

Which major chords can I play using the A-based major barre chord?

There are twelve different A-based major barre chords that you can play. The name of each A-based major barre chord is determined by the note that is played on the 5th string at the fret you are barring with your index finger. You can learn the name of the note at each fret on the 5th string to identify which major chord you are playing.

B♭/A♯   B   C   C♯/D♭   D   D♯/E♭   E   F   F♯/G♭   G   G♯/A♭   A

PRACTICE

Exercise 1

D   A   C   D

Count: 1 2 3 4   1 2 3 4   1 2 3 4   1 2 3 4

Exercise 2

E♭   B♭   F   C

Count: 1 2 3 4   1 2 3 4   1 2 3 4   1 2 3 4

Exercise 3

G   C   B♭   D

Count: 1 2 3 4   1 2 3 4   1 2 3 4   1 2 3 4

8 Strum the strings toward the floor, without strumming the 6th string.

9 Repeat steps **5** to **8** on each fret to play all possible major chords.

- These exercises show simple chord progressions that you can play by using A-based barre chords. Perform these exercises to practice switching between the chords.

- Strum each chord toward the floor each time you see the ⊓ symbol. The shape of the note indicates how long you should hold each chord: 𝅗𝅥 (4 counts), ♩ (2 counts), ♪ (1 count).

other A-based barre chords

When you are familiar with the A-based major barre chord, you can learn the A-based minor and minor 7th barre chords using the same method of barring strings.

To form an A-based minor or minor 7th barre chord, you use a combination of your middle, ring and pinky fingers to form an A minor or minor 7th chord. Then form a barre with your index finger across the first five strings. For information on the A minor chord, see page 66. For information on the A minor 7th chord, see page 74.

You can use the finger positions for these barre chords at any fret on the fingerboard to play many different minor and minor 7th chords. Like the A-based major barre chords, the note played on the 5th string by your index finger determines the name of each A-based minor and minor 7th barre chord. For information on the notes played on the 5th string, see the top of page 91.

For practice, play a chord progression that uses A-based major, minor and minor 7th barre chords.

A-based Minor Barre Chord

1 Place your middle finger on the 2nd string, just behind the second fret.

2 Place your ring finger on the 4th string, just behind the third fret.

3 Place your pinky finger on the 3rd string, just behind the third fret.

4 Press your index finger across the first five strings, just behind the first fret.

5 Strum the strings toward the floor, without strumming the 6th string.

6 Slide your fingers toward the bridge by one fret at a time, repeating step 5 to play all the minor chords.

Tip

I find the A minor chord difficult to play at the twelfth fret. What can I do?

The shape of acoustic guitars make it difficult to play the A minor chord at the twelfth fret. If you are playing an acoustic guitar, play the A minor chord as an open-position chord, instead of using a barre. To form the open-position A minor chord, see page 66. You may also want to use the E-based barre chord to play the A minor chord, as shown on page 88.

What are the advantages of playing A-based and E-based barre chords together?

By using combinations of A-based and E-based barre chords, many chords will be positioned closer together on the fingerboard than if you were only using one barre chord. For example, if you use the A-based and E-based barre chords to play the D and A chords respectively, the notes for the D and A chords are on the same fret. If you only use one barre chord, the notes for the D and A chords are five frets apart.

A-based Minor 7th Barre Chord

1 Place your middle finger on the 2nd string, just behind the second fret.

2 Place your ring finger on the 4th string, just behind the third fret.

3 Press your index finger across the first five strings, just behind the first fret.

4 Strum the strings toward the floor, without strumming the 6th string.

5 Slide your fingers toward the bridge by one fret at a time, repeating step 4 to play all the minor 7th chords.

CONTINUED...

other A-based
barre chords

You can learn the A-based dominant 7th and major 7th barre chords using the same method of barring strings as the A-based major barre chord.

To play an A-based dominant 7th or major 7th barre chord, you use a combination of your middle, ring and pinky fingers to form an A dominant 7th or major 7th chord. Then use your index finger to barre the first five strings. For information on the A dominant 7th chord, see page 69. For information on the A major 7th chord, see page 73.

Just like all other A-based barre chords, the name of each A-based dominant 7th and major 7th barre chord is determined by the note played on the 5th string by your index finger. For information on the notes played on the 5th string, see the top of page 91.

For practice, play a few chord progressions of A-based dominant 7th and major 7th barre chords. You may also want to refer to other practice examples in this book and replace the major chords with A-based major 7th barre chords.

A-based Dominant 7th Barre Chord

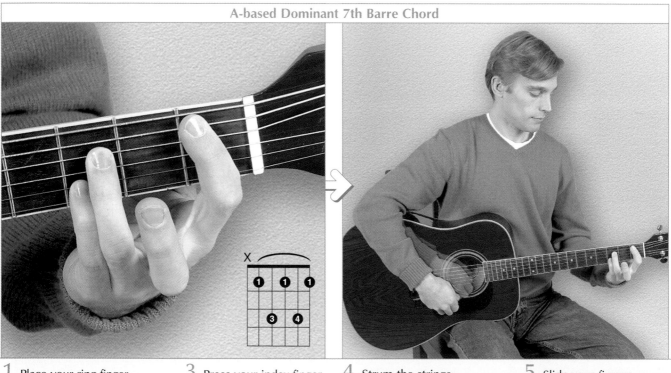

1 Place your ring finger on the 4th string, just behind the third fret.

2 Place your pinky finger on the 2nd string, just behind the third fret.

3 Press your index finger across the first five strings, just behind the first fret.

4 Strum the strings toward the floor, without strumming the 6th string.

5 Slide your fingers toward the bridge by one fret at a time, repeating step 4 to play all the dominant 7th chords.

Tip

How can I make barre chords easier to play?

Make sure the tip of your thumb is firmly pressed against the back of the neck and is closer to the bottom edge of the neck. Your thumb should also be perpendicular to the neck. In this position, your thumb acts as a pivot, allowing you to stretch your fingers as far as possible. You should also remember to curl your fingers so your fingertips press down on the strings, which helps to avoid touching other strings by accident.

My hands are sore from playing barre chords. Should I continue to play?

No. As with any chord or technique, you should never try to force yourself to play these chords if your hands ache—otherwise you may injure your hands. If you feel any pain in your hands, stop playing immediately. Because these chords are difficult, they may take time to learn. Work at learning them gradually and with time and practice, you will be able to master them.

A-based Major 7th Barre Chord

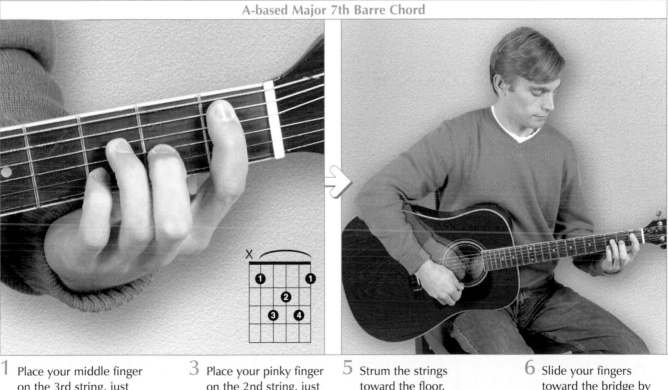

1 Place your middle finger on the 3rd string, just behind the second fret.

2 Place your ring finger on the 4th string, just behind the third fret.

3 Place your pinky finger on the 2nd string, just behind the third fret.

4 Press your index finger across the first five strings, just behind the first fret.

5 Strum the strings toward the floor, without strumming the 6th string.

6 Slide your fingers toward the bridge by one fret at a time, repeating step 5 to play all the major 7th chords.

open-position power chords

An open-position chord is a chord that is played by strumming the strings of a guitar without fretting, or pressing down, some of the strings. Open-position power chords also have at least one string not pressed down.

An open-position power chord is composed of the two or three lowest notes of its corresponding major chord. The open-position power chords are A5, which is based on the A major chord, E5, which is based on the E major chord, and D5, which is based on the D major chord. For information on the A, E and D major chords, see pages 63 to 65.

Power chords are often referred to as "5" chords because the second note of the chord is always five steps higher than the root note. For example, when playing the A5 power chord, the root note is A and the second note of the chord is E, which is five steps higher than A.

Due to their lower pitch and stripped down sound, power chords are popular in hard rock and heavy metal songs. You can hear power chords in older songs, such as "Iron Man" by Black Sabbath, and also in modern songs by bands such as Green Day and Blink 182.

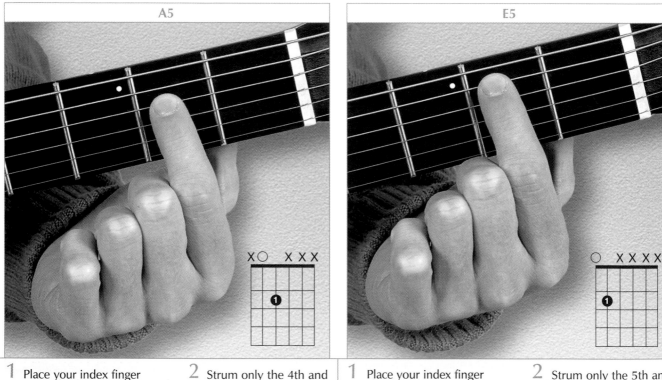

A5

1 Place your index finger on the 4th string, just behind the second fret.

2 Strum only the 4th and 5th strings toward the floor.

E5

1 Place your index finger on the 5th string, just behind the second fret.

2 Strum only the 5th and 6th strings toward the floor.

How can I play the three-string versions of the A5, E5 and D5 chords?

Tip

To play the three-string version of:

The A5 chord

Place your index finger on the 4th string, just behind the second fret, and your middle finger on the 3rd string, just behind the second fret. Then strum the 3rd, 4th and 5th strings toward the floor.

The E5 chord

Place your index finger on the 5th string, just behind the second fret, and your middle finger on the 4th string, just behind the second fret. Then strum the 4th, 5th and 6th strings toward the floor.

The D5 chord

Place your index finger on the 3rd string, just behind the second fret, and your ring finger on the 2nd string, just behind the third fret. Then strum the 2nd, 3rd and 4th strings toward the floor.

D5

PRACTICE

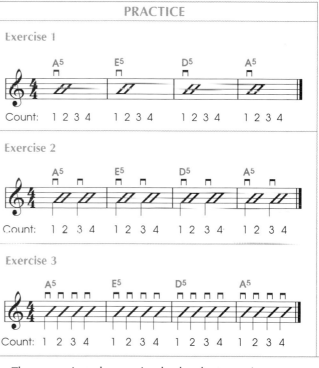

1 Place your index finger on the 3rd string, just behind the second fret.

2 Strum only the 3rd and 4th strings toward the floor.

- These exercises show a simple chord progression that you can play by using open-position power chords. Perform these exercises to practice switching between the chords.

- Strum each chord toward the floor each time you see the ⊓ symbol. The shape of the note indicates how long you should hold each chord: ⧸⧸ (4 counts), ⧸ (2 counts), ⧸ (1 count).

97

movable power chords

Movable power chords are power chords you can play on any fret on the fingerboard. This allows you to play 12 different chords using the same hand position. Movable power chords are composed of the two or three lowest notes of either the E-based or A-based major barre chords. For more information on E-based and A-based major barre chords, see pages 86 and 90.

When playing the E-based movable power chord, the chord you play depends on the name of the note played on the 6th string. When playing the A-based movable power chord, the chord you play depends on the name of the note played on the 5th string.

Power chords are considered neither major nor minor and are often referred to as 5 chords since the two notes that make up a power chord are five steps apart.

E-Based Movable Power Chord

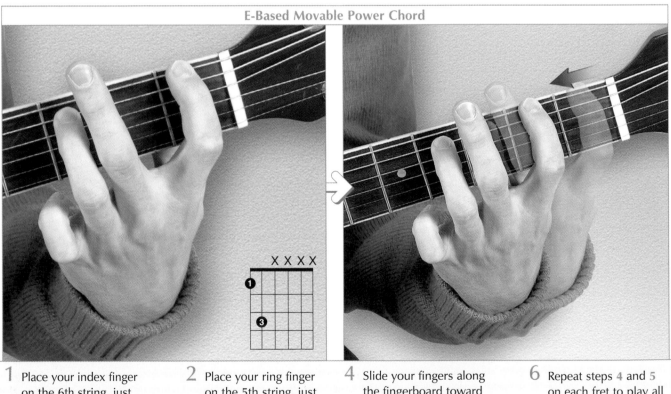

1 Place your index finger on the 6th string, just behind the first fret.

2 Place your ring finger on the 5th string, just behind the third fret.

3 Strum the 5th and 6th strings toward the floor.

4 Slide your fingers along the fingerboard toward the bridge by one fret.

5 Strum the 5th and 6th strings toward the floor again.

6 Repeat steps 4 and 5 on each fret to play all the E-based movable power chords.

Tip

How can I play the three-string version of a movable power chord?

To play the three-string version of a movable power chord, place your pinky finger underneath your ring finger on the next string, just behind the same fret. For example, to play the three-string version of the E-based movable power chord, place your index finger on the 6th string, just behind the first fret. Position your ring finger on the 5th string and your pinky finger on the 4th string with both fingers just behind the third fret. Then strum the 4th, 5th and 6th strings toward the floor.

Is there a way to mute the other strings when playing movable power chords?

Yes. When playing E-based power chords, let your index finger lightly touch the other strings you do not want to sound while pushing down on the 6th string. When playing A-based power chords, your index finger should reach over the 5th string to also lightly touch the 6th string. When you mute the strings in this manner, the strings will not sound if you accidentally strum them. You should hear only the two notes you want to play.

A-Based Movable Power Chord

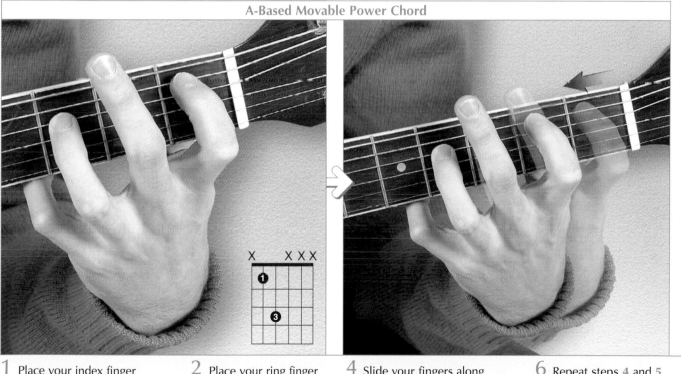

1 Place your index finger on the 5th string, just behind the first fret.

2 Place your ring finger on the 4th string, just behind the third fret.

3 Strum the 4th and 5th strings toward the floor.

4 Slide your fingers along the fingerboard toward the bridge by one fret.

5 Strum the 4th and 5th strings toward the floor.

6 Repeat steps 4 and 5 on each fret to play all the A-based movable power chords.

songs for practice

Auld Lang Syne

Robbie Burns

A♭ Minor Blues

Minor Blues

Chapter 6

Understanding how to play single notes allows you to play the melodies of songs. In this chapter, you will learn how to play single notes on each of the six strings of the guitar, as well as how to combine the notes to play scales and simple melodies. This chapter also discusses how to play melodies while keeping your fretting hand in one position on the fingerboard and how to play two notes at the same time.

Playing Single Notes

In this Chapter...

playing notes on the 1st string

You can play a single note on the guitar by simply picking a string, with or without a finger pressing on the string. The ability to play single notes allows you to play the melodies of songs, instead of simply strumming chords, and also helps you tune your guitar. For information on tuning your guitar, see page 32.

For the notes shown below, your fretting hand should be in first position. To place your hand in first position, your index finger should be over the first fret, your middle finger over the second fret, your ring finger

over the third fret and your pinky finger over the fourth fret. When playing in first position, E, F and G are the notes on the 1st string.

You should always try to keep each finger of your fretting hand over its respective fret, just an inch or less above the strings. This allows you to keep your fingers in proper position to play the next note. You should also make sure you press the strings using only the tip of your fingers.

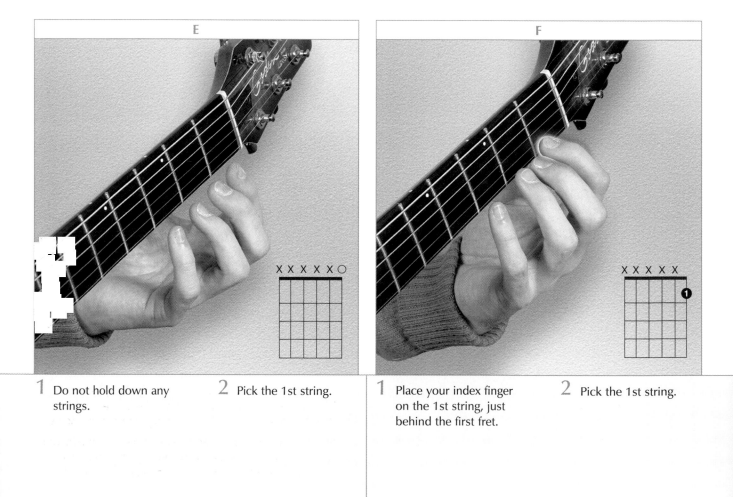

E	F

1 Do not hold down any strings.

2 Pick the 1st string.

1 Place your index finger on the 1st string, just behind the first fret.

2 Pick the 1st string.

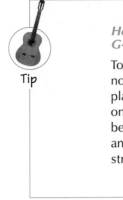

Tip

How can I play an F-sharp (F♯) or G-flat (G♭) note on the 1st string?

To play an F♯ or G♭ note on the 1st string, place your middle finger on the 1st string, just behind the second fret, and then pick the 1st string.

X X X X X
②

How can I play a G-sharp (G♯) or A-flat (A♭) note on the 1st string?

To play a G♯ or A♭ note on the 1st string, place your pinky finger on the 1st string, just behind the fourth fret, and then pick the 1st string.

X X X X X
④

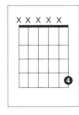

G

X X X X X
③

1 Place your ring finger on the 1st string, just behind the third fret.

2 Pick the 1st string.

PRACTICE

Exercise 1

(E)   (F)   (G)   (F)
Count: 1 2 3 4   1 2 3 4   1 2 3 4   1 2 3 4

Exercise 2

(E)   (F)   (G)   (F)
Count: 1 2 3 4   1 2 3 4   1 2 3 4   1 2 3 4

Exercise 3

(E)   (F)   (G)   (F)
Count: 1 2 3 4   1 2 3 4   1 2 3 4   1 2 3 4

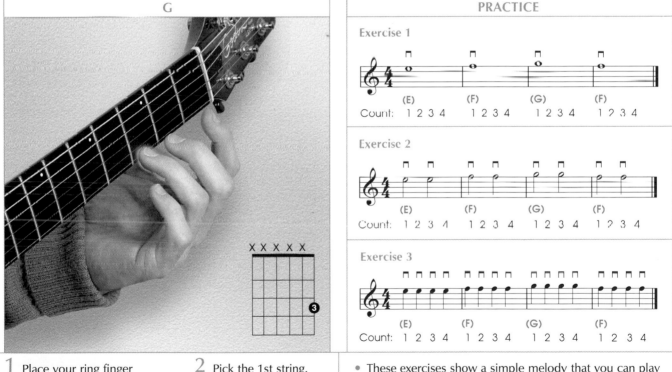

- These exercises show a simple melody that you can play by using single notes played on the 1st string. Perform these exercises to practice switching between the notes.

- Pick the 1st string each time you see the ⊓ symbol. The shape of the note indicates how long you should hold each note: ○ (4 counts), ♩ (2 counts), ♪ (1 count).

105

playing notes on the 2nd string

When playing in first position, B, C and D are the notes on the 2nd string. For information on playing in first position, see page 104.

When playing a note followed by a higher note on the same string, you can leave the finger playing the first note down on the string while you fret the higher note. This helps ensure a smooth sound between the two

notes. For example, if you play C at the first fret of the 2nd string followed by D at the third fret on the same string, leave your index finger down on the first fret while you press your ring finger on the third fret.

Practice playing the notes you have learned to play on the 1st and 2nd strings until your fingers become accustomed to finding the notes.

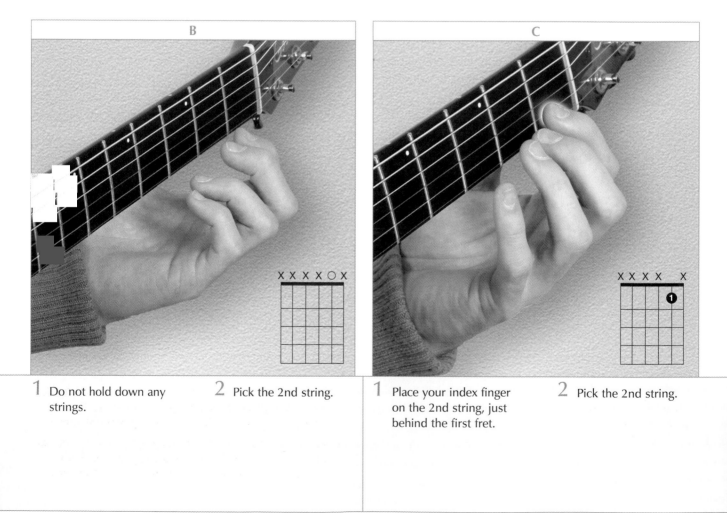

B	C
X X X X O X	X X X X X ❶

1 Do not hold down any strings.

2 Pick the 2nd string.

1 Place your index finger on the 2nd string, just behind the first fret.

2 Pick the 2nd string.

Tip

How can I play a C-sharp (C♯) or D-flat (D♭) note on the 2nd string?

To play a C♯ or D♭ note on the 2nd string, place your middle finger on the 2nd string, just behind the second fret, and then pick the 2nd string.

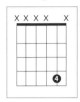

How can I play a D-sharp (D♯) or E-flat (E♭) note on the 2nd string?

To play a D♯ or E♭ note on the 2nd string, place your pinky finger on the 2nd string, just behind the fourth fret, and then pick the 2nd string.

D

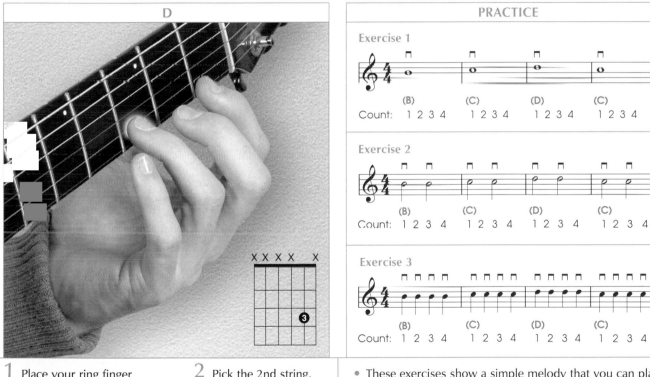

1 Place your ring finger on the 2nd string, just behind the third fret.

2 Pick the 2nd string.

PRACTICE

Exercise 1

(B)   (C)   (D)   (C)
Count: 1 2 3 4   1 2 3 4   1 2 3 4   1 2 3 4

Exercise 2

(B)   (C)   (D)   (C)
Count: 1 2 3 4   1 2 3 4   1 2 3 4   1 2 3 4

Exercise 3

(B)   (C)   (D)   (C)
Count: 1 2 3 4   1 2 3 4   1 2 3 4   1 2 3 4

- These exercises show a simple melody that you can play by using single notes played on the 2nd string. Perform these exercises to practice switching between the notes.

- Pick the 2nd string each time you see the ⊓ symbol. The shape of the note indicates how long you should hold each note: o (4 counts), ♩ (2 counts), ♩ (1 count).

playing notes on the 3rd string

When playing in first position, G, A, and B are the notes on the 3rd string. For information on playing in first position, see page 104.

Keep in mind that there is more than one way to play a note on the guitar. For example, playing the B note with your pinky finger on the 3rd string, just behind the fourth fret, is the same as playing the B note on the 2nd string without holding down the string. You can play the note in whichever way feels more comfortable and allows you to easily move from one

note to another. However, playing a note on a fretted string has the advantage of allowing you to stop the string from sounding by simply releasing your finger from the string. To stop playing a note on a string that is not fretted, you will need to mute the string. To mute a string, place your finger lightly on the string.

Practice playing the notes you have learned to play on the 1st, 2nd and 3rd strings until your fingers become accustomed to finding the notes.

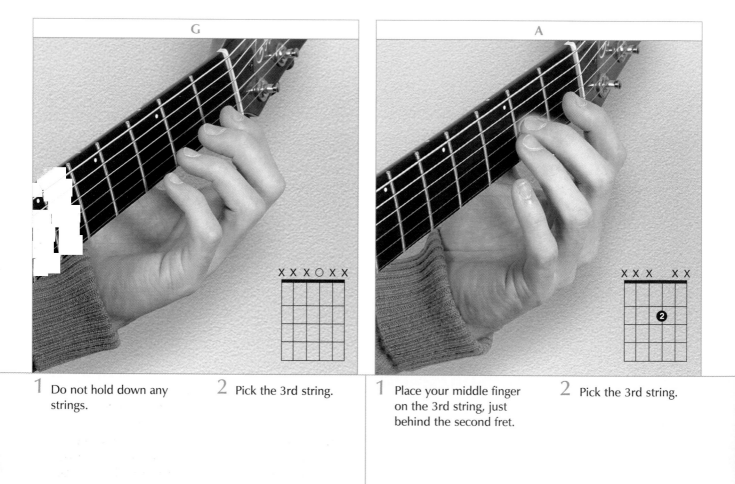

G	A
x x x o x x	x x x x x

1 Do not hold down any strings.

2 Pick the 3rd string.

1 Place your middle finger on the 3rd string, just behind the second fret.

2 Pick the 3rd string.

Tip

How can I play a G-sharp (G♯) or A-flat (A♭) note on the 3rd string?

To play a G♯ or A♭ note on the 3rd string, place your index finger on the 3rd string, just behind the first fret, and then pick the 3rd string.

x x x   x x
①

How can I play an A-sharp (A♯) or B-flat (B♭) note on the 3rd string?

To play an A♯ or B♭ note on the 3rd string, place your ring finger on the 3rd string, just behind the third fret, and then pick the 3rd string.

x x x   x x
③

B

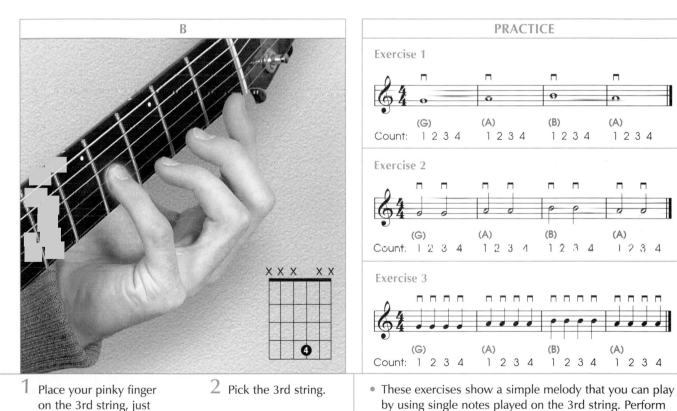

x x x   x x
④

1 Place your pinky finger on the 3rd string, just behind the fourth fret.

2 Pick the 3rd string.

PRACTICE

Exercise 1

(G)　　(A)　　(B)　　(A)
Count: 1 2 3 4　1 2 3 4　1 2 3 4　1 2 3 4

Exercise 2

(G)　　(A)　　(B)　　(A)
Count: 1 2 3 4　1 2 3 4　1 2 3 4　1 2 3 4

Exercise 3

(G)　　(A)　　(B)　　(A)
Count: 1 2 3 4　1 2 3 4　1 2 3 4　1 2 3 4

- These exercises show a simple melody that you can play by using single notes played on the 3rd string. Perform these exercises to practice switching between the notes.

- Pick the 3rd string each time you see the ⊓ symbol. The shape of the note indicates how long you should hold each note: o (4 counts), ♩ (2 counts), ♩ (1 count).

playing notes on the 4th string

When playing in first position, D, E and F are the notes on the 4th string. For information on playing in first position, see page 104.

When playing single notes, you should always try to keep your hands and shoulders relaxed. You may want to take a few deep breaths if you start to feel your hands or shoulders tensing up. To help develop good single note picking skills, you should start slowly and not rush through the picking exercises.

Remember to keep your fretting hand in first position when playing a single note so that your fingers are in the proper position to play another note. Also, try to keep your fingers just an inch or less above the strings, but not right on the strings.

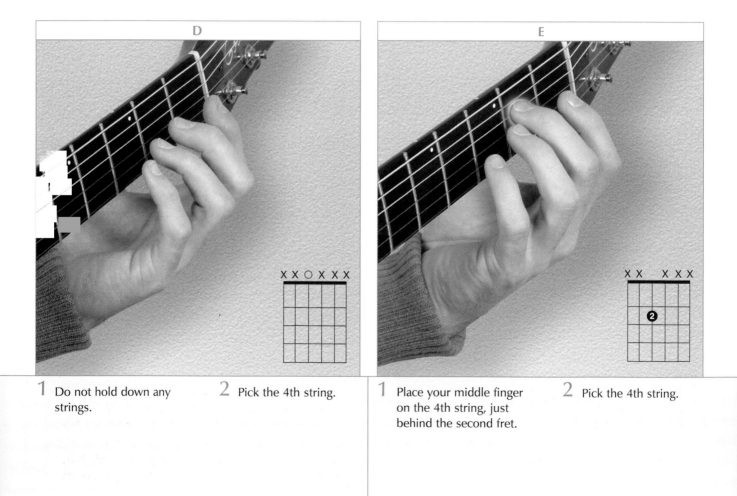

D

1 Do not hold down any strings.

2 Pick the 4th string.

E

1 Place your middle finger on the 4th string, just behind the second fret.

2 Pick the 4th string.

Tip

How can I play a D-sharp (D♯) or E-flat (E♭) note on the 4th string?

To play a D♯ or E♭ note on the 4th string, place your index finger on the 4th string, just behind the first fret, and then pick the 4th string.

How can I play an F-sharp (F♯) or G-flat (G♭) note on the 4th string?

To play an F♯ or G♭ note on the 4th string, place your pinky finger on the 4th string, just behind the fourth fret, and then pick the 4th string.

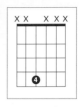

F

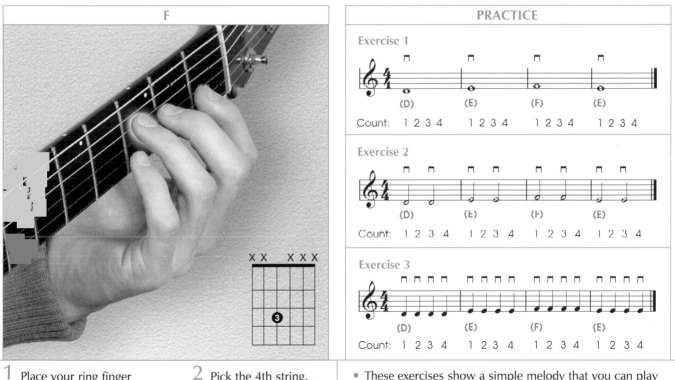

1 Place your ring finger on the 4th string, just behind the third fret.

2 Pick the 4th string.

PRACTICE

Exercise 1

(D)   (E)   (F)   (E)

Count: 1 2 3 4   1 2 3 4   1 2 3 4   1 2 3 4

Exercise 2

(D)   (E)   (F)   (E)

Count: 1 2 3 4   1 2 3 4   1 2 3 4   1 2 3 4

Exercise 3

(D)   (E)   (F)   (E)

Count: 1 2 3 4   1 2 3 4   1 2 3 4   1 2 3 4

• These exercises show a simple melody that you can play by using single notes played on the 4th string. Perform these exercises to practice switching between the notes.

• Pick the 4th string each time you see the ⊓ symbol. The shape of the note indicates how long you should hold each note: 𝅝 (4 counts), 𝅗𝅥 (2 counts), 𝅘𝅥 (1 count).

playing notes on the 5th string

When playing in first position, A, B and C are the notes the 5th string. For information on playing in first position, see page 104.

You can practice the notes you have learned on the first five strings to play the C major scale—C, D, E, F, G, A, B and C. A scale is composed of eight successive notes, in which the first and last notes are the same but are one octave apart. Try to play the notes slowly at first and then slightly increase the speed as you become more comfortable. You should make sure you always maintain a steady rhythm. Practice playing the C major scale until your fingers become accustomed to finding the notes.

If the notes you play sound fuzzy, you can try to slightly adjust your fingers on the frets until the sound becomes clearer. Remember to press the strings using only the tips of your fingers.

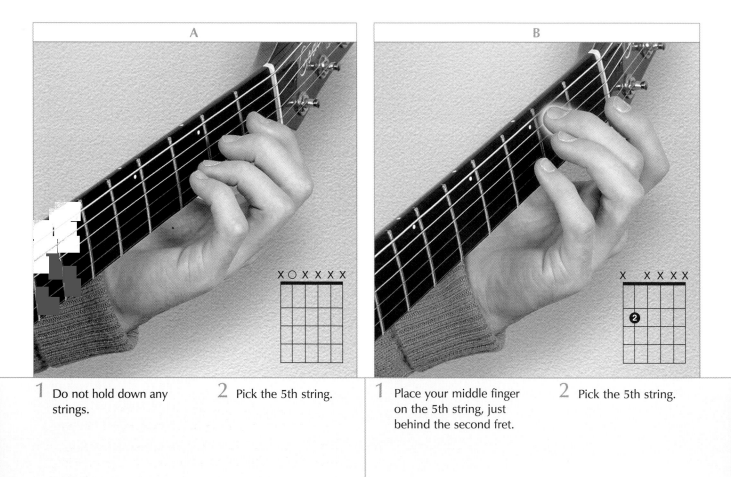

A

1 Do not hold down any strings.

2 Pick the 5th string.

B

1 Place your middle finger on the 5th string, just behind the second fret.

2 Pick the 5th string.

Tip

How can I play an A-sharp (A#) or B-flat (B♭) note on the 5th string?

To play an A# or B♭ note on the 5th string, place your index finger on the 5th string, just behind the first fret, and then pick the 5th string.

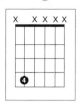

How can I play a C-sharp (C#) or D-flat (D♭) note on the 5th string?

To play a C# or D♭ note on the 5th string, place your pinky finger on the 5th string, just behind the fourth fret, and then pick the 5th string.

C

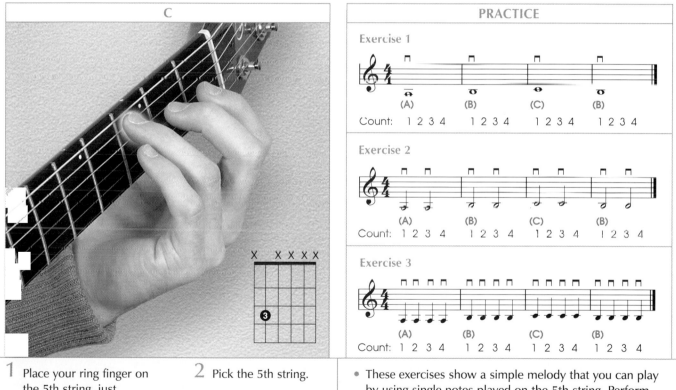

1 Place your ring finger on the 5th string, just behind the third fret.

2 Pick the 5th string.

PRACTICE

Exercise 1

Count: 1 2 3 4   1 2 3 4   1 2 3 4   1 2 3 4

Exercise 2

Count: 1 2 3 4   1 2 3 4   1 2 3 4   1 2 3 4

Exercise 3

Count: 1 2 3 4   1 2 3 4   1 2 3 4   1 2 3 4

- These exercises show a simple melody that you can play by using single notes played on the 5th string. Perform these exercises to practice switching between the notes.

- Pick the 5th string each time you see the ⊓ symbol. The shape of the note indicates how long you should hold each note: o (4 counts), ♩ (2 counts), ♩ (1 count).

playing notes on the 6th string

When playing in first position, E, F and G are the notes on the 6th string. For information on playing in first position, see page 104.

After you are comfortable playing the notes on the sixth string, you can use the notes you have learned on the sixth, fifth, fourth and third strings to practice playing a one octave G major scale. To play this scale, you begin with the G note on the sixth string. Then play the A, B and C notes on the fifth string, followed by the D, E and F-sharp (F♯) notes on the fourth string

and then the G note on the third string. Then play all the notes again in the opposite order.

You can also play a two octave G major scale to help you practice playing the notes on all six strings. Play the G major scale from the sixth string to the third string as described, and then continue the scale by playing the A note on the third string, the B, C and D notes on the second string and finally the E, F♯ and G notes on the first string. Then play all the notes again in the reverse order.

E	F
1 Do not hold down any strings. **2** Pick the 6th string.	**1** Place your index finger on the 6th string, just behind the first fret. **2** Pick the 6th string.

Tip

How can I play an F-sharp (F♯) or G-flat (G♭) note on the 6th string?

To play an F♯ or G♭ note on the 6th string, place your middle finger on the 6th string, just behind the second fret, and then pick the 6th string.

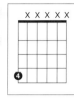

How can I play a G-sharp (G♯) or A-flat (A♭) note on the 6th string?

To play a G♯ or A♭ note on the 6th string, place your pinky finger on the 6th string, just behind the fourth fret, and then pick the 6th string.

G

1 Place your ring finger on the 6th string, just behind the third fret.

2 Pick the 6th string.

PRACTICE

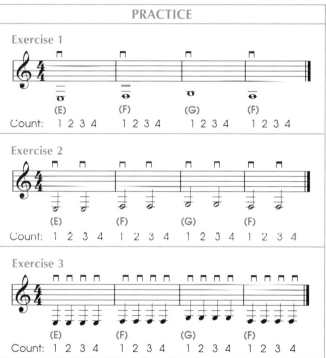

Exercise 1

Count: 1 2 3 4   1 2 3 4   1 2 3 4   1 2 3 4

Exercise 2

Count: 1 2 3 4   1 2 3 4   1 2 3 4   1 2 3 4

Exercise 3

Count: 1 2 3 4   1 2 3 4   1 2 3 4   1 2 3 4

- These exercises show a simple melody that you can play by using single notes played on the 6th string. Perform these exercises to practice switching between the notes.

- Pick the 6th string each time you see the ⊓ symbol. The shape of the note indicates how long you should hold each note: o (4 counts), ♩ (2 counts), ♩ (1 count).

finding notes
on your guitar

The following charts can help you find each note on your guitar. You can also see which note on the staff corresponds to each fret on each string. Learning the position of the notes on the fingerboard can help you read music and play in different positions.

Two adjacent notes on the same string are a half step apart and the notes are named after the letters A, B, C, D, E, F and G. You can also play sharps and flats on each string. Just keep in mind that the notes B and E do not have sharps and the

notes C and F do not have flats. For more information on sharps and flats, see page 42.

In the charts, we have only labelled frets 1 to 12 since the same pattern of notes occurs after the twelfth fret. If you play every note on the 1st string, from the open string to the twelfth fret, you would play a chromatic scale beginning and ending with the E note. A chromatic scale is a scale that contains twelve different notes, where each successive note is a half step apart.

Notes on Your Guitar

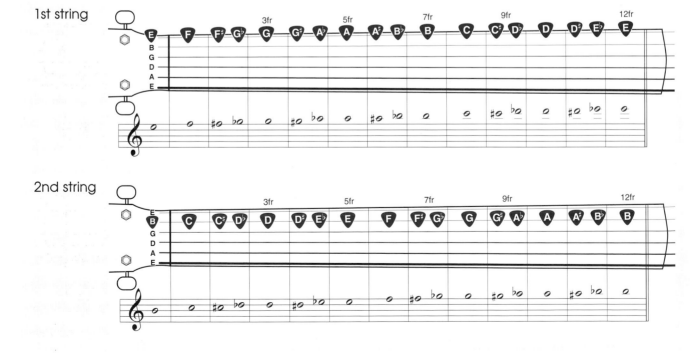

3rd string

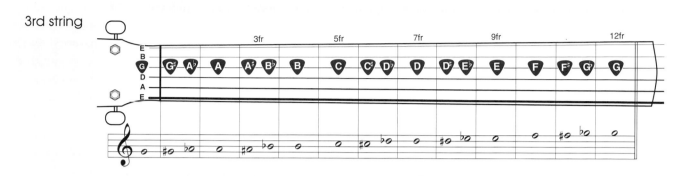

4th string

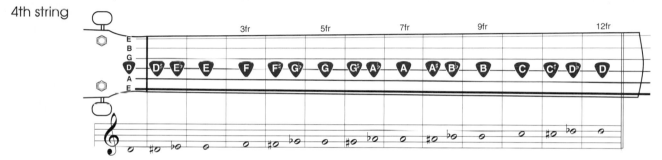

5th string

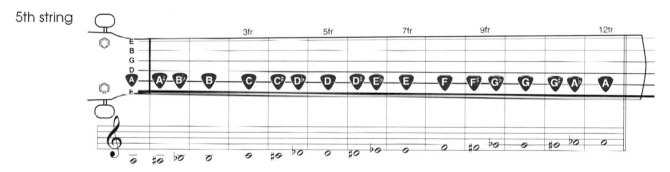

6th string

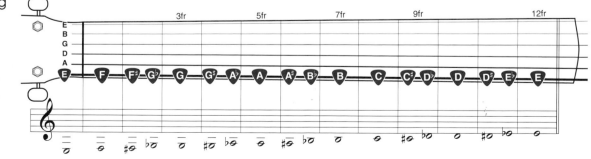

position playing

Position playing allows you to play a wide variety of notes without constantly moving your fretting hand up and down the fingerboard.

Playing in Position

To play in position, you place each finger over one of four side-by-side frets, such as the first, second, third and fourth frets. You can then play all the notes at each fret with a particular finger. For example, your index finger plays the notes at the first fret, your middle finger plays the notes at the second fret, your ring finger plays the notes at the third fret and your pinky finger plays the notes at the fourth fret.

When using this technique, the placement of your index finger determines the name of the position.

For example, when your index finger is at the first fret you are playing in first position or when your index finger is at the fifth fret you are playing in fifth position.

There is also a position called open position. When playing in open position, you play the notes in first or second position in addition to the open strings. An open string is a string you play without pressing the string down. Open position is one of the easiest positions to use for playing melodies.

Benefits of Position Playing

You can easily switch between notes when using one finger per fret. Instead of moving to several different locations on the fingerboard to play different notes, your hand remains in one location. Position playing is a relaxed method of playing guitar and can make you look like a more advanced player.

Position playing is useful when learning scales. A scale is a series of related

notes played in sequence. Once you have learned the fingering for one scale, you can move your hand to another position and play a different scale using the same finger pattern. As a result, you can learn different scales without even knowing the names of the notes you are playing. For more information on scales, see page 122.

Choosing a Position

The best position for playing is the one that lets you play all the notes of a key within the position's four frets. A key is a specific group of notes that are usually played together in a song. Trying different positions allows you to see what works best for a particular melody. You should not feel limited by the four frets of a playing position. You can always stretch your index or pinky finger one fret above or below the four frets to play additional notes.

Position Shifting

To play a song, you normally have to switch your hand between different positions, which is known as position shifting. When you shift from a lower position to a higher position on the neck, shift your index finger to the new position's first fret. When you shift from a higher position to a lower position on the neck, shift your pinky finger to the new position's fourth fret. Although this technique may take some practice to master, you should eventually be able to play so that it is impossible to tell when you switch positions.

Position Playing Tips

- When you are not using a finger to play, make sure you keep the finger above its designated fret. This ensures you do not forget where you are playing and use the wrong fingers to play notes.

- When you fret a note, keep the tip of your finger perpendicular to the string.

- Always keep your fingers no more than an inch away from the fingerboard. They should always be curled and ready to play, but not touching the strings. This can make your playing faster because you do not have to move your fingers as far.

- Keep your shoulders and your breathing relaxed at all times to avoid tensing up.

CONTINUED...

position playing

To practice playing in different positions, you can play the following examples, which include a common scale (the C major scale), a simple melody and the song "Ode to Joy." Each example is shown in three different positions for you to practice.

Position Playing Example 1
C Major Scale

In First Position

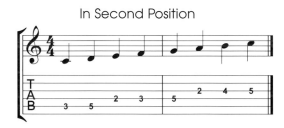

In Second Position

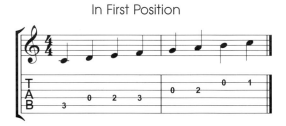

In Seventh Position

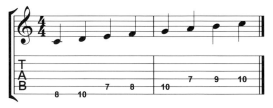

Position Playing Example 2
Simple Melody

In First Position

In Fourth Position

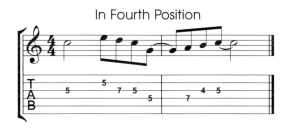

In Ninth Position

Position Playing Example 3
Ode to Joy

In First Position

In Fifth Position

In Ninth Position

playing scales

What is a Scale?

A scale is a group of related notes arranged in order of pitch. You usually start and end a scale on the same note, which is referred to as the root note.

The most common scales are major scales and minor scales, which contain seven different notes. Scales are usually played in one or two octaves. An octave refers to the group of notes that fall between two notes with the same letter name. For example, to play a one octave C major scale, you play C, D, E, F, G, A, B, C. To play the two octave scale, you play the notes, then repeat the notes at a higher pitch until the next occurrence of the root note.

The notes of a scale are determined by the root note followed by a specific sequence of semi-tones and tones. A semi-tone is the smallest interval between two notes. The change in pitch from one fret on the guitar to the next fret on the same string is one semi-tone. A tone refers to the change in pitch from one fret to two frets above or below on the same string.

The sequence of tones and semi-tones that make up the notes of a scale determine whether the scale is major or minor.

Notes in a Scale

Each of the seven different notes in a scale is represented by a roman numeral and is referred to by a degree name.

Note	Roman Numeral	Degree Name	Example (in C major scale)
1st	I	Root note *or* tonic	C
2nd	II	Supertonic	D
3rd	III	Mediant	E
4th	IV	Subdominant	F
5th	V	Dominant	G
6th	VI	Submediant	A
7th	VII	Leading tone	B

Reasons for Playing Scales

✓ Learning scales will help you understand how notes relate to each other, which will enhance your ability to play songs on the guitar. Understanding the relationship between notes allows you to determine which notes you can use in each key.

✓ Playing scales is a good finger exercise. You can play scales to help warm up your fingers before each session on your guitar.

✓ After you learn to play scales, you will be able to vary the notes of the scales to create your own solos and melodies.

Tips for Playing Scales

✓ Try to play each note at the same pace. To help you maintain a steady beat, you can tap your foot or use a device such as a metronome.

✓ Vary the picking technique you use when practicing scales. For example, you can use alternate picking, which involves picking one note toward the floor and the next note toward the ceiling.

✓ Make practicing scales a part of your daily practice routine. You should play through a couple of scales at least 4 or 5 times daily.

Playing Scales Along One String

You can play scales along one string on the guitar by moving one fret for each semi-tone and two frets for each tone in the scale. Playing along a single string clearly illustrates the relationship between the frets of the guitar and the semi-tones or tones that make up a scale.

When playing along one string, the note you begin the scale on determines the scale you play. For example, if you begin a major scale on an F note, you play an F major scale.

Playing Scales in Position

You can play scales in position to minimize the distance your fretting hand has to move to play the notes. To play in position, you place each finger over one of four side-by-side frets and then use a specific finger to play the notes at each fret. For more information on position playing, see page 118.

When you play a scale in position, you usually follow a specific pattern of notes. Once you learn the finger pattern for the notes of a scale, you can use the same finger pattern to play the scale in any key without needing to know the name of each note for every scale.

The starting note of the scale determines the scale you play. To change the starting note, you simply start playing the scale at a different fret on the starting string. For example, if you start playing the finger pattern for a major scale by playing a G note, you play a G major scale.

CONTINUED...

playing scales

The sequence of tones and semi-tones that make up the notes of a scale determine whether a scale is major or minor. Major scales are the most common type of scale. The notes that make up a major scale follow this sequence: starting note, tone, tone, semi-tone, tone, tone, tone, semi-tone. One of the most well-known major scales is the C major scale, which consists of the notes C, D, E, F, G, A, B, C.

Every major scale has a related minor scale. A minor scale contains the same notes as its corresponding major scale, but the first note of the minor scale is the sixth note of the major scale. For example, the A minor scale is the related minor scale of the C major scale since the sixth note of the C major scale is A. The notes of the A minor scale are A, B, C, D, E, F, G, A. The notes that make up a minor scale follow this sequence: starting note, tone, semi-tone, tone, tone, semi-tone, tone, tone.

You can play scales along one string or in position using several strings. For information on playing in position, see page 123.

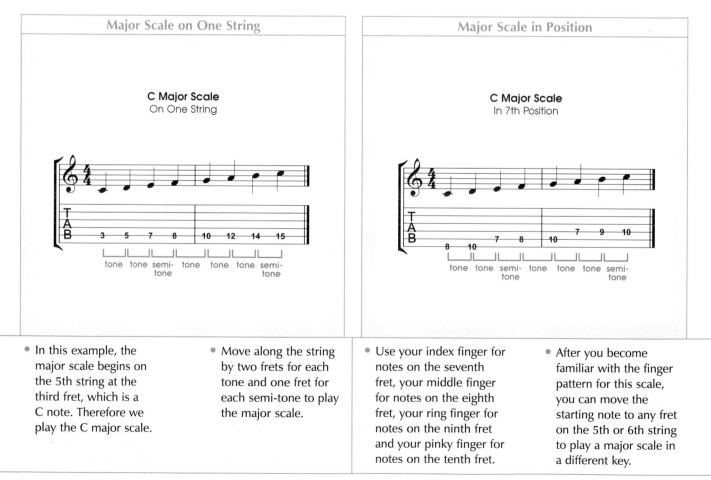

Major Scale on One String

C Major Scale
On One String

tone tone semi-tone tone tone tone semi-tone

- In this example, the major scale begins on the 5th string at the third fret, which is a C note. Therefore we play the C major scale.

- Move along the string by two frets for each tone and one fret for each semi-tone to play the major scale.

Major Scale in Position

C Major Scale
In 7th Position

tone tone semi-tone tone tone tone semi-tone

- Use your index finger for notes on the seventh fret, your middle finger for notes on the eighth fret, your ring finger for notes on the ninth fret and your pinky finger for notes on the tenth fret.

- After you become familiar with the finger pattern for this scale, you can move the starting note to any fret on the 5th or 6th string to play a major scale in a different key.

Tip

What is a harmonic minor scale?

A harmonic minor scale has the same notes as a minor scale, except the seventh note of the scale is increased by a half step. The notes that make up a harmonic minor scale follow this sequence: starting note, tone, semi-tone, tone, tone, semi-tone, 3 semi-tones, semi-tone. For example, the notes of the A minor harmonic scale are A, B, C, D, E, F, G♯, A.

What is a melodic minor scale?

A melodic minor scale has the same notes as a minor scale, except the sixth and seventh notes of the scale are increased by a half step each when the scale is played in ascending order. The notes that make up an ascending melodic minor scale follow this sequence: starting note, tone, semi-tone, tone, tone, tone, tone, semi-tone. For example, the notes of the ascending A minor melodic scale are A, B, C, D, E, F♯, G♯, A. When played in descending order, the notes that make up a melodic minor scale are exactly the same as the minor scale.

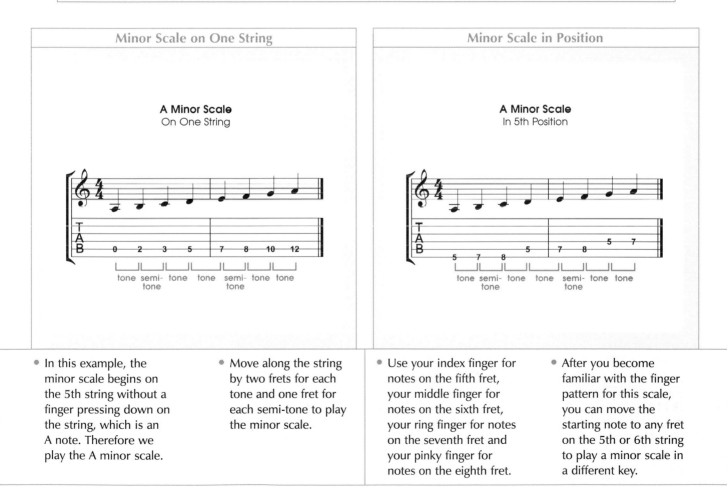

Minor Scale on One String	Minor Scale in Position

A Minor Scale
On One String

A Minor Scale
In 5th Position

- In this example, the minor scale begins on the 5th string without a finger pressing down on the string, which is an A note. Therefore we play the A minor scale.

- Move along the string by two frets for each tone and one fret for each semi-tone to play the minor scale.

- Use your index finger for notes on the fifth fret, your middle finger for notes on the sixth fret, your ring finger for notes on the seventh fret and your pinky finger for notes on the eighth fret.

- After you become familiar with the finger pattern for this scale, you can move the starting note to any fret on the 5th or 6th string to play a minor scale in a different key.

playing double-stops

A double-stop refers to playing two notes at a time. A double-stop falls between playing a single note and playing a chord, which is usually made up of 2 or more notes. Double-stops help make melodies sound richer and more pleasant than melodies that use single notes. You will find the easiest double-stops to play are on strings that are next to each other.

You will often hear double-stops used in country and 50's rock and roll music. Double-stops can be heard in songs such as "Brown Eyed Girl" by Van Morrison and "Margaritaville" by Jimmy Buffett.

There are generally two ways to play double-stops—up and down the neck and across the neck.

Playing Double-Stops Up and Down the Neck

You can play double-stops up and down the length of the neck. In this case, you will use the same two strings at the same or different frets. Use your index and middle fingers to play notes that are on the same fret or one fret apart and use your index and ring fingers to play notes that are two frets apart.

Double-stops played up and down the neck are typically played in thirds, which refer to two notes

played together that are two letter names apart, such as A-C and B-D. This results in a sweeter-sounding melody.

When playing double-stops up and down the neck, the notes of each double-stop should be in the same key as the music you are playing. For example, when you are playing a song in the key of G, the notes of each double-stop should be in the key of G.

Examples of Double-Stops
Up and Down the Neck

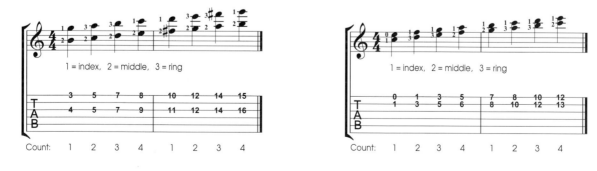

Playing Double-Stops Across the Neck

You can play double-stops across the width of the neck of the guitar. In this case, you will use different strings on one part of the neck. For example, you can play the 3rd and 2nd strings and then play the 2nd and 1st strings. Double-stops played across the neck are more frequently used than double-stops played up and down the neck. In blues and rock songs, you tend to play double-stops at the same fret using the same finger.

Examples of Double-Stops
Across the Neck

1 = index, 2 = middle, 3 = ring, 4 = pinky

1 = index, 2 = middle

Double-Stop Tips

When playing double-stops, you should strum the strings as one to create a single sound, instead of creating two separate sounds. When playing strings that are not next to each other, you may need to mute the strings you do not want to sound. To mute strings you do not want to sound, rest your fingers on the strings to prevent the strings from making a sound.

You may also want to use your thumb or a pick to play the lower-sounding note and use your middle or ring finger to pick the higher-sounding note. For example, when playing the 3rd and 1st strings, use the pick on the 3rd string and your middle finger on the 1st string.

songs for practice

I've Been Working On The Railroad

Oh, Susanna

Stephen Foster

songs for practice

Lullaby

Johann Brahms

Clementine

Chapter 7

Articulation techniques allow you to get creative with your guitar and infuse individuality into your music. As the term articulation implies, you can use these techniques to express emotions using the guitar and make the guitar "speak." Try using the articulation techniques discussed in this chapter, such as hammer-ons, pull-offs, slides and bends, to make your music more expressive and interesting.

Articulation Techniques

In this Chapter...

- Playing Hammer-Ons
- Playing Pull-Offs
- Playing Slides
- Muting Strings
- Playing Bends
- Applying Vibrato

playing hammer-ons

A hammer-on allows you to play two successive, ascending notes on the same string without picking the string to play the second note. This allows for a smoother transition between two notes, compared to picking each note individually. After positioning your index finger, you simply use another finger to hit or "hammer" the same string at a higher fret while the first note is still ringing. When playing a hammer-on, your finger should hit the string hard enough to make the note ring, without using excessive force.

When playing a hammer-on, the index finger is often used to fret the first note, while the middle or ring finger is used to hammer the second note. A hammer-on is indicated in tab notation by a curved line that connects the first and last notes. The letter "H" may appear above the curved line.

After you hammer your finger onto a string, it is important to keep your finger on the string. Do not merely hammer the string and then quickly release your finger again. You should also avoid moving your index finger along the fingerboard when you hammer your finger on the higher note.

Example of the Hammer-On Technique

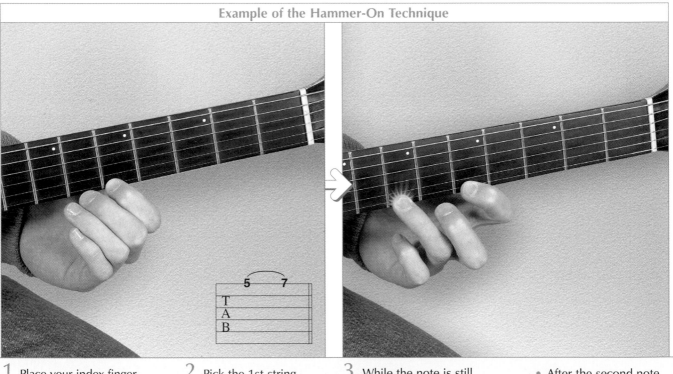

1 Place your index finger on the 1st string, just behind the fifth fret.

2 Pick the 1st string.

3 While the note is still ringing, use your ring finger to quickly hammer on the 1st string, just behind the seventh fret.

• After the second note sounds, remove your index finger from the string.

playing pull-offs

A pull-off allows you to play two successive, descending notes on the same string without having to pick the string to play the second note. To play a fretted note pull-off, position two fingers on different frets on the same string and then pick the string. While the first note is still ringing, remove your finger off the higher fret to sound the second, lower note.

A pull-off is indicated in tab notation by a curved line that connects the first and last notes. The letter "P" may appear above the curved line.

You can also perform a pull-off on an open string by first fretting the first note, picking the string and while the first note is still ringing, pulling your finger off the string to sound the open-string note.

When pulling a finger off a string, you should pull the finger slightly toward the floor. Depending on the notes you want to play, you can use whichever fingers work best for the strings and frets you need to use. For added practice, you can try playing pull-offs over the entire neck of the guitar.

Example of the Pull-Off Technique

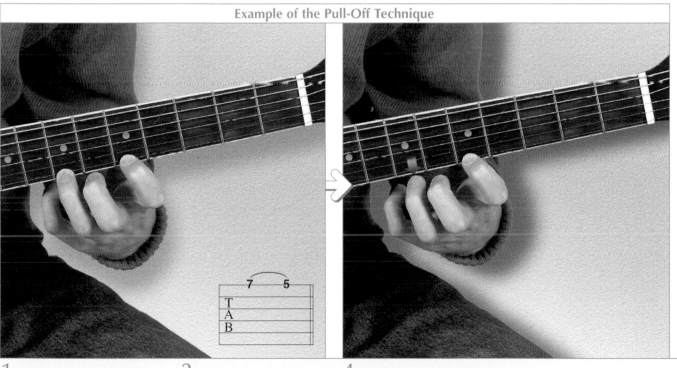

1 Place your index finger on the 1st string, just behind the fifth fret.

2 Place your ring finger on the 1st string, just behind the seventh fret.

3 Pick the 1st string.

4 While the note is still ringing, pull your ring finger off the 1st string, slightly toward the floor.

playing slides

A slide allows you to easily connect two or more notes on the guitar. You can play a slide by moving your finger to a different fret on the same string while the first note is still ringing. You can play slides with a definite or an indefinite pitch.

To play slides with a definite pitch, pick the first note and then slide your finger to a higher fret to play the last note, maintaining enough pressure to keep the string ringing throughout the slide. You can also pick the first note, slide your finger and then pick the last note.

To play slides with an indefinite pitch, slide your finger

with slight pressure at first and then increase the pressure until your finger reaches the target fret. Alternatively, you can start a slide with normal pressure and then slowly decrease the pressure as your finger slides away from the starting fret.

A slide is indicated in tab notation by a slanted line that connects the first and last notes. If there is a curved line above the slanted line, you only have to pick the first note. Otherwise, you need to pick both the first and last notes. The letters "sl" or "s" may appear above the curved line.

Example of the Slide Technique

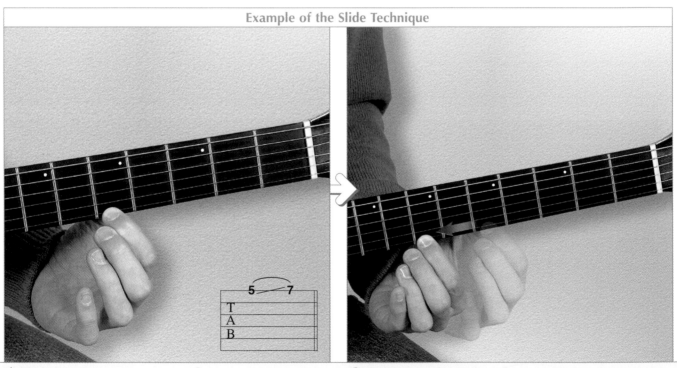

1 Place your index finger on the 1st string, just behind the fifth fret.

2 Pick the 1st string.

3 While the note is still ringing, slide your index finger along the 1st string until your index finger is just behind the seventh fret.

• You can then pick the 1st string again to play the new note.

muting strings

You can use your fretting hand or the palm of your picking hand to mute the strings on a guitar. When you mute strings, you stop them from ringing and damp the sound.

To use your fretting hand to mute strings, lay your fingers across all six strings on the neck of the guitar. This stops the strings from ringing and fully damps the sound as you strum the strings. When using your fretting hand to mute strings, do not press the strings too far down. You should only press the strings enough to prevent them from sounding. Fretting-hand muting is indicated

in tab notation by small Xs on the string lines.

To use the palm of your picking hand to mute strings, rest the side of your hand against the bridge of the guitar and pick each string to slightly damp the sound and generate a thick and heavy sound effect. The closer your picking hand is to the bridge of the guitar, the heavier the notes will sound. Palm muting is generally used for individual strings and power chords. It is specified in tab notation by the letters "P.M." above the tab staff and a dotted line to indicate how long to mute the strings.

Fretting-Hand Muting

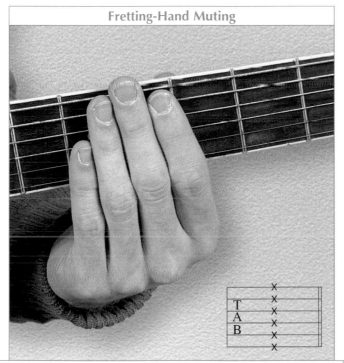

1 Lay your fingers across all six strings on the neck of the guitar.

2 Strum the strings toward the floor to hear the sound of muted strings.

Palm Muting

1 Rest the side of your hand against the bridge of the guitar.

2 Pick each string to hear the sound effect created by palm muting.

137

playing bends

Bending is the most expressive articulation technique you can perform on a guitar. To bend a note, you use a finger to stretch the string toward the 1st or 6th string, which increases the pitch of the note.

In tab notation, a curved arrow indicates a bend. A number or fraction, such as $1\frac{1}{2}$ or $\frac{1}{2}$, or the word "Full" next to the curved arrow tells you how many steps to increase the pitch of the note. For information on steps, see page 292. "Full" indicates that you should bend the note until the pitch is one step higher. The most common bends are a $\frac{1}{2}$ or full step.

You usually use your ring finger to play bends, with your index and middle fingers providing support, but when playing only a $\frac{1}{2}$ step bend, you can use only one finger—usually your index finger. You should make sure you keep the string firmly pressed against the fingerboard as you bend it.

You can also play pre-bends, which are similar to normal bends, except you bend the string before picking the note.

Example of the 3-Finger Bend Technique

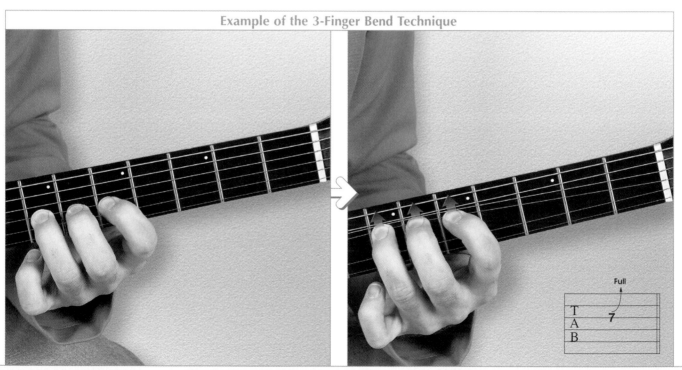

1 Place your ring finger on the 3rd string, just behind the seventh fret.

2 Place your middle finger on the 3rd string, just behind the sixth fret.

3 Place your index finger on the 3rd string, just behind the fifth fret.

• Your index and middle fingers simply help to support your ring finger.

4 Pick the 3rd string.

5 While the note is still ringing, use your ring, middle and index fingers to push the 3rd string up toward the 6th string until the note is a step higher.

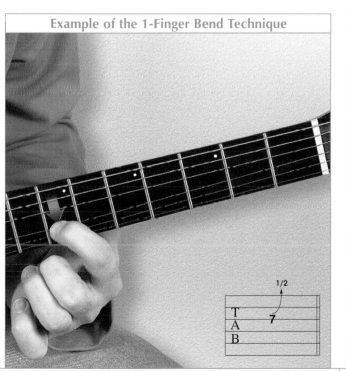

How can I tell if I'm bending the note properly?

You can play the target note normally and compare with the bent note to see if they sound the same. When bending a full step on the 3rd string, you can play the note normally by pressing down the 2nd string 2 frets closer to the nut. For example, after performing steps **1** and **2** on page 138, place your index finger on the 2nd string at the fifth fret. Pick the 2nd and 3rd strings. While the notes are still ringing, bend the 3rd string until the note on the 3rd string sounds the same as the note on the 2nd string.

Should I move only my fingers to play bends?

Instead of just bending the string using your fingers, you may want to also move your entire hand by rotating your hand at the wrist. You can use whichever method works best for you.

Can I bend more than one string at a time?

Yes. To bend multiple strings at once, position your ring finger on top of the strings you want to bend. Then keeping your finger firmly pressed to the fingerboard, push all the strings up at once to bend the strings.

Example of the 1-Finger Bend Technique

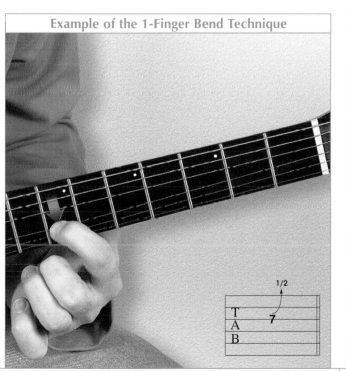

1 Place your index finger on the 3rd string, just behind the seventh fret.

2 Pick the 3rd string.

3 While the note is still ringing, use your index finger to pull the 3rd string down toward the 1st string until the note is a half step higher.

Example of the Pre-bend Technique

1 Perform steps **1** to **3** on page 138.

2 Use your ring, middle and index fingers to push the 3rd string up toward the 6th string.

3 Pick the 3rd string.

4 While the note is still ringing, use your fingers to pull the 3rd string back down to its natural position on the fingerboard.

applying vibrato

Applying vibrato infuses a sustained note with warmth and character by producing a steady fluctuation in pitch as you hold the note.

To apply vibrato, you can play any note and then bend the string sideways toward the 1st or 6th string. Then you return the string to its natural position and continue bending and releasing the string until the note stops ringing. For information on bending notes, see page 138.

You can use any finger to apply vibrato, but it is usually easiest to use your ring or index finger. The finger(s) you use and the direction you bend the string is up to you. The vibrato speed can vary, but keep your movements even throughout.

A narrow or wide wavy line above a note is used in tab notation to indicate where you should apply vibrato. A narrow wavy line (ᨆᨆᨆ) indicates a subtle, very slight fluctuation in pitch, while a wide wavy line (∿∿∿) indicates a quicker, greater fluctuation in pitch.

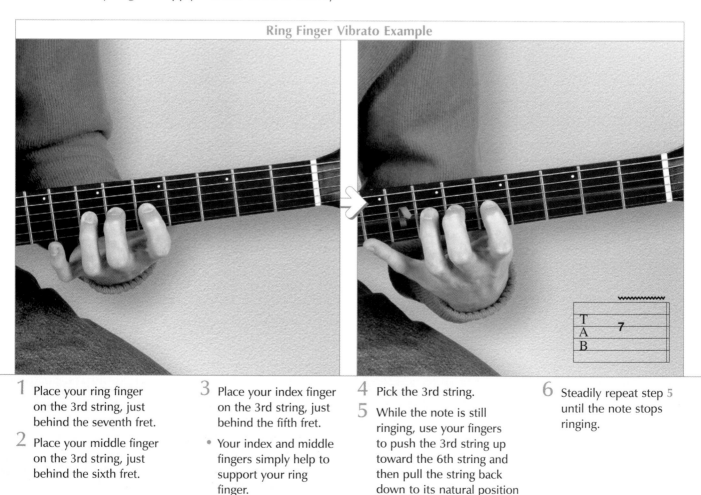

Ring Finger Vibrato Example

1 Place your ring finger on the 3rd string, just behind the seventh fret.

2 Place your middle finger on the 3rd string, just behind the sixth fret.

3 Place your index finger on the 3rd string, just behind the fifth fret.

• Your index and middle fingers simply help to support your ring finger.

4 Pick the 3rd string.

5 While the note is still ringing, use your fingers to push the 3rd string up toward the 6th string and then pull the string back down to its natural position on the fingerboard.

6 Steadily repeat step 5 until the note stops ringing.

Tip

Should I move only my fingers to apply vibrato?

In addition to moving your fingers, you can also move your entire hand by rotating your hand at the wrist. You should use the method that works best for you.

My fingers bump other strings when I apply vibrato using my ring finger. What can I do?

If your fingers bump into the strings above the string you are playing, you can mute the strings to stop them from sounding. To mute the strings, place your index finger lightly on the strings.

Are there more interesting ways to apply vibrato?

Yes. Instead of immediately applying vibrato after playing a note, you can allow the note to play for a few moments and then apply vibrato toward the end of the note. You can also incorporate vibrato with other techniques. For example, you can enhance a long vibrato by playing a descending slide at the end. For more information on slides, see page 136.

Index Finger Vibrato Example

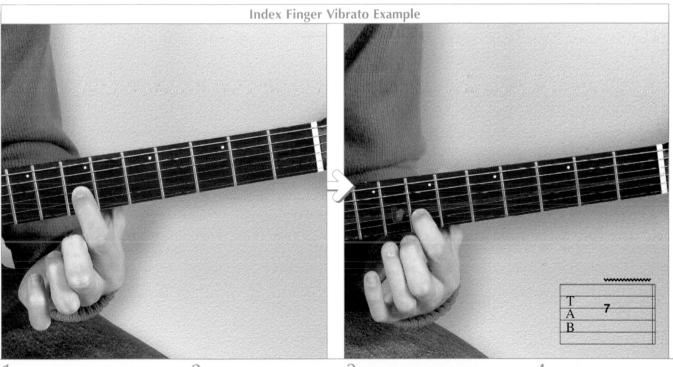

1 Place your index finger on the 3rd string, just behind the seventh fret.

2 Pick the 3rd string.

3 While the note is still ringing, use your index finger to pull the 3rd string down toward the 1st string and then push the string back up to its natural position on the fingerboard.

4 Steadily repeat step 3 until the note stops ringing.

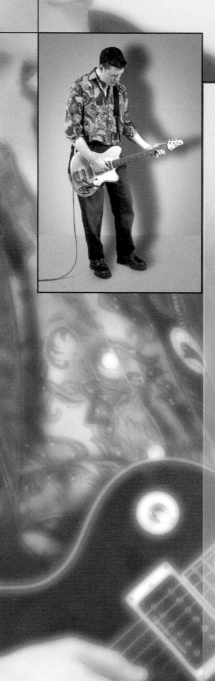

Chapter 8

The speed and energy involved in playing rock guitar is one of the most attractive features of this genre. Playing rock guitar requires the same skills as playing any other type of music. You can read this chapter to learn how to play add chords, slash chords and suspended chords. You will also learn how to use open tunings and alternate tunings to infuse flavor into your music.

Playing Rock Guitar

In this Chapter...

introduction to rock guitar

Rock Lead Guitar

Rock lead guitar usually involves playing melodies on top of accompanying instruments or beneath the vocals of a song. Rock guitar songs often also include guitar solos, in which the vocals cease and the lead guitar becomes the main sound. Rock lead guitar makes use of many articulation techniques, such as bending and hammering-on strings. For information about articulation techniques, see pages 134 to 141.

Rock Rhythm Guitar

In most cases, playing rock rhythm guitar refers to playing accompaniment to a singer or a lead instrument. Rock rhythm guitar largely involves strumming chords or playing single note riffs and double-stops on the lower-sounding strings.

Styles of Rock Guitar

Early Rock 'n' Roll

This style made the electric guitar famous in the 1950s and 1960s. In early rock 'n' roll, the lead guitar sound was very clean and undistorted. Famous lead guitarists of this style include Scotty Moore and Duane Eddy. Rhythm guitar in early rock 'n' roll often used a rhythm style and chord progression heard in many songs such as "Johnny B. Goode." Famous rhythm guitarists of early rock 'n' roll include Bo Diddley and Buddy Holly.

70's Rock

During the 1970s, heavy rock and blues-rock styles became more popular. Most 70's rock relied on thick sound layers and several amplified guitars. In 70's rock, lead guitar often involved long, virtuoso guitar solos. Great lead guitarists of 70's rock include David Gilmour and Jimmy Page. Rhythm guitar in 70's rock was similar to that of classic rock. Paul Stanley is one of the famous rhythm guitarists of 70's rock.

Classic Rock

Classic rock reached the height of its popularity in the 1960s and 1970s but is still popular today. The electric guitar riff is a major feature of classic rock lead guitar. Lead guitarists, such as Jimi Hendrix and Eric Clapton, often used distortion boxes, wah-wah pedals and bigger amplifiers to change the guitar sound. Classic rock rhythm guitar incorporated power chords and plenty of early rock 'n' roll rhythm patterns, but with a darker sound. Great classic rock rhythm guitarists include Keith Richards and Pete Townshend.

Styles of Rock Guitar (continued)

Punk Rock

Speed and energy characterized the punk rock guitar sound of the 1970s. Since punk rock was a backlash against the virtuoso guitar style of 70's rock, very little lead guitar was used. Rhythm guitar in punk bands such as the Ramones and The Clash relied on fast and loud power chords.

80's Rock (Heavy Metal)

80's heavy metal guitar used lots of gain and heavily distorted sounds. Lead guitarists of this style, such as Eddie Van Halen and Warren DeMartini, often used whammy bars, extremely fast guitar playing and fingertapping—a technique that involves tapping your fingers along the fingerboard to sound the notes. 80's heavy metal rhythm guitarists, such as Malcolm Young and James Hetfield, used lots of distortion, palm muting and power chords.

80's Rock (Pop/New Wave)

In the pop/new wave style of 80's rock, the lines between lead and rhythm guitar sounds blended together. This style used lots of delay and was more melodic than older styles of rock. This rock style did not use a lot of guitar solos. Famous guitarists of this style of 80's rock include The Edge of U2 and Johnny Marr.

Grunge Rock

Grunge rock's popularity peaked in the 1990s. Famous grunge bands include Nirvana and Soundgarden. Lead guitar in grunge rock was often blues-rock inspired. Famous lead guitarists of the grunge style include Mike McCready and Kim Thayil. Grunge rock rhythm guitarists, such as Stone Gossard and Kurt Cobain, often used alternate tunings, such as Drop-D, lots of power chords and fuzzy distortion.

Modern Rock

There are several types of modern rock. Two of the most popular include rap metal, with bands such as Korn and Limp Bizkit, and punk rock, with bands such as Green Day and Blink 182. Lead guitar in rap metal uses a lot of minor keys and odd noises, while rap metal rhythm guitar uses very low tunings to get a heavier sound. Punk rock lead guitar often uses simple, fast melodies, while punk rock rhythm guitar uses lots of palm muting, heavy distortion and power chords.

playing rock lead guitar
(minor pentatonic scale)

The minor pentatonic scale allows you to easily play solos in rock music. Playing this scale involves using a finger pattern to play notes within a small square area of the fingerboard, similar to a box. Once you learn the finger pattern for the scale, you can create rock lead solos by playing the notes in the scale in different orders.

There are many different finger patterns you can use to play notes in the minor pentatonic scale. We refer to the finger pattern used to play the basic scale as Box A. To add higher notes to the scale, use Box B. To add lower notes to the scale, use Box C.

You can play the notes of the minor pentatonic scale in any key by using the same finger pattern. The key you play a song in determines the notes you can play in that song. The note you begin the scale on determines the key you will play in. For example, if you start playing the scale on the 6th string at the fifth fret, you play an A note, so you will play the scale in the key of A. Minor pentatonic scales in the key of A are commonly used in rock music.

To add variety to your solos, you can bend notes of the scale. The most common notes for bending in the minor pentatonic scale are the note your ring finger plays on the 3rd string and the note your pinky finger plays on the 2nd string. For information on bending notes, see page 138.

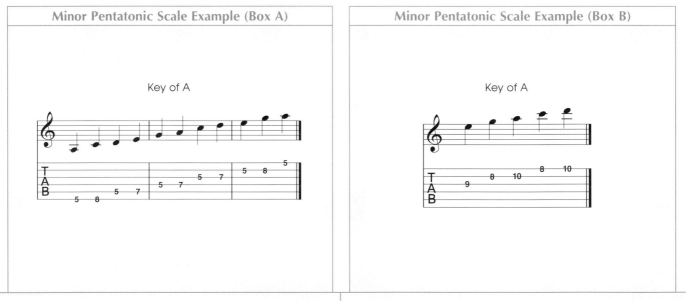

Minor Pentatonic Scale Example (Box A)	Minor Pentatonic Scale Example (Box B)
Key of A	Key of A

- We refer to the minor pentatonic scale as Box A.
- In this example, the minor pentatonic scale begins on an A note. Therefore we play the minor pentatonic scale in the key of A.

- Use your index finger for notes on the fifth fret, your ring finger for notes on the seventh fret and your pinky finger for notes on the eighth fret.

- We refer to these five notes as Box B. You can play these notes in addition to Box A to reach higher notes and add variety to your solos.
- In this example, we play Box B in the key of A.

- Use your index finger for notes on the eighth fret, your middle finger for notes on the ninth fret and your ring finger for notes on the tenth fret.

Tip

Can I play a combination of boxes A, B and C?

Yes. Combining boxes A, B and C allows you to use a wider range of notes. In the fingerboard diagram, the vertical lines represent frets and the horizontal lines represent the strings, with the 6th string on the bottom and the 1st string on the top. The root notes for the key you are playing in, which are the best notes for ending your phrases—or lines of music—on, are shown in yellow.

To play boxes A, B and C, start to play at the bottom left corner of the diagram and play one note at a time, moving from left to right. Play each note on the string before moving up to the next string.

This example shows the finger pattern for boxes A, B and C of the minor pentatonic scale in the key of A. When you become familiar with this finger pattern, you can start the scale on a different note and use the same finger pattern to play the scale in a different key.

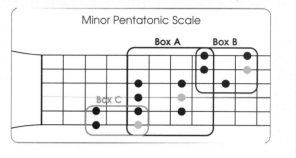

Minor Pentatonic Scale

Box A Box B

Box C

Minor Pentatonic Scale Example (Box C)

Key of A

PRACTICE

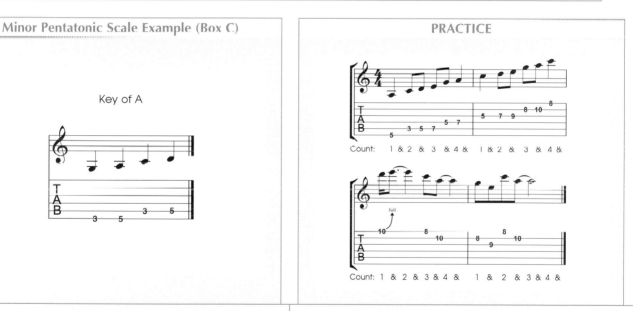

Count: 1 & 2 & 3 & 4 &   1 & 2 & 3 & 4 &

full

Count: 1 & 2 & 3 & 4 &   1 & 2 & 3 & 4 &

- We refer to these four notes as Box C. You can play these notes in addition to Box A to include lower notes in your solos.

- In this example, we play Box C in the key of A.

- Use your index finger for notes on the third fret and your ring finger for notes on the fifth fret.

- You can play this rock lead example to experience the sound of playing notes from the minor pentatonic scale in the key of A.

- You hold half notes (♩) for 2 counts, quarter notes (♩) for 1 count and eighth notes (♪) for 1/2 count. When two or more eighth notes appear in a row, they are joined with a beam (♫).

CONTINUED...

playing rock lead guitar
(major pentatonic scale)

The major pentatonic scale is popular for playing southern-rock and country-rock solos. Playing this scale involves using a finger pattern to play notes within a small square area of the fingerboard, similar to a box. Once you learn the finger pattern for the scale, you can create a solo by playing different arrangements of the notes in the scale.

There are many different finger patterns you can use to play notes in the major pentatonic scale. We refer to the finger pattern used to play the basic scale as Box A. To add higher notes to the scale, use Box B. To add lower notes to the scale, use Box C.

The finger patterns for the major pentatonic scale are the same as the finger patterns for the minor pentatonic scale, except you play the major pentatonic scale three frets closer to the headstock. For information on the minor pentatonic scale, see page 146.

To add variety to your solos, you can bend notes of the scale. The most common note for bending in the major pentatonic scale is the note your ring finger plays on the 3rd string. For more information on bending notes, see page 138.

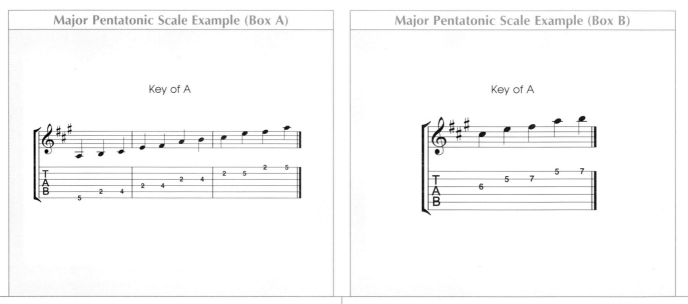

Major Pentatonic Scale Example (Box A)	Major Pentatonic Scale Example (Box B)
Key of A	Key of A

- We refer to the major pentatonic scale as Box A.

- In this example, the major pentatonic scale begins on an A note. Therefore we play the major pentatonic scale in the key of A.

- Use your index finger for notes on the second fret, your ring finger for notes on the fourth fret and your pinky finger for notes on the fifth fret.

- We refer to these five notes as Box B. You can play these notes in addition to Box A to reach higher notes and add variety to your solos.

- In this example, we play Box B in the key of A.

- Use your index finger for notes on the fifth fret, your middle finger for notes on the sixth fret and your ring finger for notes on the seventh fret.

Can I play a combination of boxes A, B and C?

Yes. Combining boxes A, B and C allows you to use a wider range of notes. In the fingerboard diagram, the vertical lines represent frets and the horizontal lines represent the strings, with the 6th string on the bottom and the 1st string on the top. The root notes for the key you are playing in, which are the best notes for ending your phrases—or lines of music—on, are shown in yellow.

To play boxes A, B and C, start to play on the 6th string at the bottom left corner of the diagram and play one note at a time, moving from left to right. Play each note on the string before moving up to the next string.

This example shows the finger pattern for boxes A, B and C of the major pentatonic scale in the key of A. When you become familiar with this finger pattern, you can start the scale on a different note and use the same finger pattern to play the scale in a different key.

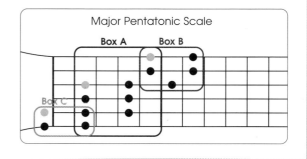

Major Pentatonic Scale

Box A   Box B

Box C

Major Pentatonic Scale Example (Box C)

Key of A

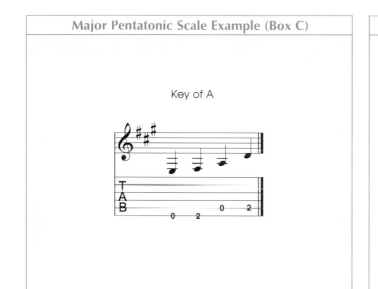

- We refer to these four notes as Box C. You can play these notes in addition to Box A to include lower notes in your country-rock and southern-rock solos.

- In this example, we play Box C in the key of A.
- Use your index finger for notes on the second fret.

PRACTICE

Count: 1 & 2 & 3 & 4 &   1 & 2 & 3 & 4 &

Count: 1 & 2 & 3 & 4 &   1 & 2 & 3 & 4 &

- You can play this rock lead example to experience the sound of playing notes from the major pentatonic scale in the key of A.

- You hold half notes (♩) for 2 counts, quarter notes (♩) for 1 count and eighth notes (♪) for 1/2 count. When two or more eighth notes appear in a row, they are joined with a beam (♫).

playing rock rhythm guitar

You usually play rock rhythm guitar when accompanying vocals or another featured instrument. Two popular examples of rock rhythm guitar are Chuck Berry style and I-VI-II-V progression.

Chuck Berry style is an early rock 'n' roll style featured in most of Chuck Berry's songs, such as "Johnny B. Goode." When playing a song using Chuck Berry style, you play the root note for each chord and then alternate between the 5th and 6th notes of the major scale for that root note. The root note is the note the chord is named after.

The I-VI-II-V progression, or 1-6-2-5 progression, is commonly used in 50's-style music, such as songs from the movie *Grease*. To play the I-VI-II-V progression, you play specific chords built on the notes of the scale for the key you are playing in. For example, when playing in the key of C, the notes of the scale are C, D, E, F, G, A, B, C—you play the major chord built on the first note of the scale (C major), followed by the minor chord built on the sixth note (A minor), then the minor chord built on the second note (D minor), and then the major chord built on the fifth note (G major).

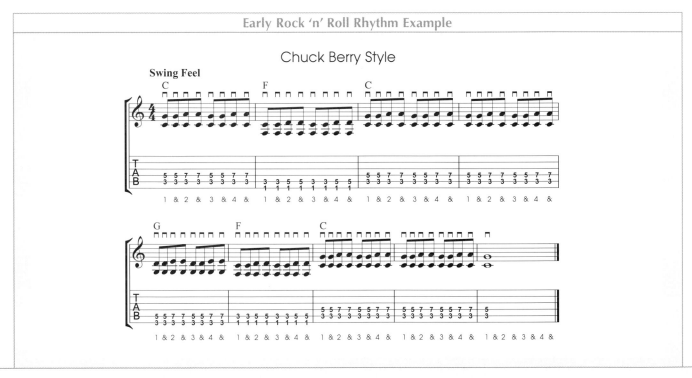

Early Rock 'n' Roll Rhythm Example

Chuck Berry Style

- This exercise shows an early rock 'n' roll rhythm chord progression in the Chuck Berry style that you can play.

- Strum each chord toward the floor each time you see the ⊓ symbol.
- You hold eighth notes (♪) for 1/2 count each. When two or more eighth notes appear in a row, they are joined with a beam (♫).

What styles are common in modern rock rhythm guitar?

Modern rock rhythm guitar usually involves playing fast-paced power chords using all downstrokes. Punk music or hard rock guitarists use frequent palm muting and heavy distortion to give the rhythm progression its unique sound. For information on power chords, see pages 96 to 99. For information on palm muting, see page 137. Some examples of bands that use rock rhythm guitar include The Ramones, Green Day and Blink 182.

What guitar strings will I use most often when playing rock rhythm guitar?

Most rock rhythms use the bass strings, which are the low-sounding 6th, 5th and 4th strings, more often than the higher-sounding treble strings, which are the 3rd, 2nd and 1st strings.

I-VI-II-V Progression Rhythm Example

50's-Style Progression

- This exercise shows a 50's-style rock rhythm chord progression that you can play.

- Pick the string toward the floor each time you see the ⊓ symbol and toward the ceiling each time you see the ∨ symbol.

- You hold eighth notes (♪) for 1/2 count each. When two or more eighth notes appear in a row, they are joined with a beam (♫).

playing suspended chords

Suspended (sus) chords are commonly used by rhythm guitarists in modern rock and provide an interesting yet incomplete sound. One type of suspended chord is written as "sus4" or "sus" and the other type is written as "sus2" or "2."

Forming suspended chords is similar to forming major and minor chords, except you replace the middle note with another note. To build a major or minor chord, you use the first, third and fifth notes of the scale. For example, to build a C chord, look at the C major scale (C, D, E, F, G, A, B, C) and form the chord using C, E, and G. To form a sus4 chord, use the first, fourth and fifth notes of the scale instead. For example, the Csus4 chord is made up of C, F and G. To form a sus2 chord, use the first, second and fifth notes of the scale. For example, the Csus2 chord is made up of C, D and G. Because the middle note in a suspended chord is different from the middle note in a regular chord, a suspended chord creates an unresolved sound.

EXAMPLES OF SUSPENDED CHORDS

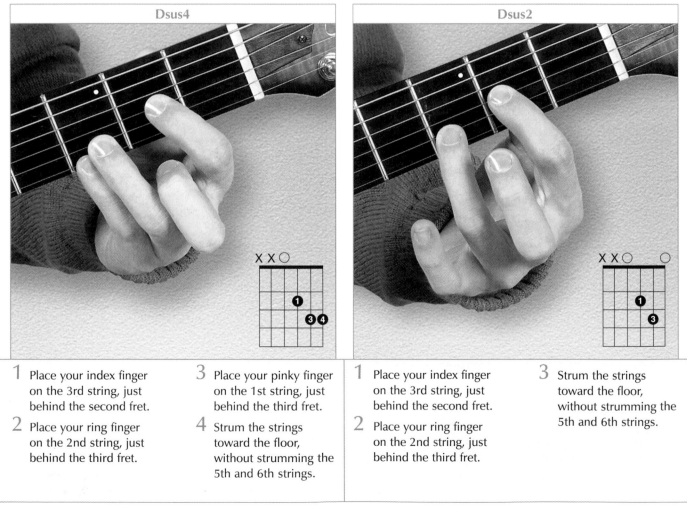

Dsus4	Dsus2

Dsus4

1 Place your index finger on the 3rd string, just behind the second fret.

2 Place your ring finger on the 2nd string, just behind the third fret.

3 Place your pinky finger on the 1st string, just behind the third fret.

4 Strum the strings toward the floor, without strumming the 5th and 6th strings.

Dsus2

1 Place your index finger on the 3rd string, just behind the second fret.

2 Place your ring finger on the 2nd string, just behind the third fret.

3 Strum the strings toward the floor, without strumming the 5th and 6th strings.

Tip

When would I use suspended chords?

You may want to play a suspended chord as a transition from a major key to a minor key. The unresolved sound of a suspended chord helps to smooth out the transition between the major and minor sounds.

Suspended chords can also be used as substitutes for major-sounding chords. If you are not sure whether to play a major or a minor chord, you can usually just substitute the equivalent suspended chord.

When should I avoid suspended chords?

You should never play a suspended chord after another suspended chord. Instead you should always move from a suspended chord to a chord that resolves the suspension. For example, you can play the suspended version of a chord, such as Dsus4, and then play the major version of the chord, such as D, next.

Dsus4 as an A-based Barre Chord

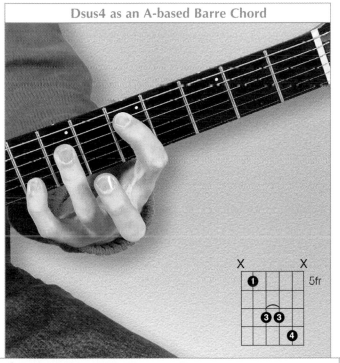

1 Place your index finger on the 5th string, just behind the fifth fret.

2 Press your ring finger firmly across the 3rd and 4th strings, just behind the seventh fret.

3 Place your pinky finger on the 2nd string, just behind the eighth fret. Use your pinky finger to mute the 1st string.

4 Strum the strings toward the floor, without strumming the 6th string.

Dsus2 as an A-based Barre Chord

1 Press your index finger firmly across the strings just behind the fifth fret, pressing down the first five strings.

2 Place your ring finger on the 4th string, just behind the seventh fret.

3 Place your pinky finger on the 3rd string, just behind the seventh fret.

4 Strum the strings toward the floor, without strumming the 6th string.

playing add chords

Add chords are commonly played by rhythm guitarists in modern and progressive rock music. To form an add chord, you simply form a major or minor chord and then add another note to the chord.

There are four common types of add chords in rock music: add2, add9, add4 and add11. The number in the chord name specifies the scale position of the note you add to the chord. For example, in Cadd2, you add the second note in the C major scale, which

is D. For information on scales, see page 122.

Add2 and add9 chords are basically the same chord because the second and ninth notes of the scale are the same, but one octave apart. Similarly, add4 and add11 chords are basically the same chord because the fourth and eleventh notes of the scale are the same, but one octave apart. Even though the added notes in the chords are one octave apart, most guitarists play the chords interchangeably.

EXAMPLES OF ADD CHORDS

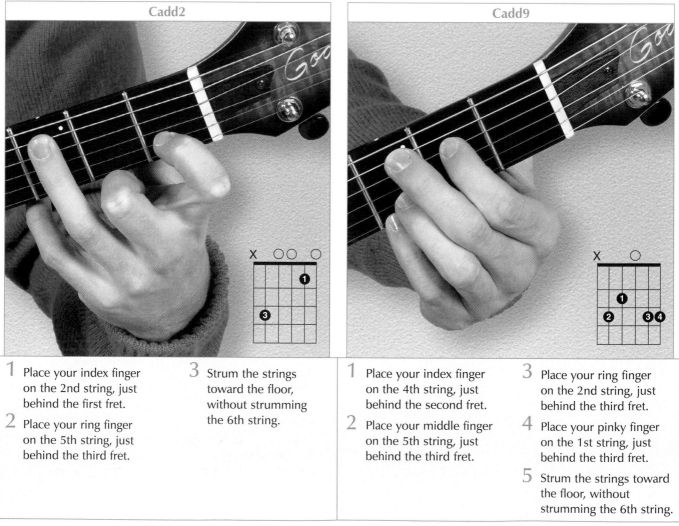

Cadd2

1 Place your index finger on the 2nd string, just behind the first fret.

2 Place your ring finger on the 5th string, just behind the third fret.

3 Strum the strings toward the floor, without strumming the 6th string.

Cadd9

1 Place your index finger on the 4th string, just behind the second fret.

2 Place your middle finger on the 5th string, just behind the third fret.

3 Place your ring finger on the 2nd string, just behind the third fret.

4 Place your pinky finger on the 1st string, just behind the third fret.

5 Strum the strings toward the floor, without strumming the 6th string.

Tip

What is the difference between add chords and suspended chords?

When you form suspended chords, you replace the middle note with another note, whereas when you form add chords, you add a note to the basic chord.

Are 9 chords the same as add9 chords?

No. Make sure you do not mistake a 9 chord, such as C9, for an add9 chord, such as Cadd9. The 9, 11 and 13 chords are variations on the related dominant 7th chord.

Can add chords help me with my playing?

Yes. Sometimes add chords can help you play more smoothly by providing a way to switch between chords more easily. For example, the C and G chords are commonly played together in the key of G, but they have very different finger shapes. Since Cadd9 is a similar finger shape to the G chord, you can substitute Cadd9 for the C chord to make it easier to switch between the C and G chords.

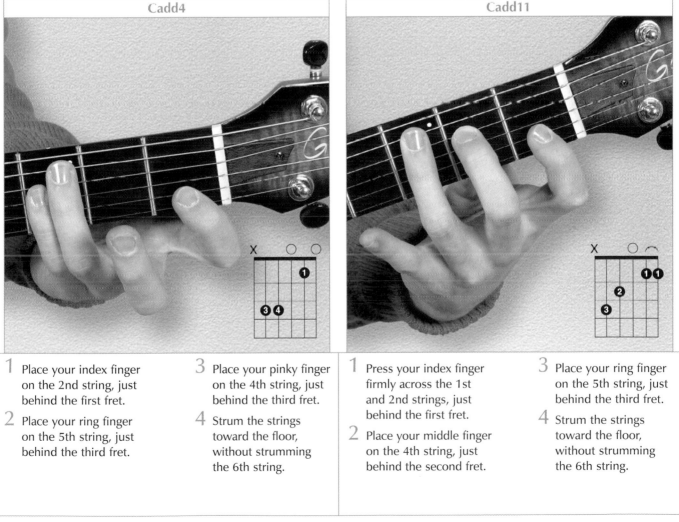

Cadd4

1 Place your index finger on the 2nd string, just behind the first fret.

2 Place your ring finger on the 5th string, just behind the third fret.

3 Place your pinky finger on the 4th string, just behind the third fret.

4 Strum the strings toward the floor, without strumming the 6th string.

Cadd11

1 Press your index finger firmly across the 1st and 2nd strings, just behind the first fret.

2 Place your middle finger on the 4th string, just behind the second fret.

3 Place your ring finger on the 5th string, just behind the third fret.

4 Strum the strings toward the floor, without strumming the 6th string.

playing slash chords

Slash chords are commonly used by rhythm guitarists in rock music to give flavor to the music. When you see a slash (/) in a chord name, such as G/B, you should play a slash chord. You can refer to a slash chord, such as G/B, as "G over B," "G slash B" or "G with a B in the bass."

To play a slash chord, you finger the chord that comes before the slash and make the note that comes after the slash the lowest note in the chord. The new lowest note, known as the bass note, can be a note that is already in the chord or any other note. Make sure you play this note on a lower-sounding string than the rest of the notes in the chord. It is important to know all the notes on the guitar so you can quickly find the nearest bass note that is paired with the chord.

Slash chords are frequently used in songs with quickly moving bass lines.

EXAMPLES OF SLASH CHORDS

G/B	C/E

G/B

1. Place your index finger on the 5th string, just behind the second fret.

2. Place your ring finger on the 2nd string, just behind the third fret.

3. Place your pinky finger on the 1st string, just behind the third fret.

4. Strum the strings toward the floor, without strumming the 6th string.

C/E

1. Place your index finger on the 2nd string, just behind the first fret.

2. Place your middle finger on the 4th string, just behind the second fret.

3. Place your ring finger on the 5th string, just behind the third fret.

4. Strum all the strings toward the floor.

Tip

Can slash chords make my playing sound smoother?

Slash chords can make chord progressions sound more gradual. For example, you can add D/F♯ in between a G chord and an E minor chord.

Is there an alternate fingering for the C/E chord?

Yes. Place your index finger on the 2nd string, just behind the first fret and your middle finger on the 4th string, just behind the second fret. Then strum only strings 1 to 4.

Is there an easier way to play slash chords?

If a slash chord has an E, A or D bass note, you can play the bass note as an open string, which means you strum the string without pressing the string down on the fingerboard. You can strum the open 6th string to play an E, strum the open 5th string to play an A and strum the open 4th string to play a D. Playing an open-string bass note makes the chord easier to play because you use fewer fingers.

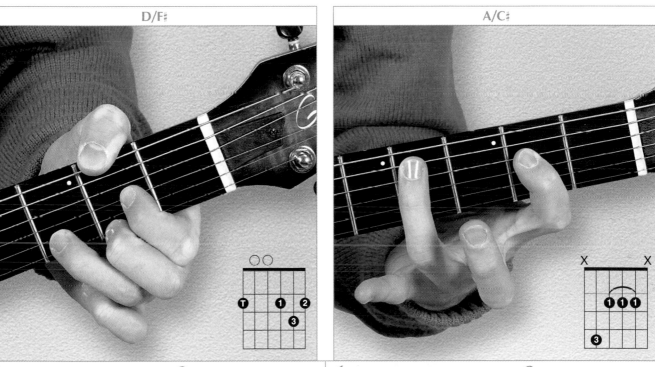

D/F♯

A/C♯

1 Place your index finger on the 3rd string, just behind the second fret.

2 Place your middle finger on the 1st string, just behind the second fret.

3 Place your ring finger on the 2nd string, just behind the third fret.

4 Place your thumb on the 6th string, just behind the second fret.

5 Strum all the strings toward the floor.

1 Press your index finger firmly across the 2nd, 3rd and 4th strings, just behind the second fret. Allow your index finger to gently rest on the 1st string so the 1st string will not sound.

2 Place your ring finger on the 5th string, just behind the fourth fret.

3 Strum the strings toward the floor, without strumming the 6th string.

using open tunings

When you strum the strings of a guitar toward the floor without fretting, or holding down, any of the strings, you play the notes E, A, D, G, B and E. This is referred to as standard tuning.

You can change the tuning of your guitar to allow you to play a chord when you strum all the strings without fretting any strings. This is referred to as open tuning. Open-D tuning, which allows you to play a D major chord, and Open-G tuning, which allows you to play a G major chord, without fretting any strings, are the two most popular open tunings.

When using open tunings, you do not play most chords the same way you play them in standard tuning. To play a chord, you can simply press down all the strings at a specific fret with your index finger. For example, if your guitar is tuned to Open-G tuning, you press down all the strings at the first fret to play a G-sharp major chord or press down all the strings at the second fret to play an A major chord.

When using an open tuning, you may need to re-tune your guitar each time you want to play a different song.

Tune Your Guitar to Open-D Tuning

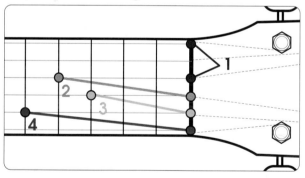

1 Lower the pitch of the 6th string until it is one octave lower than the note played on the 4th string when the string is not pressed down.

2 Lower the pitch of the 3rd string until it matches the note played on the 4th string at the fourth fret.

3 Lower the pitch of the 2nd string until it matches the note played on the 3rd string at the third fret.

4 Lower the pitch of the 1st string until it matches the note played on the 2nd string at the fifth fret.

Tune Your Guitar to Open-G Tuning

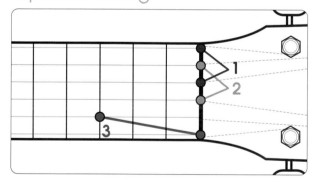

1 Lower the pitch of the 6th string until it is one octave lower than the note played on the 4th string when the string is not pressed down.

2 Lower the pitch of the 5th string until it is one octave lower than the note played on the 3rd string when the string is not pressed down.

3 Lower the pitch of the 1st string until it matches the note played on the 2nd string at the third fret.

Benefits of Open-D and Open-G Tunings

Open-D tuning allows you to easily change to other open tunings by using a capo. For each fret that you move the capo up, the chord played when you strum all the strings without fretting any strings will be one half step, or semi-tone, higher. For example, when your guitar is tuned to Open-D, you can place a capo at the first fret to make Open-D-sharp tuning or at the second fret to make Open-E tuning. For information on capos, see page 214.

When your guitar is tuned to Open-G tuning and you strum all the strings without fretting any strings, the G major chord has a richer tone than the G major chord you play in standard tuning. When using the Open-G tuning, you can play most chords the same way you play them in standard tuning except do not fret, or hold down, the 1st, 5th and 6th strings when you strum a chord.

Open-D Tuning Example

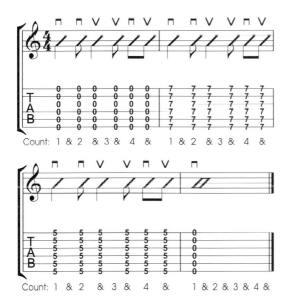

Open-G Tuning Example

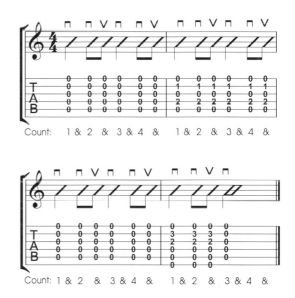

- Tune your guitar to the Open-D tuning and then play this example.

- Strum the strings toward the floor each time you see the ⊓ symbol and toward the ceiling each time you see the ∨ symbol. You hold whole notes (𝅝) for 4 counts, quarter notes (𝅘) for 1 count and eighth notes (𝅘𝅥) for 1/2 count. When two or more eighth notes appear in a row, they are joined by a beam (𝅘𝅥𝅮).

- Tune your guitar to the Open-G tuning and then play this example.

- Strum the strings toward the floor each time you see the ⊓ symbol and toward the ceiling each time you see the ∨ symbol. You hold half notes (𝅗𝅥) for 2 counts, quarter notes (𝅘) for 1 count and eighth notes (𝅘𝅥) for 1/2 count. When two or more eighth notes appear in a row, they are joined by a beam (𝅘𝅥𝅮).

using alternate tunings

When you strum the strings of a guitar toward the floor without fretting, or holding down, any of the strings, you play the notes E, A, D, G, B and E. This is referred to as standard tuning.

You can change the tuning of your guitar to achieve a different sound. An alternate tuning may allow you to more easily play chords that are normally difficult for you to finger, or may simply allow you to change a song so you can play it in a more unique way.

You can tune your guitar to an almost endless number of alternate tunings. For example, you can simply change the pitch of a single string or change the pitch of every string on the guitar.

When using an alternate tuning, you often have to relearn how to play the chords for the alternate tuning. For this reason, you should try to learn as much as you can about one alternate tuning before you try out another.

DOWN A HALF STEP TUNING

Down a half step tunings, or low tunings, are often used by bands who want to create a low, grinding sound. In addition to tuning down a half step, you can also tune down a full step or even a step and a half.

Tuning Your Guitar Down a Half Step

1 To tune your guitar down by a half step, tune your guitar as you normally would, except hold down each string at the first fret as you adjust the pitch of each string. To tune a guitar, see page 34.

Down a Half Step Tuning Example

- After you tune your guitar down by a half step, you can play this example to hear how your guitar will sound.

- Strum the strings toward the floor each time you see the ⊓ symbol and toward the ceiling each time you see the ∨ symbol. You hold half notes (♩) for 2 counts, quarter notes (♩) for 1 count and eighth notes (♪) for $1/2$ count. When two or more eighth notes appear in a row, they are joined by a beam (♫).

DROP-D TUNING

Drop-D tuning is the closest alternate tuning to standard tuning and is commonly used for playing rock rhythm guitar. This tuning allows you to produce a deeper, bolder sound. When you use Drop-D tuning, you can play any chord that does not use the 6th string the same way you would play the chord in standard tuning. For chords that use the 6th string, you must fret the 6th string two frets higher than normal.

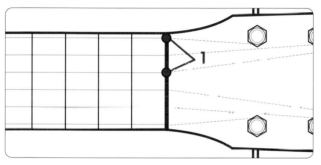

Tuning Your Guitar to Drop-D Tuning

1 Lower the pitch of the 6th string until it is one octave lower than the note played on the 4th string when the string is not pressed down.

Drop-D Tuning Example

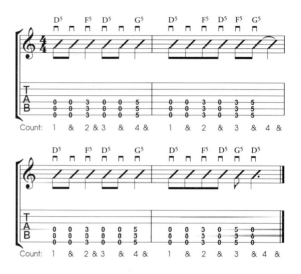

- After you tune your guitar to Drop-D tuning, you can play this example to hear how your guitar will sound.

- Strum the strings toward the floor each time you see the ⊓ symbol. You hold quarter notes (♩) for 1 count and eighth notes (♪) for 1/2 count. When two or more eighth notes appear in a row, they are joined by a beam (♫).

DOUBLE DROP-D TUNING

Double Drop-D tuning is similar to Drop-D tuning and is often used by musicians such as Neil Young. Perform the following steps to tune your guitar to Double Drop-D tuning.

1 Lower the pitch of the 6th string until it is one octave lower than the note played on the 4th string when the string is not pressed down.

2 Lower the pitch of the 1st string until it matches the note played on the 2nd string at the third fret.

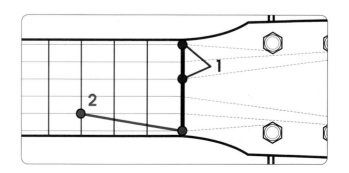

songs for practice

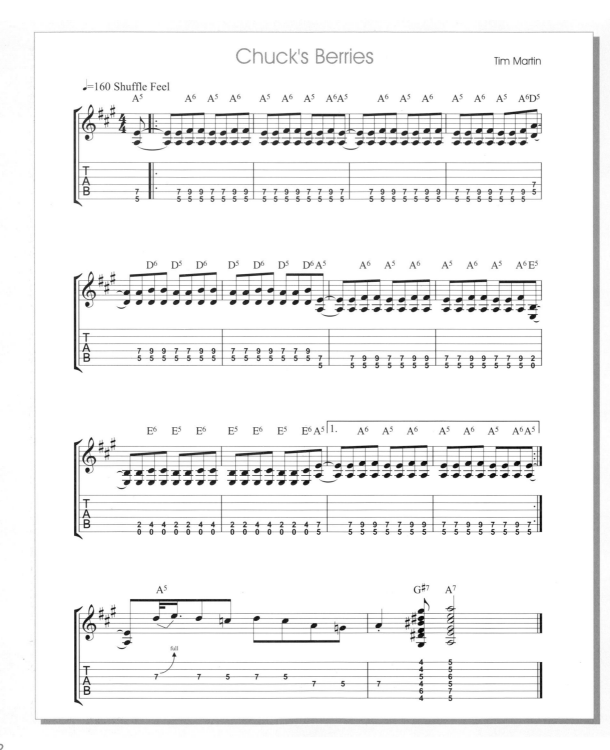

Chuck's Berries

Tim Martin

Reach For The Sun

Tim Martin

Chapter 9

Blues guitar is famous for its expressive, emotional quality and simple rhythms, which are some of the reasons the blues is one of the most common styles of music played on the guitar. This chapter explains essential blues techniques, such as the blues scale and slide guitar. You can also play the songs included in this chapter to practice the blues style.

Playing the lues

In this Chapter...

introduction to
blues guitar

Blues guitar is one of the most popular guitar styles. Blues music is known for its expressive, emotional style and lyrics as well as its simplicity. You do not require extensive guitar skills to play a simple blues tune.

The blues guitar style, which developed in the late 19th and early 20th centuries in the African American communities of Texas and the Mississippi Delta, has its roots in African folk music. Initially called plantation songs or sorrow songs, the style began to be referred to as "blues" in the 1920s.

The blues style has been influential in the development of many types of popular music and its history is closely linked to the history of rock music.

Blues songs are often played in the key of E. The key of a song determines the notes and chords you can play in that song.

Acoustic Blues

Acoustic guitars were the first instruments used to play the blues. Early musicians strummed or picked out soulful tunes on acoustic guitars with their bare fingers, foregoing the use of a pick.

Acoustic blues usually consists of open-position chords played in the key of E. An open-position chord is a chord you play without fretting, or pressing down, one or more of the strings that you play. The acoustic blues style allows you to play chords and melodies together. As you sing, you can play chords as accompaniment and then follow the singing by playing the same melody on the guitar.

Notable acoustic blues guitarists include Robert Johnson and Leadbelly.

Electric Blues

Electric blues developed in the northern urban areas of the United States, such as Chicago, after the migration of many African-Americans northward out of the rural south. Playing blues on the electric guitar developed as a mainly urban-based style, as opposed to the acoustic blues of the country.

Some notable electric blues guitarists include Buddy Guy, B.B. King and Muddy Waters. More modern electric blues guitarists include Stevie Ray Vaughan, Jonny Lang and Robert Cray.

BLUES LEAD GUITAR

Playing Blues Lead Guitar

You can play blues lead guitar by simply learning a few scale patterns and a few short phrases, or lines of music. Articulation techniques such as bending, vibrato, hammering-on, pulling-off and slides are also useful for blues lead guitar. For more information on articulation techniques, see pages 134 to 141.

You usually play blues lead guitar using the E minor pentatonic scale or the E blues scale. These scales are easy to play and include notes that give the music its sad, haunting sound. For information on the minor pentatonic scale, see page 146. For information on the blues scale, see page 170. You can also add notes from the E major pentatonic scale to enhance your blues solos. For information on the major pentatonic scale, see page 148.

Bending

Hammering-On

Blues Melodies

Example of Call and Response

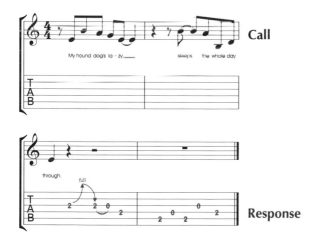

Call

Response

Playing blues lead guitar usually involves playing blues melodies. Blues melodies usually involve repeating phrases, or lines of music. For example, the blues guitarist can follow a short phrase of singing by playing the same or similar melody on the guitar in a format referred to as call and response. **"Call"** refers to the singing and **"response"** refers to the guitar playing, which essentially echoes the call. Bars of call are usually followed by an equal number of bars of response. A bar, or measure, breaks down a song into smaller, more manageable units of time. Typically, a song will have 2 bars of call followed by 2 bars of guitar response. This pattern is then repeated throughout the song.

Blues songs also often feature solo sections in which the guitarist can improvise freely.

CONTINUED...

introduction to
blues guitar

BLUES RHYTHM GUITAR

Playing Blues Rhythm Guitar

You usually play rhythm guitar to accompany vocals or another featured instrument. Playing blues rhythm guitar usually involves strumming chords and playing short, repeated sequences of notes on the low, bass strings. Blues rhythms have an easy style that requires only minimal technical skill.

12-Bar Blues

There are various blues rhythm progressions, such as 8-bar and 16-bar blues, but the 12-bar blues is the most common. A bar, or measure, breaks down a song into smaller, more manageable units of time. You can refer to page 174 to see examples of the 12-bar blues.

A 12-bar blues progression is made up of a combination of three chords built on the 1st, 4th and 5th notes of the major scale of the key you are playing in. For example, when playing a blues song in the key of E, the notes of the E major scale are E, F♯, G♯, A, B, C♯, D♯, E. To use the chords based on the 1st, 4th and 5th notes of the scale, you play the E, A and B chords.

In a basic 12-bar progression in the key of E, you play the following:

- **4 bars of E**
- **2 bars of A**
- **2 bars of E**
- 1 bar of B
- **1 bar of A**
- **2 bars of E**

You can also play the chords for a 12-bar blues progression as dominant 7th chords to produce more of a blues sound. For example, when playing a song in the key of E, you would play the E7, A7 and B7 chords. For information on dominant 7th chords, see page 68.

You can also use a combination of E-based and A-based barre chords to play a 12-bar blues progression. Dominant 7th barre chords are most commonly used to achieve the blues sound, but you can also use major barre chords if you prefer. For information on barre chords, see pages 82 to 101.

Turnarounds

A turnaround is a series of notes you play between repetitions of a 12-bar blues progression. The turnaround acts as a sort of bridge between verses, signalling the end of the progression and preparing you for going back to the beginning to repeat the progression.

The turnaround shown in this example follows a 12-bar blues progression in the key of E.

At the end of a blues song, you play an ending instead of a turnaround. You usually end the song on the same chord as the key you are playing the song in. So if you are playing in the key of E, you would end on the E chord.

Example of a Turnaround

The Blues Shuffle

Example of a Blues Shuffle

The shuffle, or swing, rhythm is common in blues music. In a blues shuffle, each beat is divided into three parts, called a triplet. In written music, a triplet is indicated by a group of three beats joined by a beam with the number 3 marked above (♪♪) or the symbol ⌐3⌐ above the notes on the staff.

When playing a triplet, you can count "one-and-ah two-and-ah three-and-ah four-and-ah." In a shuffle rhythm, you usually play notes on only the first and third parts of the triplet beat, which for example, would be on the "one" and the "ah." In other words, you play a triplet as you would play a quarter note followed by an eighth note—holding the quarter note for one beat and the eighth note for half a beat.

playing the blues scale

To play a blues scale, you play the minor pentatonic scale, except you add a flatted fifth note to the scale. For information on the minor pentatonic scale, see page 146. The flatted fifth note adds a "blues" sound to the minor pentatonic scale.

A flatted fifth note is one fret, or semi-tone, lower than the fifth note of a minor scale. For example, the fifth note in the E minor scale is B, so you play

B♭ as the flatted fifth in the blues scale in the key of E.

You can move the finger pattern for the notes of the blues scale to any fret to play in a different key. The note you start the scale on determines the key. For example, if you start the scale by playing C on the 6th string at the eighth fret, you play the blues scale in the key of C. The key of a song tells you what notes and chords you can play in the song.

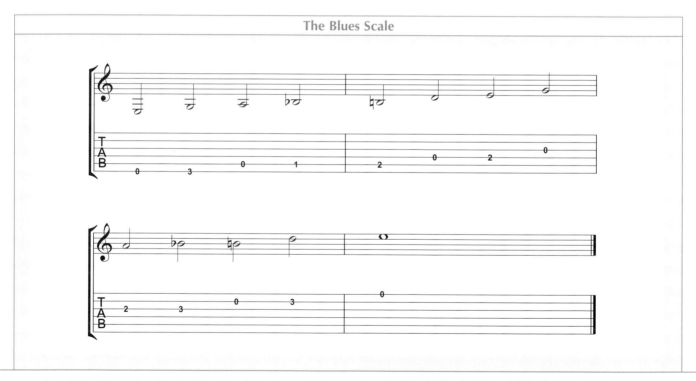

The Blues Scale

- Use your index finger for the notes on the first fret, your middle finger for the notes on the second fret and your ring finger for the notes on the third fret.

- The blues scale is essential to know if you want to play blues lead guitar.

- In this example, the blues scale begins on the 6th string without holding the string down, which is the E note. Therefore, we play the blues scale in the key of E.

adding a major third note

You can add a major third note to the blues scale to achieve a funky sound in your blues playing. For information on the blues scale, see page 170. Adding a major third note is especially effective when you are playing in a major key.

A major third note is one fret, or semi-tone, higher than the third note of a minor scale. For example, the third note in an E minor scale is G, so G♯ is the major third note that you add to the blues scale in the key of

E. The key you play a song in determines which notes and chords you can play in the song.

To play the major third note, you often hammer-on the major third note from the note that comes before it, which is usually one fret lower. For information on playing hammer-ons, see page 134.

Once you learn which note you should add to the blues scale to include the major third note, you can add the note to add interest to your playing.

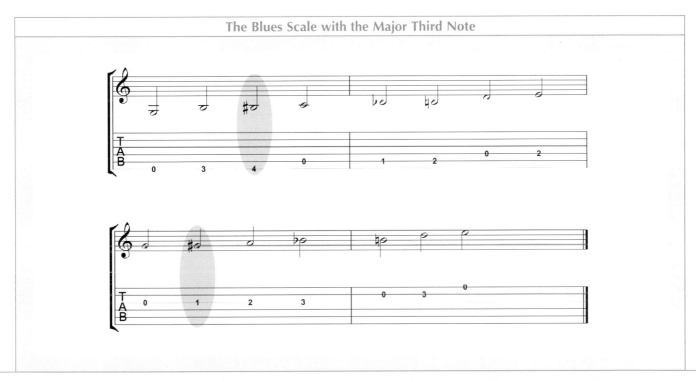

The Blues Scale with the Major Third Note

- Use your index finger for the notes on the first fret, your middle finger for the notes on the second fret, your ring finger for the notes on the third fret and your pinky finger for the notes on the fourth fret.

- In your blues guitar playing, only add the major third note occasionally as a special note.

- In this example, the blues scale begins on the 6th string without holding the string down, which is the E note. Therefore, we play the blues scale with the added major third note in the key of E.

playing slide guitar

When playing blues music, a technique often employed is the use of a slide. This technique was developed by the first blues guitarists, who slid the necks of glass bottles along the strings to mimic the sound of the human voice.

Slides can be found in various shapes, sizes and materials. A slide's material typically influences the resulting sound. For example, a glass slide creates a crisper, more subtle sound than a slide made of metal.

When using a slide, do not press down too firmly on the strings or you will create a buzzing sound. In addition to using a slide, you can press down the strings with your fingers behind specific frets to form a chord.

To play slide guitar, you can use any acoustic or electric guitar with steel strings. If you use an electric guitar, use a guitar with heavier strings and a high action. The action refers to the distance between the strings and the fingerboard. You can strum or pick the strings using your fingers, a pick or a combination of fingerpicks and thumbpicks. Each method requires a slightly different way of playing and produces a different sound.

Playing Slide Guitar Example

1 Place the slide over the pinky or ring finger on your fretting hand.

• Placing the slide on your pinky or ring finger leaves your other fingers free to fret notes while you play.

2 Position the slide directly on top of the fifth fret.

• The slide should be directly above the fret, not behind it.

• Make sure the slide is parallel to the fret and not angled across the fret.

3 Gently touch the strings with the slide.

Tip

What is the most popular type of tuning used when playing slide guitar?

Slide guitarists often use open tunings. Open tunings are useful for slide guitar because they allow you to play a chord by simply pressing the slide against all the strings at a fret. Open-G and Open-E tunings are the most popular open tunings for slide guitar. For information on open tunings, see page 158.

What variations can I perform when using slides?

You can use a sliding technique in which you place the slide a few frets higher or lower than the desired note. You then pluck the strings and gradually move the slide to the proper fret.

You can also apply vibrato to quickly raise and lower the tone. To perform this variation, pick the strings and shift your fretting hand in slight but quick movements up and down the neck.

4 Allow your fingers to rest lightly on the strings between the slide and the headstock of the guitar.

- Resting your fingers behind the slide helps to damp, or mute, the strings. Damping the strings above the slide makes it easier to play single notes clearly.

5 Strum the first two strings toward the floor.

- If the strings buzz, gently increase the pressure on the strings until the notes ring out.

6 Repeat steps 2 to 5, moving the slide to a different fret each time you perform step 2 to experience the sound of slide guitar.

songs for practice

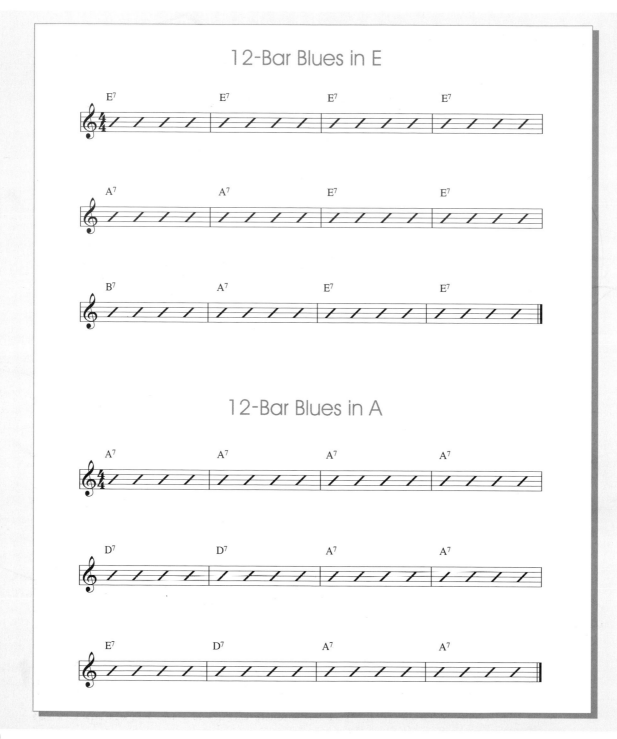

Norwood's Blues

Tim Martin

Chapter 10

The melodies of folk and country music were traditionally played around campfires and in rural villages. However, folk and country music have evolved beyond these modest beginnings to become major genres of popular music. This chapter will show you how to play some of the most common styles of folk and country music, including Carter style, Travis picking, and more.

Playing Folk and Country Music

In this Chapter...

introduction to
folk and country music

Folk music and country music are popular music forms that use the guitar.

A major hallmark of folk music is the simplicity of the music and lyrics. The simple, catchy melodies were traditionally created by the common people for an audience of their peers, making it the music of the masses. Some notable folk guitarists are Bob Dylan, Woody Guthrie and Joni Mitchell.

Country music has evolved over the years from the honky-tonk, western beat of the early years to a more blues-inspired sound. Today, country music attracts younger audiences and the influence of many other types of music, especially pop music, can be clearly heard. Some notable country guitarists are Chet Atkins, Merle Travis and Hank Williams.

Guitars Used for Folk and Country Music

Most folk guitarists use acoustic guitars because they are portable, convenient and produce natural, organic-sounding music. Acoustic instruments such as Martin guitars are commonly used.

Country music players use acoustic or electric guitars depending on the type of sound they want to achieve. Acoustic guitars are usually used for rhythm playing and electric guitars are used for playing leads. Simple, all-purpose guitars are preferred for country music. The Fender Telecaster has become the ultimate country music guitar.

Martin Guitar

Capo

Capos are commonly used when playing folk and country music. A capo is a device that clamps down across the fingerboard on a guitar to hold down all the strings at a specific fret. The capo acts as an adjustable nut that allows you to change the guitar's pitch. For more information on capos, see page 214.

A capo is useful when playing accompaniment for vocals. You can move the capo up or down until you find the best sound for the vocal range of the singer.

Thumbpicks and Fingerpicks

Thumbpicks are plastic or metal picks you can wrap around your thumb. Fingerpicks are similar to thumbpicks, except they are worn on the fingers. Country and folk players often use thumbpicks in addition to plucking with their fingers to produce a strong sound. Some players prefer to use fingerpicks, which give a slightly brighter sound than just your fingertips. You can also use a thumbpick and fingerpicks together.

Guitar Techniques

Folk and country guitarists often use arpeggio and open tuning techniques. An arpeggio is a chord in which each note, or string, is played separately. To play an arpeggio, you fret the strings for the chord and then pluck each string individually so that the sound of each note is sustained. For more information on arpeggio style, see page 194.

Open tuning involves tuning your guitar to allow you to play a chord when you strum all the open strings. An open string is a string you play without fretting, or holding down the string. For more information on open tuning, see page 158.

Fingerpicking

Fingerpicking is a common technique used for playing folk and country music. Fingerpicking involves using the thumb and fingers to pluck or strum the guitar strings instead of using a pick. You play the three lowest-pitched bass strings by plucking downward with your thumb and the higher-pitched treble strings by plucking upward with your fingers. For more information on fingerpicking, see page 27.

You can also use a pick in addition to plucking with your fingers. This technique is popular among folk and country guitarists, but it is difficult to master.

playing the
bass note strum style

The bass note strum style is a different way of playing chords that involves plucking a bass note and then strumming a chord. This style is used in folk and country music and is a great way to accompany a singer.

To play the bass note strum style, place the fingers of your fretting hand on the appropriate frets to form a chord. With your picking hand, use your thumb to strike the bass, or lowest, note of the chord on a thicker, lower-sounding string. Then use the back of your index, middle and ring fingernails to strum the other notes of

the chord on the thinner, higher-sounding strings. You can also use a pick to play the bass note strum style.

To make things more interesting, you can play the alternating bass note strum style. To do this, play a chord using the bass note strum style and then play the chord using the bass note strum style again, except choose a different, usually higher, note for the bass note. You can then alternate between the two bass notes.

Bass Note Strum Style Example

- In this example, we play the bass note strum style with a C chord.

1 Place your index finger on the 2nd string, just behind the first fret.

2 Place your middle finger on the 4th string, just behind the second fret.

3 Place your ring finger on the 5th string, just behind the third fret.

4 Pick the 5th string toward the floor with your thumb.

5 Strum the 1st, 2nd and 3rd strings toward the floor with the back of the nails of your index, middle and ring fingers.

- You can also use a pick instead of your fingers in steps 4 and 5.

Tip

Is there a way to add variety when using the bass note strum style?

Yes. You can add variety to the bass note strum style by adding an upstroke that uses your index finger to strike the 1st or the 1st and 2nd strings toward the ceiling after you play a chord using the bass note strum style. When playing this variation, you need to maintain a constant rhythm of down and up strumming. Here is an example of this variation with a C chord.

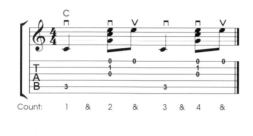

What are the commonly used alternating bass strings for the basic chords?

Here is a list of basic chords with the alternating bass strings you can use when playing the bass note strum style. For strings you would not normally hold down when playing a chord, such as the 6th string for a B7 chord, the fret at which you need to hold down a string for the bass note is included in brackets.

Chords	Alternating Bass Strings
A, Am, A7	5, 4 **or** 5, 6
B7	5, 6 (second fret) **or** 5, 4
C, C7	5, 6 (third fret) **or** 5, 4
D, D7, Dm	4, 5 **or** 4, 3
E, Em, E7	6, 5 **or** 6, 4
F	4, 5 (third fret) **or** 4, 3
G, G7	6, 5 **or** 6, 4

Bass Note Strum Style Example

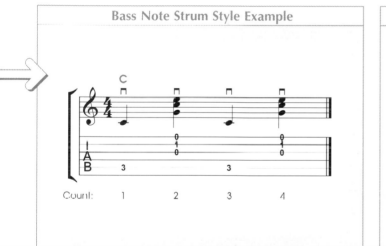

- This exercise shows the bass note strum style with a C chord. Perform the exercise to practice the bass note strum style.

- Pick or strum the string(s) toward the floor each time you see the ⊓ symbol. You hold each quarter note (♩) for 1 count.

Alternating Bass Note Strum Style Example

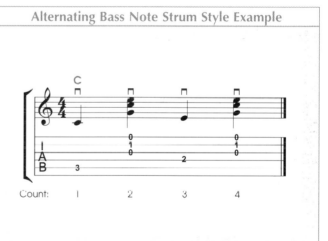

- When playing the alternating bass note strum style, you alternate between two bass notes.

- This exercise shows the alternating bass note strum style with a C chord. Perform the exercise to practice the alternating bass note strum style.

- Pick or strum the string(s) toward the floor each time you see the ⊓ symbol. You hold each quarter note (♩) for 1 count.

playing in carter style

The Carter style of playing guitar is typically used in folk and country songs, although you can play any type of song in Carter style. This style of playing guitar was named after the famous country group, the Carter Family. The Carter style is often used when playing solo since it allows you to play lead (single notes) and rhythm (chords) on the guitar at the same time.

To play in Carter style, you play a melody on the lower-sounding strings using your thumb or a pick.

When a note in a melody is longer than a quarter note, you can use the back of the nails of your index, middle and ring fingers, your thumb or a pick to strum a chord on the higher-sounding strings.

When playing in Carter style, put more emphasis on playing the melody on the thicker strings and play the accompanying chords on the thinner strings more softly.

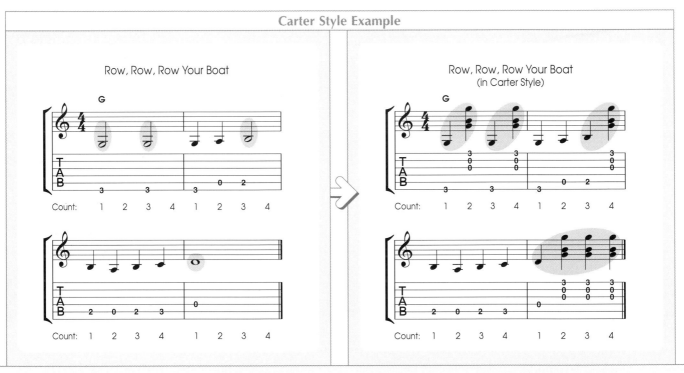

Carter Style Example

- This exercise shows the basic melody of "Row, Row, Row Your Boat." Perform the exercise to play the song.
- You hold whole notes (o) for 4 counts, half notes (♩) for 2 counts and quarter notes (♩) for 1 count.

- This exercise shows "Row, Row, Row Your Boat" in Carter style. Perform the exercise to play the song.
- In Carter style, each time a note longer than a quarter note (♩) appears in the basic melody, a chord strum is added.

playing with
travis picking

Travis picking is typically used in folk and country music, although it can be used in playing any type of music. This style of fingerpicking was named after renowned country guitarist Merle Travis.

To play music using Travis picking, you use your thumb to continually alternate between playing two bass notes on the thicker, or lower-sounding, strings. While your thumb plays the bass notes, your index, middle and sometimes ring finger play the melody by picking the thinner, or higher-sounding, strings. Since the melody and bass accompaniment are played simultaneously,

it may take some time before you become comfortable with this style of fingerpicking.

When playing music using Travis picking, your thumb usually alternates between playing the root note and the 5th of the chord. The root note is the note the chord is named after, such as C for a C major chord, and the 5th of the chord is the highest note of the three notes that make up a chord. For a list of bass notes you can use for the basic chords, see the top of page 181.

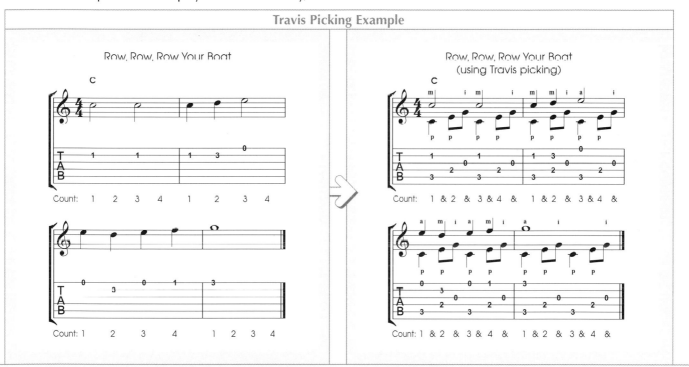

Travis Picking Example

- This exercise shows the basic melody of "Row, Row, Row Your Boat." Perform the exercise to play the song.

- You hold whole notes (o) for 4 counts, half notes (𝅗𝅥) for 2 counts, quarter notes (𝅘𝅥) for 1 count and eighth notes (𝅘𝅥𝅮) for ½ count. When two or more eighth notes appear in a row, they are joined with a beam (𝅘𝅥𝅮𝅘𝅥𝅮).

- This exercise shows "Row, Row, Row Your Boat" using Travis picking. Perform the exercise to play the song.

- When using Travis picking, your thumb (p) alternates between two bass (thicker) strings while your index (i), middle (m) and ring (a) fingers play the melody on the treble (thinner) strings.

songs for practice

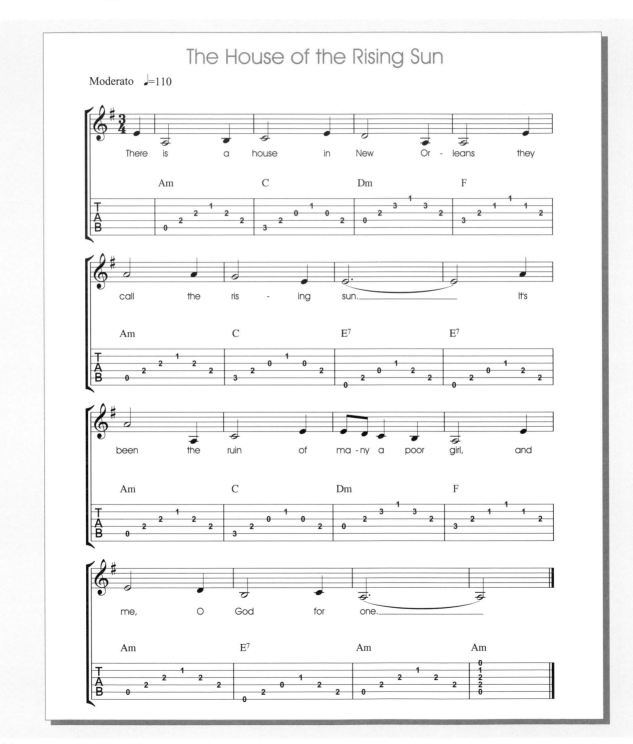

The House of the Rising Sun

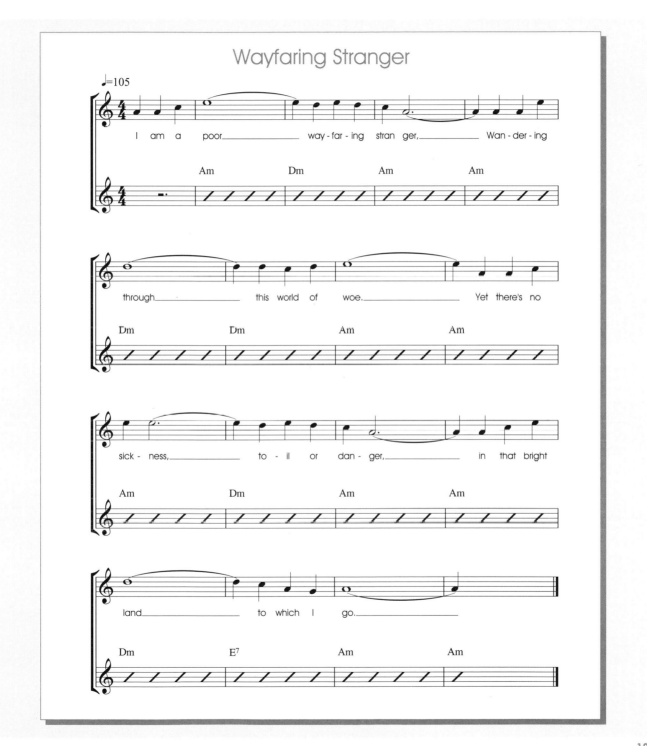

Wayfaring Stranger

Chapter 11

Although classical guitar is considered by some to be straight-laced and uninventive, many musicians agree that learning classical guitar techniques can help you incorporate some interesting touches into your music. You can read this chapter to learn about the classical style, including techniques such as free strokes, rest strokes, arpeggio style and counterpoint. There is also a practice song included to help you improve your playing.

Playing Classical Guitar

In this Chapter...

introduction to classical guitar

Classical guitar is a unique and long-established method of playing the guitar. Classical guitarists use a classical guitar and play classical music, such as music by Fernando Sor or Bach. Classical guitarists also use a distinct playing style, which involves using a combination of fingers and fingernails to strike the strings, rather than using a pick.

Many of the techniques used in classical guitar stem from various practices of composers and artists of the past. Classical guitar techniques are ideal for playing classical music, but you can also incorporate these techniques when playing other types of music, such as rock or country, to achieve a more unique sound.

History of Classical Guitar

Classical guitar has been around for several centuries. England's King Charles II was a guitar player and France's King Louis XIV had guitarists at his court. With royal interest in the instrument, the guitar became quite popular.

By the 19th century, the guitar had evolved into a 6-stringed instrument. The 19th century also brought changes that made the guitar the size and shape we recognize today. Between 1850 and 1890, Antonio de Torres Jurado produced a guitar that had a deeper body than

former guitars. The increased depth of the body helped improve the tone and volume of the guitar. The posture and hand position for playing the guitar also became more formalized in the late 19th century.

The early 20th century guitarist, Andrés Segovia, was responsible for making the guitar a popular instrument. He revolutionized the guitar by developing standardized finger notation in written guitar music and making written music more accessible to guitar players. Largely due to his efforts, the guitar became a respected and established instrument.

Classical Guitars

The classical guitar is similar to an acoustic guitar, but a classical guitar has a smaller body, wider neck and nylon strings. The nylon strings help produce a more mellow sound and are easier on your fingers than the steel strings on an acoustic guitar. Although the strings on a classical guitar are nylon, the bass strings are wrapped in metal.

Classical Guitar   Acoustic Guitar

Classical Playing Position

When you play classical guitar, you must sit in a formal playing position. This position is beneficial for playing the complex fingerings required by classical guitar.

To play the classical guitar properly, sit up straight on the edge of a chair and rest the body of the guitar over your left leg if you are right-handed and over your right leg if you are left-handed.

Hold the neck of the guitar at an angle so that the head of the guitar is at eye level when you turn your head to the side. You can maintain the correct angle of the guitar by resting your foot on a stool that is 4 to 6 inches high. There are stools specially designed for playing classical guitar. Rest the stool under your left foot if you are right-handed and under your right foot if you are left-handed.

You should also tilt the guitar slightly away from your body so the guitar can vibrate freely. The classical playing position allows your hands to move freely and helps you better play quick changes with your picking hand.

CONTINUED...

introduction to classical guitar

Hand Positions for Classical Guitar

Fretting Hand Position

The fretting hand position is very structured in classical guitar. You should arch your fingers at a 90-degree angle around the fingerboard and position your fingertips perpendicular to the strings. Also, keep your thumb straight and pressed against the back of the neck of the guitar, opposite your index finger. Your hand should remain in this position when moving to various positions along the neck of the guitar. When playing classical guitar, it is important to move your arm and hand together to ensure that you maintain the proper fretting hand position.

Picking Hand Position

The picking hand position is important when playing classical guitar to allow for maximum vibration of the strings and for producing the traditional classical guitar sound. In the proper position, you should rotate your wrist so that your index, middle and ring fingers are perpendicular to the strings. To move your picking hand into the proper position, place your thumb on the 6th string, your index finger on the 3rd string, your middle finger on the 2nd string and your ring finger on the 1st string. Then slide your thumb $1^1/_2$ inches to the left.

Picking Hand Fingernails

The length of your fingernails on your picking hand will affect the tone of the guitar. With short nails, you can use the flesh on your fingers to produce a mellow, soft tone. If you have long nails, you can use them to produce a metallic, sharp tone. Most guitarists use a combination of both flesh and nails to pick the strings, which produces a well-rounded tone.

In most cases, the best length for your picking hand fingernails is to have half moons just above your fingertips. If your nails are weak, you can use artificial nails, but they are not as flexible as natural fingernails.

Classical Guitar Notation

Classical guitar music has some unique notations you should be aware of when playing classical guitar. There are notations for the fingers you should use to play each note and for barre chords. The direction the stems point is also unique to classical guitar.

Fingerings

In classical guitar notation, the letters "p," "i," "m" and "a" indicate the first letter of the Latin names for your fingers. The following chart indicates the fingers each Latin name represents.

Letter	Latin Name	Finger
p	*pollex*	thumb
i	*index*	index
m	*medius*	middle
a	*annularis*	ring

The pinky finger is not often used in classical guitar, but if you do see it in the notation, the finger is represented by the letter "C," "X" or "E."

Barre Chords

If you need to play a barre chord, you will see a symbol that consists of a "C" followed by a roman numeral, such as "V." The "C" indicates you barre all six strings and the roman numeral indicates the fret where you place your index finger to form the barre. If a C with a line through it (¢) is displayed, you do not need to barre all six strings. The dashed line that follows this symbol indicates how long you need to hold down the barre. For more information on barre chords, see page 82.

Stems

Also unique to classical guitar notation are the stems on the notes. The stem usually points down on notes you play with your thumb and points up on the notes you play with your index, middle and ring fingers.

Numbers

A number in a circle next to a note indicates which string you should use to play the note. Other numbers may also be included to indicate which finger you should use to fret a note. Since classical guitar notation traditionally does not include tablature, these numbers specify how certain notes should be played. For information on tablature, see page 30.

Example of Classical Guitar Notation

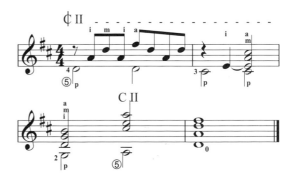

playing free strokes

Free stokes are useful for making strings ring as much as possible and for playing arpeggios. For information on playing arpeggios, see page 194. When playing free strokes, your finger or thumb does not rest on the next string.

To play a free stroke, you strike a string with your finger using an upward movement or with your thumb using a downward movement. After striking the string, your finger or thumb should be positioned slightly above the next string. You should not let your finger or thumb rest on or hit the next string. Your finger or thumb should gently press the string toward the body of the guitar before pulling slightly toward the next string. In classical guitar, your thumb plays free strokes most of the time.

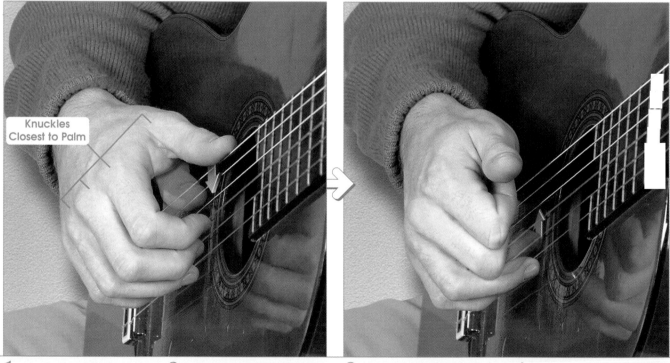

Knuckles Closest to Palm

1 Strike the 6th string with your thumb, using a downward movement. Do not allow your thumb to rest on any other string.

2 Strike the 3rd string with your index finger, using an upward movement. Do not allow your index finger to rest on any other string.

- Move your thumb or finger only from the knuckle closest to your palm.

3 Strike the 2nd string with your middle finger, using an upward movement. Do not allow your middle finger to rest on any other string.

4 Strike the 1st string with your ring finger, using an upward movement. Do not allow your ring finger to rest on any other string.

playing rest strokes

You can play a rest stroke to accentuate and enhance the sound of a string. For example, if you want to emphasize the top note when you play three or four notes at a time, you could use a rest stroke to play the top note.

To play a rest stroke, you strike a string straight across and allow your finger or thumb to rest on the next string. You should gently press the string toward the body of the guitar before pulling slightly toward the next string. When using your finger to strike a string, your finger will come to rest on the next lower-sounding string. When using your thumb to strike a string, your thumb will come to rest on the next higher-sounding string.

When playing rest strokes, your palm should stay perfectly still and your finger should move toward your palm. To get the most powerful sound, try to move your thumb or finger only from the knuckle closest to your palm.

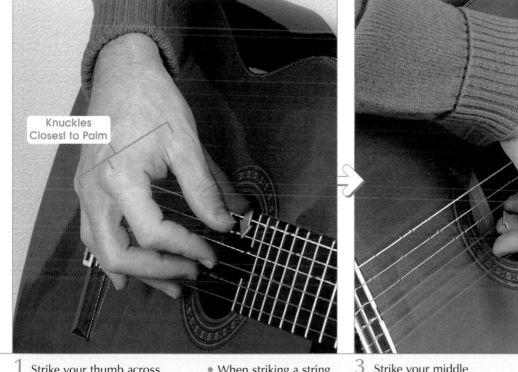

Knuckles Closest to Palm

1 Strike your thumb across the 6th string. Allow your thumb to rest on the 5th string.

2 Strike your index finger across the 3rd string. Allow your index to rest on the 4th string.

• When striking a string, make sure you move your thumb or finger only from the knuckle closest to your palm.

3 Strike your middle finger across the 2nd string. Allow your middle finger to rest on the 3rd string.

4 Strike your ring finger across the 1st string. Allow your ring finger to rest on the 2nd string.

playing arpeggio style

Classical guitar music often contains arpeggios. An arpeggio is a chord in which each note, or string, is played separately.

To play an arpeggio, you hold down the strings that form the chord and then pluck each string individually so that the sound of each note is sustained. You usually play the notes from lowest to highest sounding and then from highest to lowest sounding. You will also usually use the free stroke technique in which a finger does not rest on another string once it has plucked a string. For more information on playing free strokes, see page 192.

There are various finger patterns for playing arpeggios. Commonly played patterns include p(thumb)-i(index)-m(middle)-a(ring) and p-i-m-a-m-i.

When reading a chord on tablature for classical guitar, the numbers are written from left to right, rather than in a vertical line. For more information on tablature, see page 30.

Playing Arpeggio Style

- In this example, we play an arpeggio based on an A minor chord in the p-i-m-a pattern.

1 Place your index finger on the 2nd string, just behind the first fret.

2 Place your middle finger on the 3rd string, just behind the second fret.

3 Strike the 5th string with your thumb (p).

4 Strike the 3rd string with your index finger (i).

5 Strike the 2nd string with your middle finger (m).

6 Strike the 1st string with your ring finger (a).

playing
counterpoint

Counterpoint, also called contrapuntal style, is a major component of playing classical guitar. Throughout the Baroque era, counterpoint was very popular. Classical guitarists still use this distinct playing style today. When you play counterpoint, you play multiple melodies at once.

Music that contains counterpoint normally has bass (low) and treble (high) parts. You usually play the bass with your thumb and play the treble with your index, middle and ring fingers.

Playing counterpoint may take some practice. The fingers and thumb of your picking hand need to work together, but at the same time, work independently. As a beginner, you may find the coordination required difficult to master.

Music that uses counterpoint often includes canons, also called rounds. In a canon, a line of music begins and then is repeated a few moments later.

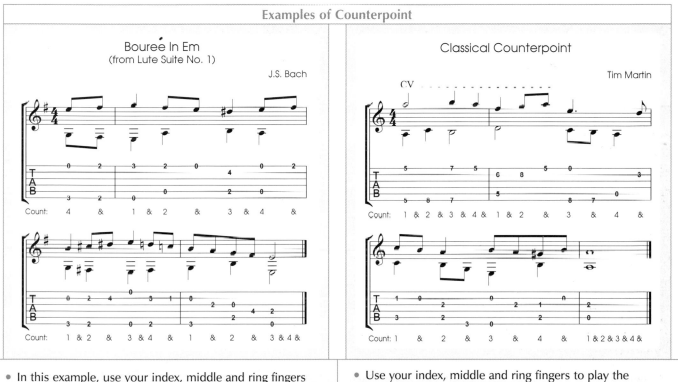

Examples of Counterpoint

Bouree In Em
(from Lute Suite No. 1)

J.S. Bach

Classical Counterpoint

Tim Martin

- In this example, use your index, middle and ring fingers to play the notes on the 1st, 2nd and 3rd strings. Use your thumb to play the notes on the 4th, 5th and 6th strings.
- You hold half notes (♩) for 2 counts, quarter notes (♩) for 1 count and eighth notes (♪) for ¹⁄₂ count. When two or more eighth notes appear in a row, they are joined with a beam (♫).

- Use your index, middle and ring fingers to play the notes on the 1st, 2nd and 3rd strings. Use your thumb to play the notes on the 4th, 5th and 6th strings.
- In this example, **CV** at the top of the musical notation indicates that you should play a barre chord (indicated by C) by pressing your index finger across all 6 strings, just behind the fifth (V) fret. For information on barre chords, see page 82.

songs for practice

1

Spanish Romance

Anonymous

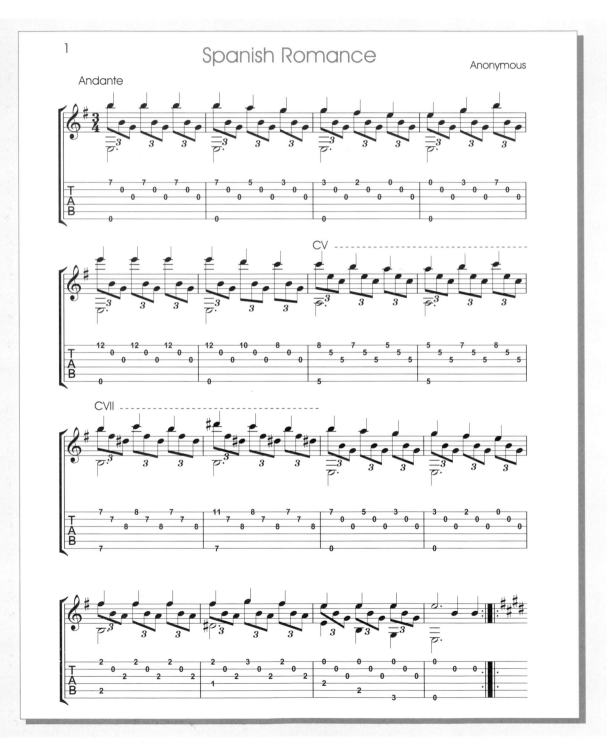

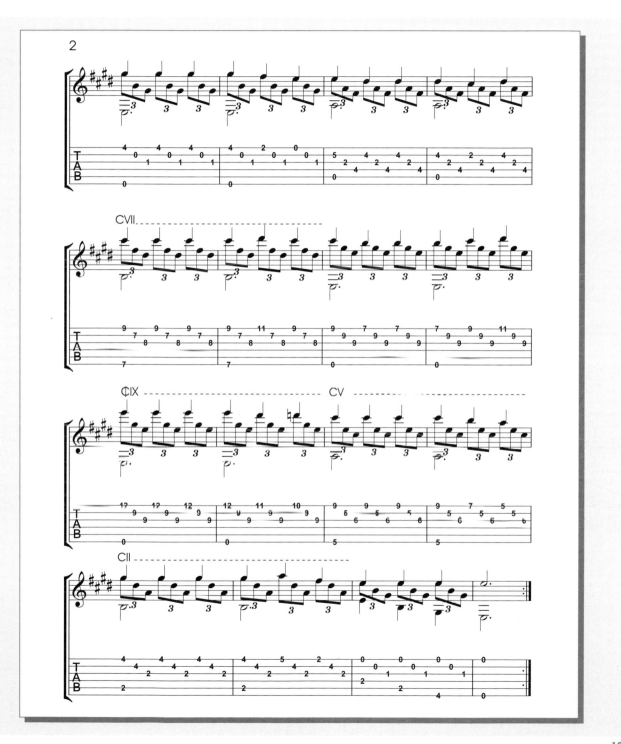

Chapter 12

You should consider your options carefully before deciding on the guitar you want to buy. This chapter provides information to help you choose the guitar that best suits your needs. You will learn about the different types of guitars, what to look for when buying a guitar, good places to purchase a guitar, as well as specific features you should consider when buying an electric guitar.

Buying a Guitar

In this Chapter...

Introduction to Buying a Guitar

Types of Guitars

Test a Guitar

Guitar Construction

Electric Guitar Considerations

introduction to
buying a guitar

It is important to carefully consider your options before buying a guitar.

You should first consider your budget, taking some time to figure out how much you can afford to spend on a guitar. If the guitar will play a major role in your life and you plan to use it frequently, you may want to buy a higher quality instrument. A used guitar is also an option if you have limited funds. Used guitars usually do not include a manufacturer's warranty, but some stores may offer a limited warranty.

How the guitar feels and sounds is also important. Your goal is to buy the best quality guitar that is within your budget. You should try different guitars to see how each one feels and sounds. If you are not sure what to look for, it is a good idea to ask someone who has experience with guitars to accompany you when you go shopping.

Shop Around

Make sure you shop around at different stores and test various types of guitars before making your purchase. If a store offers a discount on a guitar you like, you should still check the prices at other stores for the same guitar. It is also a good idea to find out the manufacturer's suggested retail price of a guitar before you visit a store. This price is usually preset by the manufacturer and is available to the public. You can check the company's Web site or call the company for information.

Consider Location

You should take the location of the store into account when buying your guitar. It is generally better to purchase the guitar at a music store in your neighborhood so it will be convenient to return to the store for any follow-up issues, such as repairs to the guitar. Most retailers will match their competitors' prices, so if you find a better price farther from home, your local store may be willing to match the price.

Mail Order or Online

You can also buy a guitar through a mail order service or from an online retailer. Mail order and online music retailers often offer better prices, but you should make sure you try the guitar in a store before you buy. Keep in mind that each guitar is slightly different, so even if the guitar you purchase online is the same make and model as the one you tested in a store, it might sound or feel different. When purchasing by mail order or online, check the return policy to ensure the retailer allows sufficient time to try the guitar and will refund your money if you are not happy with the purchase. Also, find out how warranty repairs and adjustments will be performed. When the guitar is delivered, make sure you check it carefully for damage.

Left-Handed Guitars

Since most guitars are built for right-handed people, left-handed guitars are usually harder to find and more expensive to purchase.

You can obtain an authentic left-handed guitar at a store that specializes in left-handed guitars or by placing a special order at a music store. As an alternative, you can reverse the strings on a right-handed guitar to make it suitable for playing left-handed.

Acoustic guitars are more easily converted for left-hand playing than electric guitars. When you reverse an electric guitar, the knobs and controls may end up in an awkward position and may hamper your hand position when you play. The shape of the body of the guitar may also be designed only for right-handed people and may not be comfortable to play when reversed.

When you reverse the strings on a guitar, you may have to replace the nut on the guitar as well. Each slot on the nut is cut to fit a specific guitar string.

Some notable left-handed guitar players include Kurt Cobain, Jimi Hendrix and Paul McCartney.

types of guitars

There are three main types of guitars:
acoustic, classical and electric.

Acoustic

Acoustic guitars are portable and can be played anywhere. Unlike electric guitars, acoustic guitars do not require an amplifier or a power source, which makes them ideal for people who simply want to strum their favorite tunes.

Acoustic guitars mainly differ in the size and shape of their bodies. The size and shape of an acoustic guitar's body determines how the guitar sounds and feels. A guitar with a larger body will produce a louder sound than one with a smaller body. You can add a pickup to any acoustic guitar to connect it to an amplifier. You should choose the guitar size and shape that feels most comfortable to you.

Classical

Classical guitars are specialized instruments used primarily to play classical or flamenco music. While similar to an acoustic guitar in appearance, a classical guitar has a smaller body, a wider neck and nylon strings instead of steel strings. Classical guitars also produce a more mellow sound than acoustic guitars.

Electric

Electric guitars are smaller than acoustic and classical guitars and usually cost less than comparable acoustics, since they are easier to build. However, you will need additional equipment to play an electric guitar, such as an amplifier and speakers.

The body of an electric guitar can be solid, or it can be partially or completely hollow. Electric guitars use steel strings that are usually lighter than the steel strings used on acoustic guitars.

test a guitar

Before you buy a guitar, you should try out the guitar to test how well it plays. You should test the sustain, action and intonation of the guitar to determine if the guitar is of high quality or if you should avoid buying the guitar.

Sustain

Sustain is how long a note plays before fading away. To test the sustain, hold down a string, pick the string and keep holding the string down until the note fades. You should use this process to test the sustain of all the notes on the fingerboard. Listen to ensure the sustain is equal for all the notes. If some notes play with reduced sustain, you should avoid buying the guitar.

Action

Action refers to the height of the strings off the fingerboard, which is established by the height of the strings over the nut and the bridge. To test the action, hold down the 1st string just behind the first fret and then pick the string. If the note sounds dead or produces a buzzing sound, there may be a problem with the action. For example, a buzzing sound may indicate the string is too close to a fret. Perform this test playing all the notes on all six strings, especially the notes in the middle of the neck that are usually more difficult to fret.

As you play the notes on each string, notice whether you can press the strings down easily. Strings that are too high may be difficult to hold down, which will make it challenging for your hand to quickly change chords and notes.

Intonation

Intonation indicates whether the guitar plays notes in tune. To test the intonation, hold down a string just behind the twelfth fret and pick the string. Then play the string without holding the string down. You can tell if the intonation is correct if the note sounds one octave higher when you are holding the string down. Perform this test on all six strings. If you are not capable of distinguishing the sound between octaves, use an electronic tuner or bring an experienced guitarist with you to the store.

guitar construction

You should consider how a guitar is constructed before deciding to buy a guitar.

Body

Inspecting the body of a guitar can tell you how well the guitar was made. To make sure there are no loose parts, pick up the guitar and lightly tap the back and top while listening for rattling sounds. Check the body for stains, unevenly applied varnish, nicks or scratches and look for gaps or cracks in the wood, especially between the neck and body.

Type of Solid Wood

Different types of wood have slightly different sound characteristics. The type of wood may also affect the price of the guitar, since rarer woods are generally more expensive.

Most acoustic and classical guitars have a spruce or cedar top. Spruce-top guitars produce a slightly brighter sound, while cedar-top guitars give a darker, warmer sound.

Electric guitars are usually made from woods such as mahogany, maple or ash.

Spruce	Cedar	Mahogany

Solid Wood versus Laminated Wood

You will need to choose between solid and laminated wood when buying an acoustic or classical guitar. To tell if the top of the guitar is made of solid wood, you can examine the edge of the sound hole to make sure the grain of the wood runs over the edge instead of just along the top.

Unlike solid wood guitars, which are made from whole pieces of wood, laminated wood guitars are made from thin layers of wood glued together and covered with veneer. Solid wood guitars provide much better sound quality than guitars made with laminated wood, but are more expensive. However, laminated wood is more durable and resistant to cracking than solid wood.

A guitar made entirely of solid wood is ideal, but since the top of the guitar is most important in producing sound, make sure at least the top is solid wood even if the sides and back are not.

Neck

You should examine the construction of the neck and how it attaches to the body of the guitar. On acoustic and classical guitars, the neck is usually glued on to the body. The neck of an electric guitar can be attached in three different ways. The neck can be attached by bolts, glued on, or the piece of wood used to build the neck can continue through the body, resulting in no visible neck joint.

To check if the neck is warped or bent, hold the guitar with the headstock pointing toward you and look down the neck toward the bridge. The neck should be fairly straight, except for a slight curve in the fingerboard halfway down the neck. To check the curvature, hold down the thickest string at the first and fifteenth fret. The middle of the string should not touch the frets in the middle of the neck. Then check the thinnest string in the same way.

Ebony (black), rosewood (dark brown) and maple (light brown) are used most often for the fingerboard of an electric guitar, since these woods produce a hard, smooth fingerboard that gives a richer, brighter tone. The fingerboards of most acoustic and classical guitars are made from rosewood or ebony.

Decorative Elements

Some guitars have additional features that are purely esthetic, such as mother-of-pearl inlays, sound hole etchings or gold-plated hardware. Keep in mind that these features increase the cost of the guitar, but do not affect the guitar's sound quality.

Hardware

Some of the more expensive guitars have upgraded hardware that are of higher quality or nicer design, such as knobs, tuners and switches that are gold-plated instead of chrome-plated.

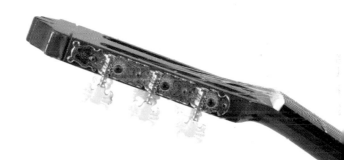

You should check that all the knobs, switches and tuners work correctly. Turn each tuning machine slightly to ensure the tuning machine turns easily and will adjust the tension of the attached string. On electric guitars, check the knobs and other hardware to make sure all the parts are firmly in place.

electric guitar
considerations

Before you buy an electric guitar, there are specific features of the guitar that you should test thoroughly. You should also consider what type of bridge and pickups you need. You may notice when you are shopping for an electric guitar that better electronics tend to increase the price of electric guitars.

Test an Electric Guitar

To test an electric guitar, try the following:

✓ Plug the guitar into an amplifier so you can hear the guitar's full sound. Make sure the amplifier's controls are not enhancing the sound of the guitar.

✓ Listen to the sound produced when the guitar is positioned close to the amplifier. The sound should be fairly quiet.

✓ Note the scale length, which is the length of the string between the nut and the saddle. A longer scale length makes the strings tighter and harder to bend. This quality is a matter of personal preference.

✓ Test the volume and tone controls to determine if they work properly. You should not hear any buzzing or crackling when adjusting the controls.

✓ Test the pickups, ensuring each string has a clear sound and plays at the same volume through the amplifier. You should also use the pickup selector switch when testing the pickups. This switch allows you to listen to each pickup individually so you can make sure each one is working properly.

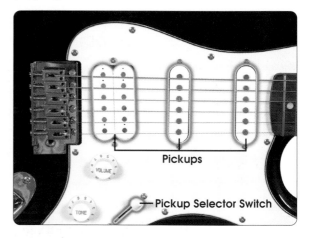

Pickups

Pickup Selector Switch

✓ Play a few bends to determine if there are any problems with the neck or frets. For information on playing bends, see page 138.

✓ Try out the guitar with some distortion on the amplifier. This may lead you to detect some hidden electronic problems, such as pickup and connection problems.

Types of Bridges

The bridge connects the strings to the body of the guitar. There are three main types of bridges—fixed, fulcrum and floating.

Fixed Bridge

A fixed bridge stays in place and does not have a tremolo bar. A tremolo bar allows you to adjust the tension and pitch of the strings on the guitar. An electric guitar with a fixed bridge will stay in tune longer.

Fulcrum Bridge

You can also choose a fulcrum bridge, also often called a knife-edge style bridge. On this type of bridge, you can usually only push the tremolo bar down, but vigorous use of the tremolo bar can cause the guitar to go out of tune.

Floating Bridge

The third type of bridge is a floating bridge, in which you can pull up or push down the tremolo bar. Even with vigorous use of the tremolo bar, the guitar tends to stay in tune. However, this type of bridge requires a lot of maintenance.

Types of Pickups

A pickup is a magnet that senses the strings' vibrations. The pickup converts these vibrations into electrical currents that an amplifier can use to produce sound. Most electric guitars have two or more pickups. It is important to choose an electric guitar with high-quality pickups. There are two main types of pickups—single-coil and dual-coil.

Single-coil Pickups

Single-coil pickups are pickups with one coil. Guitars with the name brand Fender are commonly equipped with single-coil pickups. Although single-coil pickups may produce a humming noise, they provide a clearer tone than dual-coil pickups. Single-coil pickups are popular with country, rock and blues guitarists.

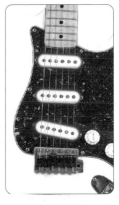

Dual-coil Pickups

Dual-coil pickups, also called humbucking pickups, are pickups that use a combination of two single coils. Guitars with the name brand Gibson often come with dual-coil pickups. Primarily used by hard rock and jazz players, dual-coil pickups can produce a louder and fuller sound than single-coil pickups.

Many guitars tend to have multiple pickup options, which makes these guitars more versatile. For example, some guitars have combinations of dual and single-coil pickups.

Chapter 13

Some accessories, such as strings and amplifiers for electric guitars, are essential to playing the guitar. Other accessories are more optional. These accessories are generally additional equipment that you can use to enhance your music, protect your guitar or make the guitar easier to play. This chapter discusses some common accessories you will use when playing the guitar.

Guitar Accessories

In this Chapter...

amplifiers and speakers

To obtain the full sound of an electric guitar, you need an amplifier. An amplifier connects to the guitar through a cable that plugs into the output on the guitar and into the input on the amplifier. In addition to increasing the volume of the guitar, the amplifier has controls you can use to adjust the sound quality. You will also need a speaker to hear the sound the amplifier and guitar produces. Most amplifiers have built-in speakers.

Before you buy an amplifier, consider how loud you will usually play and how you will use the amplifier. Try to buy the best amplifier you can afford, as the quality of the amplifier is crucial to the sound of your electric guitar.

Amplifier Power

Amplifier power is measured in watts and indicates how loud the amplifier will play. Keep in mind that a high wattage does not mean the amplifier is high quality.

The amount of power you require should be determined by where you are playing. If you are practicing by yourself, 5 to 15 watts is adequate. If you are playing at home or practicing with friends, 15 to 20 watts should be suitable. When performing on stage, an amplifier between 50 to 100 watts is commonly used. On some amplifiers, you can turn a switch to adjust the wattage, such as between 50 and 100 watts.

At high volume levels, a lower-watt amplifier produces distortion faster than a higher-watt amplifier. With some types of music, such as rock, a lower-watt amplifier can be beneficial since you may often want to play with distortion. In contrast, some guitarists prefer a higher-watt amplifier to maintain a clearer sound.

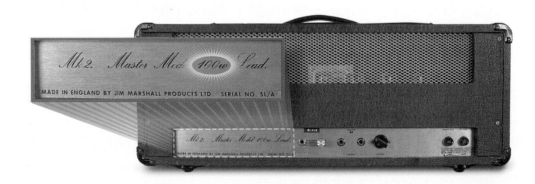

Tube versus Solid-state Amplifiers

Tube Amplifier

Solid-state Amplifier

You can choose either a tube amplifier or a solid-state amplifier. A tube amplifier uses older technology, which involves using a vacuum tube to produce sound. Solid-state amplifiers use microchips to produce sound. Although the tube variety is older and more difficult to maintain, many guitarists prefer the warm sound they produce.

A beginner normally chooses a solid-state amplifier, since this type of amplifier is more reliable and less expensive. A beginner is also less likely to notice the difference between the sound of the tube and solid-state amplifiers. In contrast, advanced guitarists often choose a tube amplifier for the best sound.

Practice versus Performance Amplifiers

You can choose a practice or a performance amplifier. A practice amplifier is less expensive, smaller and offers less wattage than a performance amplifier. Expect between 10 to 15 watts of power from a practice amplifier. Purchasing a practice amplifier is often a practical choice for a beginner with a low budget.

A performance amplifier typically provides 50 to 100 watts of power. With more power, the guitar can produce a louder, clearer sound. A performance amplifier is also bigger and of higher quality than a practice amplifier.

Even though performance amplifiers typically have higher levels of power, you may find low-power performance amplifiers. A low-power performance amplifier is useful for recording purposes.

Practice Amplifier

Performance Amplifier

CONTINUED...

amplifiers and speakers

Amplifier Simulators

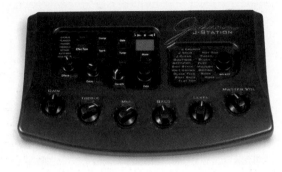

Instead of an amplifier, you can purchase an amplifier simulator, which simulates the sound of a regular amplifier. You can listen to the sound from a simulator through headphones, a stereo or even your computer. Simulators are advantageous because they are compact, easy to use and allow you to record music directly onto your computer or a tape machine. However, since the device only simulates an amplifier, the quality of the sound is not as good.

Amplifier Features

Amplifiers have a wide variety of features you should consider. An amplifier usually has three tone controls for adjusting bass, middle and treble frequencies. As with your stereo, adjusting the bass allows you to make deeper sounds and adjusting the treble allows you to create brighter sounds.

Amplifiers also often come with channels that allow you to switch between sounds. For example, one channel may provide clean sounds, whereas another channel may provide distortion. If an amplifier has multiple channels, there is usually a foot pedal you can use to easily change channels when playing.

Volume controls on an amplifier allow you to change the volume of each channel, adjust the amount of distortion and change the overall volume.

You can also find amplifiers that have a special sound effect, called reverb, which is built in to the amplifier. This effect makes it sound as if you are playing the guitar in a bigger room.

Also, consider if you want an amplifier that comes with a headphone jack. You can use a headphone jack so you do not bother others in your household when you are practicing, such as late at night. By using headphones, you will eliminate any effect the speaker has on tone quality, allowing you to hear the natural sound of your amplifier.

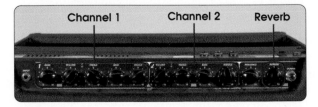

Testing Amplifiers

It is a good idea to test the amplifier you want to purchase. Take your guitar along with you to the store so you can hear the difference between different types of amplifiers. Also, listen for any crackling or buzzing because that could indicate a problem with the amplifier. In addition, test each control to determine its capability and that it works properly. To determine the amplifier's capability, test each control at a variety of settings.

Speakers

In order for an amplifier to produce sound, It must be connected to a speaker. The amplifier and speaker are usually sold as one unit, known as a combo. If you only have an amplifier without a speaker, the amplifier is called a head. If you use a head, you need to connect the head to an individual speaker cabinet, which is a box that contains a speaker. The speaker cabinets most guitarists choose contain 10 or 12-inch speakers.

When purchasing a speaker cabinet, you need to consider the speaker's impedance value. Impedance value is measured in electrical resistance called ohms. Most guitar speakers are available in 4, 8 or 16 ohms, with 8 ohm speakers being the most commonly used.

Make sure the impedance value of your speaker cabinet is the same as the impedance value of

the amplifier, which is also measured in ohms. Otherwise, you can damage both the speaker cabinet and the amplifier. For example, if the amplifier's impedance value is 8 ohms and the speaker's impedance value is 4 ohms, the amplifier will tend to overwork until both the amplifier and speaker blow out.

Speaker Cabinet

capos

A capo is a device that clamps down across the fingerboard at any fret on a guitar. Holding down all the strings at a certain fret will make the capo act as a new nut on the guitar to temporarily shorten the strings. With seemingly shorter strings, the guitar will have a higher pitch.

Types of Capos

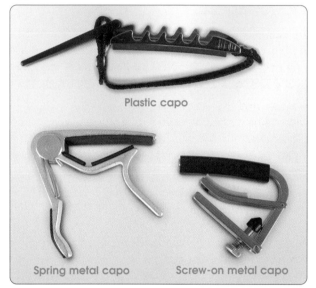

Plastic capo

Spring metal capo   Screw-on metal capo

There are many different types of capos available. Elastic band or plastic capos are less expensive, but tend to wear out quickly and may cause the strings to buzz. More expensive capos are made of metal, which last longer and are easier to position on the neck than elastic band or plastic capos. A metal capo can either clamp with a spring or screw-type mechanism. A screw-on capo is useful if you want to have more control over how tightly the capo attaches to the guitar.

Guitarists who often use capos usually select a more expensive capo. More expensive capos are easier to put on, move up and down the neck more easily and usually do a better job of holding the strings down.

Using a Capo

When attaching a capo to your guitar, you place the capo just behind the desired fret. Make sure the capo is not directly over the fret or too far away from the fret. For each fret you move the capo up, the notes will be one half step, or one semi-tone, higher. For example, if you place the capo at the second fret and you play the fingering for a G chord, you will actually be playing the higher A chord.

Check the Tuning

Keep in mind that using a capo can sometimes cause the guitar strings to no longer be in tune. Each time you attach or remove a capo, you should check the tuning of the guitar.

Play in a Different Key

A capo allows you to immediately play a song in a different key. You can play a song with fingerings you use for the original key, but with the capo acting as a new nut, the song will sound as if it is played in a new key. For example, you can play a song in the key of B-flat by placing the capo at the third fret and using chord fingerings from the key of G.

Benefits of Capos

Using a capo is beneficial when you are playing with vocal accompaniment. You can move the capo along the fingerboard to raise the pitch of the notes to play in a key comfortable for the singer. For example, if the singer's voice is best suited to the key of A, you can use a capo to change the key of a song from G to A, while still using the original fingering.

The capo can also be useful if you are playing with another guitarist. For example, you can both play a song using the same chords, but each place the capo at different frets to add tonal variety to the song.

You may find that some songs are easier to play when using a capo. A capo allows you to play chords closer to the bridge on a guitar using fingerings that you would normally play closer to the nut. Considering that frets are closer together toward the bridge on the guitar, your fingers may not have to stretch as far apart to play some chords.

If you do not like using barre chords, in many cases you can use a capo instead. For more information on barre chords, see page 82.

cases

The most important accessory you can purchase for your guitar is a sturdy case. A guitar case protects the instrument against damage from scratches, humidity, direct sunlight and extreme hot or cold temperatures. You should always place the guitar in its case when traveling or when storing the guitar for extended periods of time.

Cases vary in shape and size, but there are three basic types of cases—the hard case, the soft case and the gig bag. When choosing a case, keep in mind that you get what you pay for. Expensive cases offer better protection than cheaper ones.

Hard Case

A hard case, also called a hard shell case, provides the best protection for your guitar. Hard cases are more expensive than other types of cases, but if you are buying a high-quality guitar or will be traveling often, it is a good idea to invest in a hard case.

Hard cases are usually made from particle board or plywood, which is covered in a decorative material such as nylon or leather. Cases can also be made from hard plastic. The cases contain padding inside that holds the guitar in place and a lining of fake fur or foam to protect the guitar's finish.

Some hard cases, also called flightcases, are made with reinforced metal corners and aluminum side panels to offer extra protection, but these cases are heavy and costly.

When choosing a case, you should ensure the guitar fits snugly inside the case and will not move around.

Soft Case

Soft cases are typically made from a stiff material, such as cardboard. These cases provide basic protection from scratches and dings, but will puncture and collapse much more easily under pressure than hard cases. A soft case is a useful alternative when you cannot afford a hard case or when your guitar is not of the highest quality.

Gig Bag

Gig bags offer the least amount of protection for your guitar. These cases are zippered bags, commonly made from plastic, leather, nylon, or other fabric. Most gig bags have a shoulder strap and some have a foam lining for additional protection and outside pockets you can use to store music, picks or strings. You should make sure the inside of the zipper on a gig bag is covered so it does not come into contact with the guitar.

Because gig bags are lightweight and compact, they are ideal for students and professional musicians who frequently play at local venues. You can also find expensive gig bags that provide better protection than soft cases, while maintaining the portability of traditional gig bags.

picks

A pick, also called a plectrum, is a flat, triangular-shaped piece of plastic you can use to strum or pluck the strings of a guitar. A pick is a useful, inexpensive tool that can enhance your guitar playing.

Strumming with a pick produces a brighter, more vivid tone from the guitar than strumming with your fingers. When you first start playing the guitar, you may find it easier to use a pick and then try using your fingers as you gain experience.

Since picks are small and easily lost, you should make sure you maintain a good supply.

Types of Picks

Picks are available in many different materials, sizes, shapes, colors and thicknesses.

Although thick picks are usually more rigid than thin picks, you may find flexible picks that are thick and inflexible picks that are thin. The flexibility of a pick largely determines the type of sound the pick produces. Hard picks emit a crisp, full-bodied sound while floppy picks emit a more subdued sound. Metal picks are a good choice if you want a pick that is really hard.

Keep in mind that a particular style of music might work best with a specific type of pick. Thin, large picks are a favorite with acoustic players, since they strum through the strings with minimal resistance and help create an airy sound. However, jazz players prefer thicker, smaller picks for their response and accuracy.

Some picks have additional features, such as a non-slip surface that makes the pick easier to grip with your fingers. However, the thickness and size are the most important features you should consider when choosing a pick, so do not allow the color to influence your decision. You should try a variety of picks to determine which one works best for you.

Rough Edges

You should check that your picks do not have rough edges, which can get caught on the guitar strings as you play. If you find rough edges, try smoothing the edges with sandpaper or a nail file.

Holding a Pick

You should hold the pick firmly between your thumb and index finger so that only the tip of the pick sticks out. Be careful to hold the pick tightly enough so it does not slip between your fingers as you play. You can prevent your free fingers from getting in the way by folding the fingers into your hand or stretching them out.

Fingerpicks and Thumbpicks

Fingerpicks are plastic or metal picks you can attach to each finger. Thumbpicks are similar to fingerpicks, except they are worn on the thumb. Guitar players often use thumbpicks in addition to plucking with their fingers to produce a strong sound. Since fingerpicks tend to get caught in guitar strings, guitarists do not use them often, but they are popular with banjo players.

Use Picks or Fingers

You usually play an electric guitar with a pick, since it is difficult to play fast-paced solos with your fingers. However, many rock players sometimes pick with their fingers to achieve specific effects. Classical guitarists usually play without a pick, using their thumbs and fingers to pluck the strings instead.

electronic tuners

Using an electronic tuner is the most efficient way to tune your guitar. An electronic tuner allows you to accurately tune strings without relying solely on your ears, which makes them ideal for beginners.

An electronic tuner tunes your guitar to concert pitch, which is especially useful if you plan to play with other instruments. Concert pitch refers to a standard used for tuning instruments where the A note is tuned to the frequency of 440 Hz (A-440).

Types of Electronic Tuners

There are two main kinds of electronic tuners:

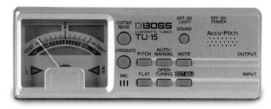

Guitar/Bass Tuners

Guitar/Bass tuners can identify only the five pitches used in standard tuning (E, A, D, G, B). Guitar/Bass tuners usually detect notes automatically, but most also have a manual mode, which allows you to select the note you want if the tuner is unable to detect the correct note automatically. The tuner may have trouble detecting the correct note if the string is extremely out of tune.

Chromatic Tuners

Chromatic tuners can detect any note—not just standard guitar notes—which means they can be used to tune most other instruments as well. These tuners are useful when you do not want to use standard tuning for your guitar or you want to tune your guitar to better complement your singing voice. For example, you can tune your guitar so each string is a half step lower in pitch, such as E-flat, A-flat, D-flat, G-flat, B-flat and E-flat.

Using an Electronic Tuner

If you are tuning an electric guitar, you can plug the guitar into the tuner. If you are tuning an acoustic or classical guitar, you can position the guitar near the tuner's built-in microphone. When you pick a string, the tuner indicates the note you are closest

to and whether the note you played is flat (too low) or sharp (too high) in relation to the closest note. Most tuners have a moving needle or light display indicator. You can turn the tuning machine for the string until the tuner indicates the string is in tune.

stands

A guitar stand is a good accessory if you use your guitar frequently and want to keep it constantly on hand instead of storing it in a case. You can use the stand to hold the guitar instead of leaning the guitar against a wall or placing it on the floor. A stand is especially useful when you are playing live and want to put the guitar aside temporarily.

Keep in mind that a guitar left on a stand may get accidentally bumped or knocked over, causing damage to the guitar. A guitar on a stand is also susceptible to temperature and humidity fluctuations, which can cause the guitar to crack, swell or warp. Leaving the guitar on a stand for long periods can result in dust build-up, which can cause the controls on an electric guitar to crackle. Although a stand is useful for temporary storage, if you will not use your guitar for a few days, you should make sure you store the guitar in its case.

Types of Stands

A stand can support the guitar either at the bottom of the guitar's body or at the top of the guitar's neck. The part of the stand that holds the neck of the guitar is usually adjustable so you can change the stand to accommodate the height of the guitar.

Most guitar stands hold only one guitar, but you can obtain stands that can hold several guitars. Although most stands can accommodate all types of guitars, some models may be able to fit only acoustic and classical guitars or only electric guitars.

Some stands are small and collapsible, allowing you to fold them to a compact size that can fit into a bag for easy transport. All guitar stands are padded to prevent the stand from scratching the guitar.

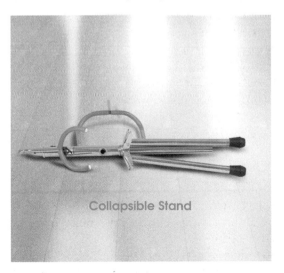
Collapsible Stand

straps

A guitar strap can help you properly position the guitar. A strap positions the guitar in front of your body and allows your hands to move freely. Your shoulder bears most of the weight of the guitar when you use a strap.

If you plan to stand while playing the guitar, you will need a guitar strap. You may also want to use a guitar strap if the guitar is awkward to hold while seated. In some cases, a guitar can tilt to one side if one side of the guitar is heavier than the other side.

When buying your strap, look for one that is sturdy, comfortable and durable. You should purchase the best guitar strap you can afford.

Types of Straps

The materials used to make straps vary greatly. You can find straps made of leather, nylon, woven fabric or plastic. If you tend to sweat a lot while playing the guitar, avoid leather straps that can bleed and stain your clothing. You should also avoid cheap plastic straps, which tend to break easily.

Straps also come in various styles. Since wearing a strap is similar to wearing a piece of clothing, you should be happy with the style of the strap. Some stores can design personalized straps for you.

Padded Strap

A strap can come with or without padding. A padded strap can be more comfortable and ease the pressure on your shoulder. If you play for long periods of time or if you play a heavy electric guitar, a padded strap may be especially useful.

Attach a Strap to a Guitar

To attach a strap to your acoustic guitar, loop one end of the strap over the pin at the bottom of the guitar. The strap attaches to the pin like a button on a shirt. Some acoustic guitars have another pin on the heel of the guitar to attach the other end of the strap. If your acoustic guitar does not have a second pin, your strap most likely comes with a shoelace style or leather string you can use to tie the strap to the guitar. Make sure you tie the string under the guitar strings on the headstock. Unlike acoustic guitars, electric guitars always have two pins for attaching the strap. Once you have attached the strap to the guitar, make sure the strap is adjusted to a comfortable height and is not twisted.

You can attach small devices to your strap that lock the strap to the pins on the guitar. You can also purchase straps with built-in locking devices.

Tips for Using Straps

If you have more than one guitar, you should have a separate strap for each guitar. This prevents you from having to constantly switch and adjust the strap for each guitar.

Never use a strap with large holes that loop over the pins. Your strap should always securely hold the guitar.

strings

The strings are an integral part of a guitar, as they allow you to produce music by strumming, plucking or bending them in various ways. To ensure your guitar always performs at its best, you should make sure your strings are in good condition and are appropriate for the type of guitar and the style of music you are playing.

When to Change Strings

You should replace your guitar strings regularly to prevent accidental breakage and ensure the best sound quality. How often you should replace the strings depends on how frequently you play and the rate at which residue builds up on the strings, but most novice players will usually need to replace the strings every three months. Many professional guitar players change the strings before each performance.

If you are not sure when to change the strings, you can watch for signs of deterioration, such as visible dirt on the strings, or strings that sound dull.

Since new strings sound brighter than older strings, you should change all the strings on the guitar at the same time. Changing guitar strings is a fairly simple task, so most people will be able to change the strings on their own.

Set   Box

String Sets

Strings are inexpensive and can be purchased individually, in sets or in boxes. Buying a set or box is usually cheaper than buying individual strings. You should try to keep a full set of strings handy in case you need to replace a broken string in an emergency.

Nylon Strings

Nylon strings produce a softer tone than steel strings and are used on classical and flamenco guitars.

The 1st, 2nd and 3rd strings on the guitar are usually made from one nylon strand, while the thicker 4th, 5th and 6th strings are made from nylon strands wrapped with wire. One advantage of nylon strings is the softer material, which is easier on your fingers than steel strings. Unlike steel strings, which have a ball at one end that secures

the string to the bridge of a guitar, nylon strings are usually tied to the bridge of a guitar. However, you can obtain specialty nylon strings with ball ends.

Keep in mind that you should never use nylon strings on a guitar that requires steel strings, or steel strings on a guitar that requires nylon strings. Nylon strings will not create enough tension on a steel string guitar to play notes properly and the extra tension of steel strings can damage a guitar made for nylon strings.

String Tension

Nylon strings are available in various tensions. The tension indicates the resistance the string offers when fretting or strumming and is the key factor you should consider when choosing strings. A higher tension string provides more resistance than a lower tension string. The way string tensions are indicated depends on the manufacturer, but there are usually four options available, such as extra hard, hard, normal and soft. The string tension you should use depends on your preference. You can try different tensions to determine what works best for you.

CONTINUED...

strings

Steel Strings

Most electric and acoustic guitars use steel strings. However, the term "steel string guitar" is usually used to refer to a steel string acoustic guitar, to differentiate between the steel string acoustic and the nylon string acoustic guitar.

Although they are called steel strings, these strings are often made from materials other than steel, such as nickel. The 1st and 2nd strings, which are thinner, single strands of metal, are generally made from nickel

or stainless steel. The thicker 3rd, 4th, 5th and 6th strings are wound with different types of wire, such as nickel or bronze. On most electric guitars, the 3rd string is made from a single strand of unwound metal.

Steel strings sound louder and sharper than nylon strings, but are tougher on your fingers. Keep in mind that you should never put steel strings on a guitar made for nylon strings, since the tension of the strings can break the guitar.

Sound Characteristics of Material

The different types of material used to wrap steel strings have different sound characteristics. This means nickel wound strings will sound different and produce a slightly different volume than bronze wound strings. Bronze wound strings tend to sound brighter and richer than nickel wound strings.

Electric guitars use nickel wound strings more often, while acoustic guitars more often use bronze wound strings. The type of material you should choose depends on your preference. You can experiment with steel strings wound in different types of materials to determine which material you prefer.

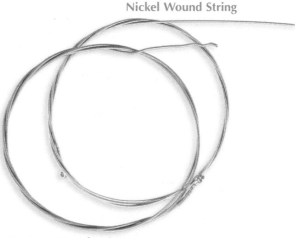

Nickel Wound String

Bronze Wound String

Steel Strings (Continued)

String Gauge

The gauge, or thickness, is the most important factor to consider when purchasing steel strings.

The gauge of a string determines the quality of the sound and how easily the string can be played. In general, lighter gauge strings are more flexible and easier to play, but produce a thinner sound, do not hold notes as long and tend to break more often. Heavier gauge strings are harder to play, but produce a more powerful tone.

Strings are available in sets ranging from extra light to heavy. The gauges of strings are specified in fractions of an inch, such as 0.010 inch. Gauges often vary depending on the brand, but in general, 008s are extra light, 009s are light, 010s are normal and gauges higher than 010s are heavy. The gauge of the high E-string is used to refer to the entire set of strings. For example, a 012-set, which is a favorite with acoustic guitarists, contains a high E-string that is 0.012 inch thick. In contrast, electric guitarists tend to use 010-sets or 009-sets.

When you change the string gauges on your guitar, you may need to adjust the intonation of the guitar and the height of the strings.

Style of String Winding

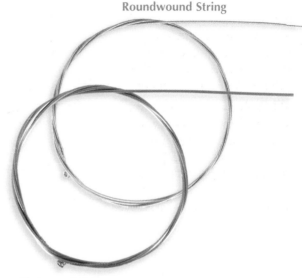

Roundwound String

Flatwound String

The thicker bass strings on the guitar can be wound in different ways. There are two main types of string winding—roundwound and flatwound.

Roundwound strings, which are wound with regular round wire, are the most common. You can recognize these strings by their ridges and the clean, bright, distinct sound they produce. Flatwound strings are specialty strings, which are perfectly smooth and produce very little squeaking when your fingers slide along the strings. These strings are preferred by jazz players for their dull, thick sound and heavy gauge, but are less suitable for rock or blues.

introduction to effects

You can produce many interesting and unusual sound effects with an electric guitar. Rock and blues guitarists invariably use effects in their playing. Using effects is a great way to add vibrancy and character to the sound of your guitar playing.

Electric guitars produce a signal that is passed on to an amplifier and then turned into sound. This signal can be electronically manipulated in different ways to produce a wide variety of sound effects. Effect units, which perform these manipulations, come in the following formats: effect pedals, multi-effects units, rack-mounted effects and effects built in to amplifiers.

Effect Pedals

The most common format of effects is effect pedals, or stomp boxes. You place effect pedals on the floor and then step on them to turn the effects on or off, leaving your hands free to continue playing.

Using effect pedals allows you to be selective in which effects you want to buy, since you can buy them individually. This flexibility can be to your advantage because you can easily set up a personalized system of effects.

Effect pedals are usually battery-powered devices, which can be convenient, but they tend to drain batteries quickly. Whenever a cable is plugged in to an effect pedal's input jack, the pedal will use up its battery, even when the effect is turned off. For this reason, you should unplug effect pedals when you are not using them and always carry spare batteries around with you when performing in front of an audience. You can use a power adapter with most effect pedals, which allows you to plug the pedals in to an electrical outlet, preventing you from having to use a battery altogether.

Always remember to turn down the volume on your amplifier or turn the amplifier off entirely before you unplug cables for your effect pedals—otherwise you will hear a loud pop and you may damage your amplifier.

Effect Pedals

Effect Pedals (continued)

Organizing Effect Pedals

Pedalboard

Since you may end up with many different individual effect pedals, you will probably want to organize them using a pedalboard. A pedalboard is a durable, flat surface where you can position your effect pedals and their power supplies. Pedalboards help protect your pedals and also keep all your pedals together so you can set them up quickly and easily when you perform.

Make sure you find a pedalboard that will fit all of your effect pedals. Keep in mind that some effect pedals are irregularly shaped and not all pedalboards will accommodate them. The pedalboard you choose should also be relatively lightweight and easy to carry around with you.

You should ensure that your pedalboard has enough electrical power for your pedals to work properly. If you are using batteries instead of a power adapter, you should consider how you will access the batteries for your effect pedals. You may find you want to use Velcro, instead of a more permanent adhesive, to attach your pedals to the pedalboard. Using Velcro allows you to easily access the batteries if they are located on the bottom of the effect pedals.

If you do not want to buy a pedalboard, you can create your own pedalboard by using a flat piece of wood and some Velcro. When you create your own pedalboard, make sure your effect pedals are positioned close enough together so that they can be easily reached, but far enough apart that you do not end up stepping on more than one pedal by accident.

CONTINUED...

introduction to effects

Multi-Effects Units

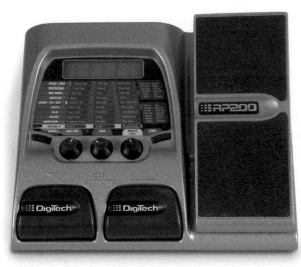

Multi-Effects Unit

Multi-effects units are programmable devices that usually include a number of pedals, which enable you to use many different types of effects. These devices allow you to program each pedal to activate one or more effects when you step on it. For example, you can step on a single pedal to switch from using flanger, delay and distortion effects to using chorus, reverb and compression effects. If you were using individual effect pedals, you would have to step on each pedal to turn some effects off and other effects on in the span of a millisecond to achieve the same result. You can also program a pedal to recall a specific setting for an effect when you step on it.

Multi-effects units are extremely convenient, which contributes to their appeal. Since all the effects you need are combined into one device that all use the same power supply, it will take you less time to set up when you are performing than if you had to plug in each individual effect pedal. Generally, multi-effects units have the same capabilities as individual effect pedals. However, many people think individual effect pedals produce better sound, so you may sacrifice quality for ease of use when you use a multi-effects unit instead of individual pedals.

If you begin to use a lot more effects and decide to invest in a multi-effects unit, you should still hold on to your individual effect pedals. You can easily hook your individual effect pedals up to your multi-effects unit and use both in your playing. Keeping your individual effect pedals can also be useful if you are playing outside of your home and would rather bring along a few individual effect pedals than a heavier and more awkward multi-effects unit.

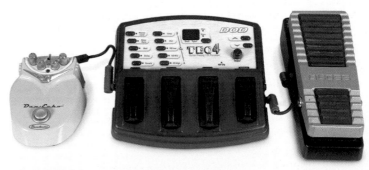

Effect Pedal   Multi-Effects Unit   Effect Pedal

Rack-Mounted Effects

Rack-mounted effects are programmable effects that are mounted in a rack cabinet, which is a cabinet-like unit. You can usually control the effects by stepping on a single pedal or a series of pedals you set up on the floor.

Rack-mounted effects are more expensive and specialized than effect pedals. Each rack-mounted effect can produce one or more effects and they usually have better sound quality and more features than other effect formats. You can buy each rack-mounted effect you want to use separately, which allows you to set up a customized system of effects. You can also buy rack-mounted effects as a single unit that includes many different effects.

Individual rack-mounted effects are placed in a cabinet because they are more delicate than other effect formats. Since a rack cabinet is always protecting the effects, rack-mounted effects are also more durable. You may be able to position the rack cabinet a considerable distance away from the foot pedals, which is useful when you are performing because you can keep the "brains" of the effects positioned safely at the back of the stage.

Due to the higher quality and cost of rack-mounted effects, professional guitarists tend to prefer this effect format.

Rack-Mounted Effects

Effects Built in to Amplifiers

Many amplifiers include built-in effects that you can use. Some amplifiers include all possible effects, while others include only a few effects. Although effects that are built in to amplifiers are convenient, you are limited in what you can do with the majority of these effects. Usually, you cannot change many of the features and parameters for each built-in effect, so you are not able to customize each effect to your liking. For example, you may not be able to change the delay time for the delay effect. Moreover, you cannot typically mix and match effects that are built in to amplifiers. Usually, only certain combinations of built-in effects, such as delay and chorus, are available for you to use simultaneously.

Amplifier with Built-in Effects

types of effects

Electric guitars produce a signal that is passed on to an amplifier, which boosts the sound volume and adjusts the sound quality. This signal can be manipulated in many different ways to produce certain sound effects. The main types of effects are ambient, gain-based, tone-based, modulation, pitch and volume-based effects.

Ambient Effects

You can use ambient effects to help make your music sound richer, more natural and add ambience to the music. Electronic ambience is almost always added to recorded music, which is often recorded in a dead, soundproof environment, to add acoustic life back into the music. Musicians can also enhance their music when playing live by adding electronic ambience.

Delay

Delay, also called echo, repeats the notes that you play to create either an echo effect, a feeling of acoustic space or a rhythm of repeated notes. These extra notes are delayed after the original note and can be heard distinctly on their own. You can adjust the length of the delay between the original note and the repeated notes and you can also change the number of times the note is repeated. Delay allows you to create effects such as slap-back echo, where a note is only repeated once quickly after the original note and at the same volume. The band U2 uses delay in their song "Pride (In the Name of Love)."

Reverb

Reverb, which is short for reverberation, produces an echo-like effect. This effect helps to give the music a more realistic sound as if the sound was naturally bouncing off walls. You can adjust the reverb to make it sound like you are playing in different sized rooms, such as playing in a garage or in a church.

Gain-Based Effects

Gain-based effects produce distortion that can have a hard-edged or fuzzy effect. These types of effects cause the guitar signal to sound overdriven, broken up or distorted.

Overdrive

Overdrive produces a warm, rounded tone and sounds more natural than the other gain-based effects. Blues or blues-rock musicians, such as Stevie Ray Vaughan and Eric Clapton, use this sound in their music.

Distortion

Distortion is a more drastic effect than overdrive, producing a harsher, yet brighter tone. You will find distortion used in the music of bands like AC/DC and Black Sabbath.

Fuzz

Fuzz sounds very edgy and hazy and is the most extreme gained-based effect. Fuzz produces a bright, almost buzzing tone. The guitar legend Jimi Hendrix, along with bands like Nirvana, use this sound in their music.

Tone-Based Effects

Tone-based effects involve adjusting the treble (high), mid-range and bass (low) frequencies in your guitar's sound.

EQ

EQ, an abbreviation for equalizer or equalization, balances the treble, mid-range and bass frequencies in your sound. Treble frequencies have a bright, clear sound and bass frequencies have a deep, booming sound. EQ is sometimes referred to as a filter because it filters out certain frequencies, while allowing other frequencies to pass through to achieve a desired balance between treble and bass.

Wah-Wah

A wah-wah, or wah, pedal serves as a frequency filter, allowing the bass and treble frequencies to fluctuate in your sound. When you press down on a wah-wah pedal while playing notes, you add vowel-like characters to the notes, almost sounding like a person saying "wah." You will find this effect in Jimi Hendrix's song "Voodoo Chile."

CONTINUED...

types of effects

Modulation Effects

Modulation effects change your guitar's tone in interesting and sometimes unusual ways.

Chorus

Chorus is an effect that makes one guitar sound like several guitars. Chorus multiplies the notes you play and then plays the copies with the original notes to produce a full, sparkling sound. The guitarist for The Police, Andy Summers, uses chorus a lot in his playing, such as in the song "Walking on the Moon."

Rotating Speaker Simulator

A rotating speaker simulator simulates the sound of a Leslie speaker, which is popular with Hammond organ players. The sound produced by a rotating speaker simulator is similar to the sound produced by chorus, but rotating speaker simulators allow you to change the speed of the effect as you play. Some units offer only fast and slow speed options, while others allow you to change the speed anywhere between fast and slow. You can produce the sound of Stevie Ray Vaughan's song "Cold Shot" with a rotating speaker simulator.

Flanger

Flanger is similar to chorus, but is a more metallic-sounding effect. This effect sounds a bit like a jet airplane taking off, producing a whirling, whooshing sound. Flanger multiplies the notes you play and then plays the copies of the notes slightly out of sync with the original notes. You can find this effect in the song "And the Cradle Will Rock" by Van Halen.

Phase Shifter

A phase shifter, also called a phaser, is similar to flanger, but produces a softer and fuller sound. Like flanger, a phase shifter duplicates the notes you play and then plays the copies, offsetting them very slightly from the original notes, but less so than flanger. This effect creates a subtle, sweeping sound.

Pitch Effects

Pitch effects add notes, or pitches, to a guitar signal as opposed to affecting the guitar signal, like many of the other types of effects.

Pitch Shifter

A pitch shifter creates a note that is higher or lower in pitch than the note you played and then sounds both notes simultaneously. When the two notes sound at the same time, a harmony is created. The most basic pitch shifters only create a note a fixed distance higher or lower than the original note. Intelligent pitch shifters allow you to specify the key of the song, such as B minor, so the pitch shifter will automatically determine which note to add based on the key you specified.

Octave Divider

An octave divider, also known as an octaver, adds a note that is one or two octaves above or below the note you are playing. A note played an octave above or below the original note has the same letter name as the original note, such as C, but is 12 semi-tones higher or lower in pitch. This effect produces a thick sound, like a guitar and bass guitar playing in unison. An octave divider is not as versatile as a pitch shifter because it only allows you to add notes that are one or two octaves above or below the original note, whereas pitch shifters allow you to add notes that are any interval above or below the original note.

CONTINUED...

types of effects

Volume-Based Effects

Volume-based effects allow you to adjust and play with the volume of your guitar's sound.

Volume Pedal

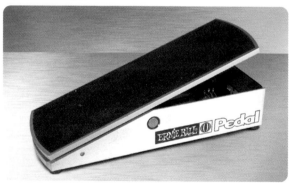

The volume pedal is not exactly an effect, but it does affect your guitar's sound. The volume pedal is just like the volume control on your guitar, but it allows you to use your foot to control the volume, enabling you to keep your hands free to continue playing. You can turn up the volume by pushing the pedal forward and turn down the volume by pushing the pedal back. The volume pedal allows you to easily turn up your volume when you start to play a solo or gradually change the volume as you play to create dramatic effects.

Compressor

A compressor boosts quieter signals and lowers louder signals to maintain an even volume level of your notes. This effect also results in your notes sounding smoother and taking longer to fade out.

Noise Gate

When you are using one or more effects and momentarily not playing your guitar, you may hear a hiss-like sound coming from the speakers. You can use a noise gate to stop this sound. A noise gate allows you to specify what volume level a note has to reach before the noise gate allows the note to be heard. One disadvantage to a noise gate is that sometimes as notes begin to fade out, the noise gate will kick in and cut off the notes before you intended.

Tremolo

Tremolo changes the volume of your sound quickly and repeatedly to produce a wavering or fluttering sound, as if your notes are passing through an electric fan. You will find this effect in R.E.M.'s song "What's the Frequency, Kenneth?"

connecting effects

The signal an electric guitar produces when you pick or strum strings can be manipulated to create specific effects before being passed on to an amplifier. To create special effects, you connect effect pedals between the guitar and the amplifier.

You can connect one or more effect pedals in a chain formation with the guitar at one end and the amplifier at the other. You can connect any number of effects, but keep in mind that too many effects will degrade the sound quality.

To connect the effects, you can use extra guitar cords. When connecting multiple effects, consider using short patch cables instead. This will avoid creating a jumble of tangled full-length guitar cords.

The signal from the string goes from one effect pedal to the next in the chain until the amplifier emits the final sound. The order of the effect pedals influences the sound produced. For example, if there is a delay effect pedal before a wah-wah effect pedal, the wah-wah effect will be applied to the delayed signal. You can vary the order of the pedals to change the final sound.

To get started, you can try the following order for your effect pedals.

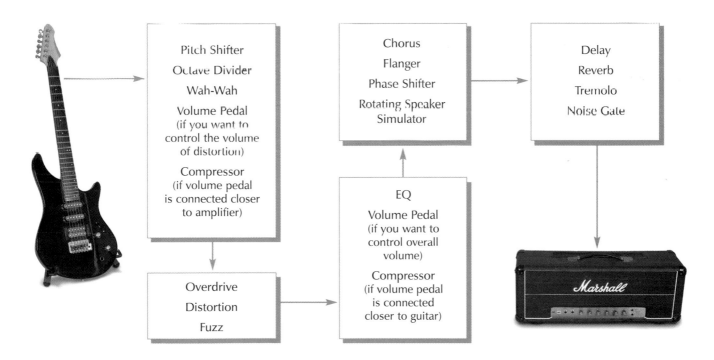

237

Chapter 14

To keep your guitar in good condition, you should perform regular maintenance on your guitar. This chapter shows you how to clean, restring and protect your guitar. You will also learn how to fix loose or broken parts and adjust the action, pickup height and intonation of a guitar to improve its sound. This chapter also discusses repairs for which you should consult a professional.

Guitar Care and Maintenance

In this Chapter...

clean your guitar

You should get into the habit of cleaning your guitar regularly to help maintain its appearance and sound quality.

Clean the Strings

Each time you play the guitar, natural oils and sweat are transferred from your fingertips to the guitar strings. Cleaning the strings regularly prevents a build-up on the strings, which deteriorates the sound quality and makes the strings wear out faster.

You should clean the strings after each session, using a clean, dry, lint-free cloth to wipe each string from end to end. You can fold the cloth around each string using your thumb and index finger and then move the cloth up and down to clean the string. To clean the back of the strings and the front of the fingerboard, gently drag the cloth between the strings and the fingerboard.

For extra cleaning, you may want to use a string lubricant, which can clean as well as help prevent corrosion so your strings last longer.

Clean the Fingerboard

You can wipe the fingerboard using a clean, dry cloth each time you change the strings of the guitar. If the fingerboard is made of ebony or rosewood, you can also apply a bit of lemon oil to help remove dirt and grease. The color of the fingerboard usually indicates whether it is ebony (black) or rosewood (dark brown). Lemon oil also moistens the wood to prevent over-drying, but be careful not to use too much, since excessive moisture can cause the frets to pop out of the fingerboard. If the fingerboard has a synthetic varnish, you should use only soap and water to clean it. A very shiny finish usually indicates that a synthetic varnish has been applied to the fingerboard.

You can use a toothbrush or a pointed object such as a toothpick or nail file to carefully remove built-up dirt from the edges of the frets and the nut.

Clean the Body

You should use a soft, lint-free, 100 percent cotton cloth to wipe dust from the body of the guitar after each use. The cloth can be dry or slightly moist. For a more thorough cleaning, use soap and water or a guitar cleaner to help remove fingerprints and stains.

You can also apply polish to the body of the guitar to restore the natural luster. To prevent polish from seeping into the wood and marring the guitar's finish, never apply liquid or spray polish directly to the surface of the guitar. Instead, soak the polish into a cloth and then use the cloth to apply the polish. You should also check the manufacturer's instructions to ensure that you use the correct polish for the type of finish on your guitar. Also, try to restrict polishing to once a month, as polish can build up on the guitar's surface if applied too often.

To remove dust from inside the body of the guitar, you can blow through the sound hole or use a vacuum cleaner with an appropriate attachment.

When cleaning the body of the guitar, make sure you avoid getting guitar cleaner on the strings as this can damage the strings.

Clean the Hardware

Cleaning the guitar hardware helps to keep these parts working properly and prevents rust or discoloration. The guitar hardware includes metal parts such as the tuners and the bridge of an electric guitar.

It is usually enough to dust the hardware with a soft cloth, especially if the metal is gold-plated. To remove the dirt in the crevices of the volume and tone knobs, a soft toothbrush or an artist's brush is useful. However, you can also use a mild, non-abrasive polish or cleaner for nickel or chrome-plated parts. A can of contact cleaner spray is handy for lubricating electrical parts as well as tone and volume controls.

Keep in mind that the pickups of an electric guitar are very sensitive to liquid. You should use only a dry cloth or brush to clean the pickups.

protect your guitar

Store a Guitar

You should always keep your guitar in its case when it is not in use. If you will not use the guitar for an extended period, store the guitar in its case in an area where there will be very little fluctuation in temperature. Very cold or very hot temperatures can cause the guitar to crack, swell or warp and affect the guitar's performance.

If you use the guitar frequently and want to keep it constantly on hand, you should use a floor stand. Keep in mind that even a guitar on a stand can be exposed to possible damage.

Protect a Guitar When Traveling

You should keep the guitar in a sturdy case when traveling. For information on guitar cases, see page 216. Before transporting the guitar, you should loosen the strings slightly to decrease the tension on the guitar.

When traveling by car or bus, keep the guitar inside the vehicle instead of in the trunk or luggage compartment where the temperature can drop or rise drastically. When traveling by airplane, arrange to carry your guitar on board instead of placing it in the cargo hold. If you put your guitar in the cargo hold, use a flightcase to provide extra protection. Even when using a hard case, avoid placing heavy objects on top of the guitar.

Prevent Temperature and Humidity Fluctuations

You need to maintain a stable, comfortable environment for your guitar to keep it in good condition. In general, an environment that is comfortable for you will be comfortable for your guitar.

To avoid sudden temperature changes, when you bring a cold guitar indoors, allow the guitar to gradually warm up to room temperature in its case.

Too little moisture can cause a guitar to crack and too much moisture can cause swelling and warping. Typically, the moisture level should be around 47 percent relative humidity. You can use a guitar humidifier to prevent the wood of your acoustic or classical guitar from drying out. For information on guitar humidifiers, see page 244.

common
guitar problems

Problem	Solution
The volume of the strings on an electric guitar is too quiet or too loud.	Move pickups closer to or further away from the strings. See Adjust the Height of Pickups on page 257.
Controls on an electric guitar crackle.	Clean the inside of the controls to remove dust and dirt. See Fix Crackling Controls on page 262.
Output jack on an electric guitar is loose.	Tighten the output jack. See Tighten Loose Connections on page 260.
Strap pin is loose.	Tighten the screw inside the strap pin. See Fix Strap Pins on page 264.
Strap pin falls out.	Use a flat toothpick and some wood glue to re-insert the strap pin. See Fix Strap Pins on page 264.
Strings break or sound dull.	Change the strings on the guitar. See Restring a Guitar on page 248, 250 or 252.
Strings buzz or are difficult to fret.	Change the height of the strings off the fingerboard. See Adjust the Action on page 256. If adjusting the action does not fix the problem, you may need to have a repair professional adjust the neck of the guitar.
Strings do not remain in tune as you play at different frets along the fingerboard.	Adjust the saddles that hold each string in place on the bridge to move the saddles away from or toward the nut. See Adjust the Intonation on page 258.
Volume or tone control is loose or falls off the guitar.	Securely fasten the control to the guitar. See Tighten Loose Connections on page 260.

For problems that will require a repair professional, see page 266.

tools for maintaining a guitar

You should inspect your guitar to determine the tools you need to maintain your guitar. Organizing your own personal guitar kit is a worthwhile investment, especially since most of the tools you will need are available for less than 10 dollars each.

Allen Wrench

To restring some electric guitars, you will need an Allen wrench. Many electric guitars also require an Allen wrench for adjusting the height of the saddle to change the action. Action refers to the height of the strings off the fingerboard.

Guitar Humidifier

Your acoustic or classical guitar may need a guitar humidifier to prevent the wood from drying out, which could lead to splitting or cracking. A guitar humidifier is particularly useful if the top of the guitar is made of solid wood, rather than laminated wood, since solid wood tends to dry out easily. Some guitar humidifiers rest inside the sound hole, while others are placed in your guitar case. Typically, the moisture level should be around 47 percent relative humidity. A moisture level that is too high can also harm your guitar.

Screwdriver

A screwdriver is a useful tool for tightening or removing screws on any type of guitar. For example, you may need to use a screwdriver to change the height of the pickups on an electric guitar or to tighten the end pins used to attach a strap to a guitar. For most repairs, you will need either a Phillips-head screwdriver or a flat-head screwdriver.

Electronic Cleaner

Electronic cleaner, also called contact cleaner, is used to clean the electronic parts of an electric guitar. For example, you can use cleaner to clean the volume and tone controls or pickup selector switch. If the volume and tone controls or pickup selector switch are crackling or periodically cut out, cleaning may alleviate these problems.

Pliers

On an electric or acoustic guitar, you may need a pair of pliers to remove bits of broken string or to remove the bridge pins that fasten the strings to the body of the guitar. You can also use pliers to tighten the output jack and the tone and volume control bolts on an electric guitar.

String Winder

A string winder, also called a peg winder, is useful when changing the strings on your guitar, since the tool makes it quick and easy to turn the tuning machines several times. Most string winders also have a groove that allows you to easily remove a bridge pin from an acoustic guitar.

Lemon Oil

Lemon oil is useful for cleaning fingerboards, particularly those made of ebony or rosewood. Using the lemon oil will remove dirt and grease, as well as moisten the wood to prevent over-drying. Do not use too much lemon oil, since excessive moisture can cause the frets to pop out of the fingerboard.

Cloth

You will need a soft, lint-free cotton cloth for cleaning the strings, body, fingerboard and hardware on your guitar. Wipe your guitar after each use to remove dust, sweat, dirt and body oils.

String Cleaner

String cleaner, also called string lubricant, can help prevent corrosion and remove the oils your fingertips leave on the strings. To use string cleaner, you simply wipe the cleaner on the strings after each use to remove any dirt, oil or perspiration.

Guitar Polish

You can use guitar polish to clean the body of a guitar. Choosing a polish designed specifically for a guitar is advisable, since it offers the best protection of the guitar's finish. To avoid a build-up of polish, do not polish your guitar more than once a month.

Wire Cutters

Wire cutters are useful when you are restringing your guitar and need to cut away excess string. You can also use wire cutters to dig out the end of a string that is lodged in a tuning machine post.

remove old strings

Replacing your guitar strings regularly helps prevent accidental breakage and ensures the best sound quality. You should change the strings when you notice signs of deterioration, such as visible corrosion or dirt on the strings, or strings that sound dull.

To remove an old string from a guitar, you first remove the string from the tuning machine. You can use a string winder to loosen the string quickly and easily, but if you do not have a string winder, you can loosen the string manually. To avoid cutting your fingers on

the end of the string, you can use a pair of pliers to carefully pull the string from the tuning machine.

After removing the string from the tuning machine, you must then remove the string from the bridge. The way you remove the string from the bridge will depend on the type of guitar. As you remove a string, be careful to avoid scratching the guitar with the ends of the string. Some people save the old strings to use in an emergency, but it is better to keep a set of new strings handy instead, since strings are fairly cheap.

Acoustic Guitars

- To remove an old string, you must first remove the string from the tuning machine.

1 To remove a string from the tuning machine, use a string winder to quickly turn the string's tuning machine to loosen the string.

- If you do not have a string winder, you can turn the string's tuning machine manually.

2 Once the string is loose, you can pull the string off the tuning machine post.

1 To remove a string from the bridge, use the groove on the string winder to remove the string's bridge pin from the bridge. Then pull the string out of the bridge pin's hole.

- If you do not have a string winder, you could use a pair of pliers to remove the bridge pin for the string, but be careful not to scratch the guitar.

Tip

Is there a faster way to remove an old string?

Yes. You can loosen the string a bit and then cut the string close to the tuning machine. This allows you to work with a shorter piece of string that you can easily unravel from the tuning machine post without having to unwind the string completely. You should be careful to avoid scratching the guitar with the ends of the string. This method is useful when you do not want to reuse the old string.

How often should I replace the guitar strings?

How often you should replace the guitar strings depends mainly on how frequently you play. Many professional players change the strings before every show. Novice players usually need to replace the strings every three months.

Should I replace all the guitar strings at once?

Yes. New strings sound brighter than older strings, so replacing all the guitar strings at the same time ensures that all the strings have the same sound quality.

Classical Guitars

1 To remove a string from the bridge, untie the string and then pull the string through the bridge.

Electric Guitars

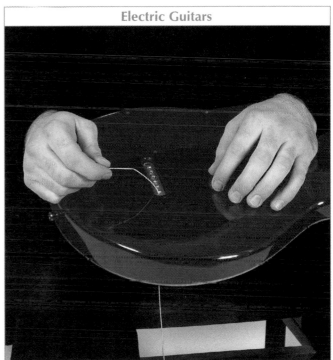

1 Trim the end of the string that was wrapped around the tuning machine post with wire cutters to allow the string to easily pass through the bridge.

2 To remove the string from the bridge, turn the guitar onto its back and then pull the string through the bridge.

● On some guitars, you do not need to turn the guitar over to pull the string through the bridge.

restring an acoustic guitar

Once you have removed an old string from an acoustic guitar, you can add a new string to the guitar.

When adding a new string, you first attach the string to the bridge and then to the tuning machine. To attach the string to the bridge, you insert the ringed end of the string into the hole for the bridge pin, then reinsert the bridge pin into the hole to secure the string.

To attach the string to the tuning machine, you wrap the end of the string around the tuning machine post to keep the string in place and then use a string winder to wind the string onto the post. If you do not have a string winder, you can turn the tuning machine manually, but this will take longer and be harder on your wrists. You should wind the string until it is in tune and then trim the unused string close to the post.

The string should wind around the tuning machine post at least three times. If you find that the string wraps around too many or too few times, you can unwind the string, adjust the amount of slack and then wind the string again.

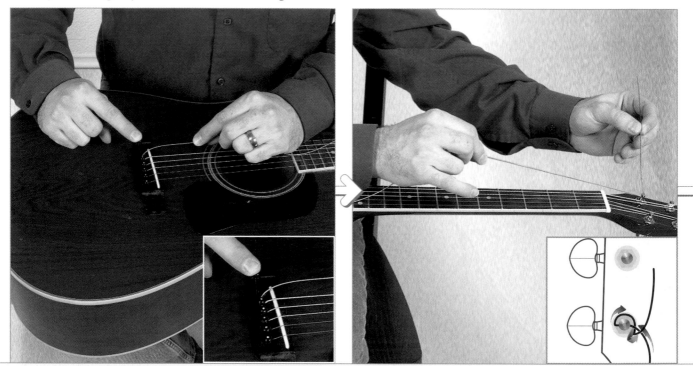

1 Remove the old string you want to replace. To remove an old string, see page 246.

2 To secure the new string to the bridge, insert the end of the string that has a small ring inside the hole that held the bridge pin.

3 Push the bridge pin firmly into the hole with its groove facing the tuning machines. The string should fit into the groove of the bridge pin.

4 Pull gently on the string to ensure the string is firmly in place.

5 To secure the string to the tuning machine, insert the string through the hole in the tuning machine post. Leave enough slack in the string so you can wind the string around the post several times.

6 Bend the string at a 90-degree angle so the string will not slip out of the hole.

7 Wrap the string around the tuning machine post as shown in the above diagram to secure the string to the post.

Tip

How can I make sure the new string will remain in tune?

New strings can go out of tune very easily because they stretch after they are attached to a guitar. To ensure the string stays in tune longer, hold the bridge in place with one hand and grasp the string with your other hand. Lightly stretch the string up and down its entire length. Then check the tuning of the string and retune if necessary. Repeat this process 5 or 6 times until the string stops going out of tune when you stretch it. For more information on tuning a guitar, see page 32.

Why should I wind the string down the tuning machine post?

Winding the string from the top to the bottom of the tuning machine post creates a greater angle at the nut, which enhances the tone the string produces and increases the amount of time the note will ring. Winding the string down the post also helps fasten the string more securely so it will not slip off the post when you play.

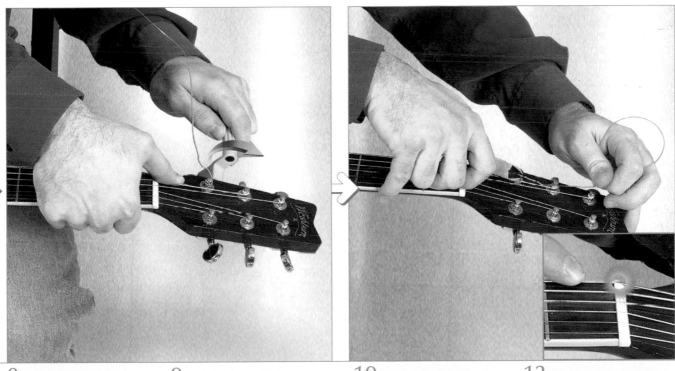

8 Hold the string down with your thumb just before the nut to keep the string tight. You want the string to wind down the tuning machine post.

9 For the three thicker strings, turn the string's tuning machine away from the guitar's body until the string is in tune. For the three thinner strings, turn the string's tuning machine toward the guitar's body.

10 As you tighten the string, make sure the string fits snugly into its groove on the nut.

11 Trim the extra string close to the tuning machine post with wire cutters.

12 Stretch and tune the string until the string stops going out of tune when you stretch it. For more information, see the first tip above.

restring a classical guitar

You can restring a classical guitar after removing an old string from the guitar. Since the bridge and tuning machine posts of a classical guitar are different from an acoustic guitar, you restring a classical guitar in a slightly different way.

You first attach a string to the bridge and then to a tuning machine. To attach a string to the bridge, you thread the string through the hole in the bridge and tie the string securely to the bridge. You should make sure

the string's knot is behind the back edge of the bridge.

Classical guitars use nylon strings, which are less stiff and easier to work with than steel strings, but can be a bit more difficult to attach to the tuning machine posts. To attach a string to a tuning machine post, thread the string through the hole in the post. You can wrap the string around the post to ensure it will not slip out of the post. Wind the string onto the post until the string is in tune. Then trim the excess string close to the post.

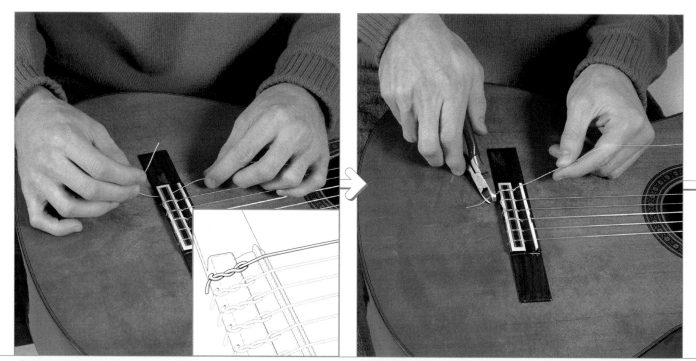

1 Remove the old string you want to replace. To remove an old string, see page 246.

2 To secure the new string to the bridge, insert one end of the string through the appropriate hole in the bridge until about two inches of the string protrudes from the hole.

3 Tie the end of the string around the bridge as shown in the above diagram.

4 Pull the ends of the string to tighten the knot. Make sure the knot is behind the back edge of bridge, rather than on top of the bridge.

5 Trim any extra string close to the bridge with wire cutters to ensure the extra string does not hit the top of the guitar.

How can I make sure a new string will remain in tune?

New strings stretch after they are attached to a guitar, which will cause them to go out of tune. To ensure a string stays in tune longer, you can manually stretch the string after you attach it. Holding the bridge in place, grasp the string and lightly stretch the string up and down its entire length. Then check the tuning of the string and retune if necessary. Repeat this process until the string stops going out of tune when you stretch it. For more information on tuning a guitar, see page 32.

Can I use a different knot to tie the string to the bridge?

Yes. You can use any knot you prefer as long as the knot will fasten the string securely to the bridge. The following diagram shows another knot you can use.

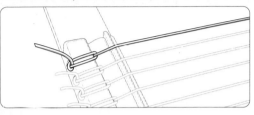

Tip

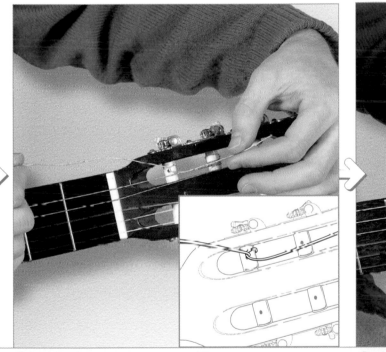

6 To secure the string to the tuning machine, insert the string through the hole in the tuning machine post. Leave enough slack in the string so you can wind the string around the post several times.

7 Wrap the string around the tuning machine post as shown in the above diagram to ensure the string is securely fastened to the post.

8 Hold the string down with your thumb just before the nut to keep the string tight.

9 Use a string winder to turn the string's tuning machine away from the body until the string is in tune. Make sure the string fits snugly into its groove on the nut.

• You can also turn the string's tuning machine manually.

10 Trim the extra string close to the tuning machine post with wire cutters.

11 Stretch and tune the string until the string stops going out of tune when you stretch it. For more information, see the first tip above.

restring an electric guitar

You need to restring an electric guitar more frequently than an acoustic guitar, but an electric guitar is easier to restring.

After removing an old string, you secure the new string first to the bridge and then to the tuning machine. To secure the string to the bridge, you thread the string through the appropriate hole in the back or the top of the guitar until the ringed end of the string is anchored to the bridge.

To attach the string to the tuning machine, you thread the string through the tuning machine post, leaving enough slack so the string can wind around the post at least 3 times. Wrap the end of the string around the tuning machine post to keep the string in place and then wind the string onto the post using a string winder or by manually turning the tuning machine. Wind the string until it is in tune and then trim the unused string close to the post. You should wind the string from top to bottom to help secure the string and create better tone and sustain.

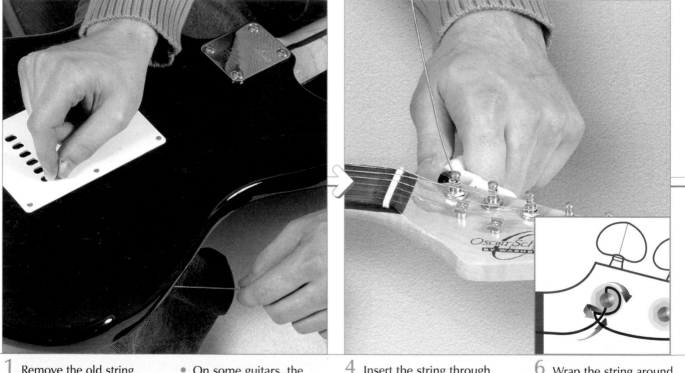

1 Remove the old string you want to replace. To remove an old string, see page 246.

2 To secure the new string to the bridge, turn the guitar onto its back. You will see a hole in the bridge for each string.

• On some guitars, the holes are on the top of the guitar.

3 Push the end of the string that does not have a small ring through the correct hole until the end of the string with the ring is anchored to the bridge.

4 Insert the string through the hole in the string's tuning machine post. Leave enough slack in the string so you can wind the string around the post several times.

5 Bend the string at a 90-degree angle.

6 Wrap the string around the tuning machine post as shown in the above diagram.

7 Hold the string down with your thumb just before the nut to keep the string tight.

Tip

What else should I consider when restringing my guitar?

If your guitar has string retainers, you should run the string under the string retainer before securing it to the tuning machine. A string retainer is a device usually found on the headstock of guitars that have all the tuning machines on one side. The string retainer pulls down some or all of the strings closer to the headstock, which increases the angle of the string with the nut, resulting in improved tone and sustain.

How can I make sure a new string will remain in tune?

New strings stretch after they are attached to a guitar, which will cause them to go out of tune. To ensure a string stays in tune longer, you can manually stretch the string after you attach it. Grasp the string and lightly pull the string up and down along its entire length. Then check the tuning of the string and retune if necessary. Repeat this process about 5 or 6 times until the string stops going out of tune. For more information on tuning a guitar, see page 32.

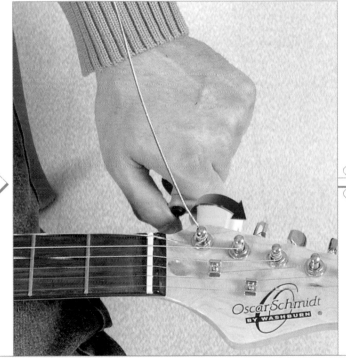

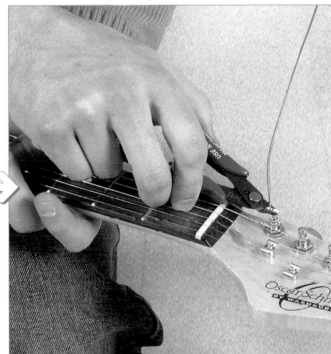

8 If all the tuning machines are on one side of the guitar, turn the string's tuning machine away from the body if they are on the left side and toward the body if they are on the right side.

• If the tuning machines are on both sides of the guitar, turn the string's tuning machine away from the body for the three thicker strings and toward the body for the three thinner strings until the string is in tune.

9 As you tighten the string, make sure the string fits snugly into its groove on the nut and saddle.

10 Trim the extra string close to the tuning machine post with wire cutters.

11 Stretch and tune the string until the string stops going out of tune when you stretch it. For more information, see the second tip above.

CONTINUED...

restring an electric guitar

Instead of a standard nut, some electric guitars have a locking nut that uses screws to clamp the strings into place at the top of the guitar neck. Locking nuts, which allow you to bend strings or use the tremolo bar vigorously without putting the strings out of tune, are usually found on guitars that have a floating bridge. A floating bridge allows you to pull up or push down a tremolo bar to change the angle of the bridge, which adjusts the tension, and thereby the pitch, of the strings. Floating bridges are common on electric guitars used to play rock music.

It will take longer to restring a guitar with a locking nut than to restring a guitar that uses a standard nut. In addition to removing an old string from the tuning machine and the bridge, you also need to release the string from the locking nut. Also, when adding a string, you need to make sure the new string is secured at the locking nut.

Keep in mind that it is best to change one string at a time on a guitar with a floating bridge.

Remove a String from an Electric Guitar with a Locking Nut

Tuning Machines

Locking Nut

1 Loosen the screw on the locking nut for the string you want to remove.

2 To remove the string from the tuning machine, use a string winder to quickly turn the string's tuning machine to loosen the string.

- If you do not have a string winder, you can turn the string's tuning machine manually.

3 Once the string is loose, cut the string with wire cutters just behind the locking nut, toward the tuning machines.

4 Pull the string off the tuning machine post.

5 Pull the other end of the string through the bridge.

Tip

The strings on my guitar are also clamped in at the bridge. How do I remove and add strings?

To remove an old string from the bridge, loosen the Allen screw for the string at the bridge. Then lift the string out of its slot in the bridge.

To secure a new string to the bridge, you may need to snip the ring off the string and position the end of the string in the correct slot in the bridge. Then tighten the Allen screw to clamp the string into place.

How can I keep the other strings from going out of tune when I change one string?

When you are changing a string on a guitar with a floating bridge, the bridge tends to move up and down, affecting the tension of the other strings and causing them to go out of tune. To ensure the other strings remain in tune when changing a string, you can place a solid object, such as a stack of cards, under the bridge to keep the bridge stable.

Add a String to an Electric Guitar with a Locking Nut

Locking Nut

Fine-Tuning Mechanisms

1 To secure the new string to the bridge and to a tuning machine, perform steps **2** to **11** starting on page 252.

• Make sure you push the string through the appropriate slot of the locking nut.

2 To lock the string in place at the locking nut, tighten the screw for the string on the locking nut. When you tighten the screw, the string may go slightly out of tune.

3 To fine-tune the string, adjust the fine-tuning mechanism for the string on the bridge until the string is in tune.

adjust the action

If you notice that the strings of your guitar buzz or are hard to play, you may need to adjust the action. The action refers to the height of the strings off the fingerboard. The closer the strings are to the frets, the easier they are to play, but if the strings are too close, they will start to buzz. You can adjust the action on an electric guitar yourself, but you should have a professional adjust the action on an acoustic guitar.

To adjust the action, you change the height of the strings by adjusting the height of the saddles that hold the strings off the fingerboard. Depending on your guitar, you may be able to adjust the height of each string separately, or adjust the height of the three strings at each end of the bridge as a unit. All the strings do not need to be the same height. Experienced players often position the thicker bass strings higher than the thinner treble strings to give them more room to vibrate and allow them to produce a thicker sound.

After you change the action, you should check to make sure the guitar is still in tune. To check the intonation of a guitar, see page 258.

- On many guitars, each saddle has two adjustment screws, one on either side of each saddle. You can adjust these screws to change the height of each string individually.

1 To raise a string, tighten a screw to raise a saddle. To lower a string, loosen a screw to lower a saddle. Make sure you adjust the screws equally on either side of a saddle.

- On some guitars, you will find one screw on each side of the bridge. Adjusting one screw will affect the height of the three thicker strings. Adjusting the other screw will affect the height of the three thinner strings.

1 To raise the strings, tighten a screw to raise the bridge. To lower the strings, loosen a screw to lower the bridge.

adjust the height of pickups

A pickup is a magnet on an electric guitar that senses the vibrations of the strings. The pickup converts these vibrations into electrical currents that an amplifier can use to produce sound.

Most guitars have two or more pickups. Adjusting the height of the pickups allows you to change the guitar's output. Moving the pickups closer to the strings produces a higher output that is perfect for distortion, but if you prefer a cleaner sound, you can lower the pickups to reduce output and avoid distortion.

Most pickups have a screw on either side that you can use to adjust the pickup. Tightening a screw raises the pickup closer to the strings and loosening a screw lowers the pickup away from the strings.

Both sides of a pickup do not need to be the same height. Most people position the thicker bass strings further away from the pickups than the thinner treble strings, since bass strings are louder and need more room to vibrate. You should adjust the pickups so that every string outputs the same volume. Also, make sure each pickup produces equal volume.

- You will usually find one screw on each side of a pickup that allows you to adjust the height of the pickup.

1 To raise a pickup to move it closer to the strings, tighten a screw. To lower a pickup to move it further away from the strings, loosen a screw.

Test Pickup Height

- The pickup can be set at any height you want, but the strings should never touch any pickups.

1 To test the pickup height, hold down the 1st string at the last fret and make sure the string does not hit any pickups.

2 Repeat step 1 with the 6th string.

adjust the intonation

The intonation of a guitar refers to whether the strings remain in tune as you play at different frets along the fingerboard.

To adjust the intonation of an electric guitar, you adjust the saddles that hold each string in place on the bridge. If a guitar does not have adjustable saddles, as is the case with acoustic, classical and some older electric guitars, the intonation cannot be adjusted, but a repair professional may be able to help fix the problem.

To test a string's intonation, compare the note produced by lightly touching the string directly at the 12th fret to the note produced with your finger pressing down behind the 12th fret. The pitch of the notes should be identical.

If the pitches do not match, you need to adjust the string's intonation. If the fretted note is sharp (too high), move the saddle away from the nut to lengthen the string. If the fretted note is flat (too low), move the saddle toward the nut to shorten the string. You can use an electronic tuner or ask an expert for help if you cannot tell the difference between the notes.

Test the Intonation

1 To test the intonation of a string, very lightly place your index finger on the 1st string, directly at the twelfth fret. Do not press the string down on the fret.

2 Pick the string and listen to the note.

3 Place your index finger on the 1st string, just behind the twelfth fret.

4 Pick the string and listen to the note.

• The string should produce the same pitch in steps 2 and 4. If the pitches do not match, you need to adjust the string's intonation.

5 Test the intonation of the other strings by repeating steps 1 to 4 for each string.

Tip

Do I need to tune a string after adjusting the intonation?

Yes. After adjusting the intonation of a string, you should tune the string. To tune a string, see page 32. Then test the intonation of the string again and readjust the intonation if necessary. Then tune the string again. Keep tuning and adjusting the intonation for each string until you are satisfied with the string's sound quality.

The frets on my guitar are worn. Can this affect the intonation of my guitar?

Yes. Worn frets can affect the intonation of your guitar. As the frets on your guitar wear out, the location where a string hits the fret will change over time. This will affect the sound the string produces. You will need to fix or replace the frets as they wear out to maintain the quality of the guitar's sound.

Adjust the Intonation

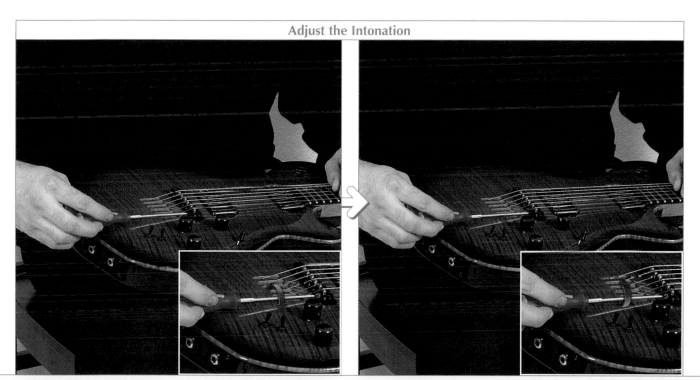

• To adjust the intonation of strings on your guitar, you can tighten or loosen the screws at the back of the bridge. You will find a screw for each string.

1 If the string's pitch in step 4 is sharp (too high), you can tighten the screw for the string to move the saddle away from the nut.

2 If the string's pitch in step 4 is flat (too low), you can loosen the screw for the string to move the saddle toward the nut.

tighten loose connections

A number of connections on your guitar can loosen over time and eventually require tightening. Loose connections are more often a problem on electric guitars, which have more mechanical parts and screws.

Rattling noises on your guitar usually indicate a loose connection. When you hear a rattle, lightly touch each part you think might be rattling as you strum the guitar. If the noise stops when you touch a specific part, that part is probably the source of the rattle.

When tightening a loose output jack, you should make sure the wires attached to the jack do not spin as you turn the bolt, since this might cause the wires to break off the jack. You can hold the inside of the jack as you tighten the bolt to ensure that you turn just the bolt.

You can securely re-attach a volume or tone control knob by widening the shaft of the knob or tightening the screw on the side of the knob. If the knob jiggles, you can tighten the bolt under the knob.

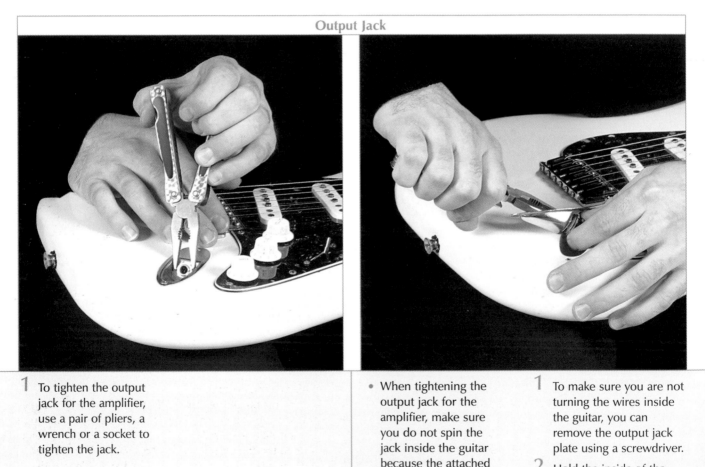

Output Jack

1 To tighten the output jack for the amplifier, use a pair of pliers, a wrench or a socket to tighten the jack.

- When tightening the output jack for the amplifier, make sure you do not spin the jack inside the guitar because the attached wires could break off the jack.

1 To make sure you are not turning the wires inside the guitar, you can remove the output jack plate using a screwdriver.

2 Hold the inside of the jack firmly as you tighten the jack.

Tip

What other loose connections do I need to tighten on a guitar?

All connections on the guitar have screws that can loosen over time. You should tighten all the connections periodically to make sure all the parts are secure.

Pickup selector switch – The pickup selector switch usually has one screw on either side or one bolt in the middle of the switch. You should check that the bolt or screws are tight.

Plates on back and sides – You should check to make sure the screws that attach the covering plates to the guitar are tightened properly.

Tuning machines – Many acoustic and electric guitars have screws that attach tuning machines to the guitar. You should make sure these screws, which are located on the back of the headstock of the guitar, are not loose.

Bolt-on necks – On many guitars, the neck is screwed on to the body of the guitar. These screws can loosen as you play and should be tightened regularly. You should never remove the screws from the bolts, since this will require you to reset the neck.

Volume and Tone Controls

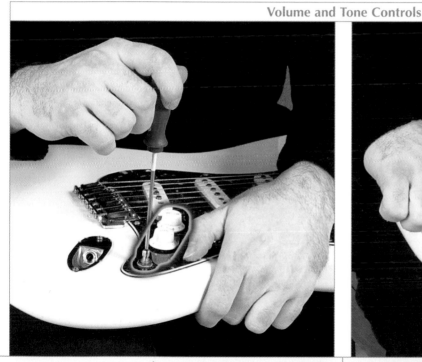

- If a volume or tone knob falls off, the knob needs to be securely fastened to the guitar.

1 On many guitars, you need to insert a screwdriver between the prongs of the knob's shaft to push the prongs slightly apart and then re-attach the knob.

- On other guitars, re-attach the knob and then tighten the screw on the side of the knob.

- If the volume or tone knob spins uncontrollably or jiggles up and down, the bolt that secures the knob to the top of the guitar needs to be tightened.

1 Remove the knob from the guitar and then use a pair of pliers, wrench or a socket to tighten the bolt for the knob. You may need to first loosen the screw on the side of the knob to remove the knob.

fix crackling controls

Dust and dirt can affect the controls on an electric guitar, causing them to crackle or cut out completely. You can usually fix a crackling control by cleaning the inside of the control.

The pickup selector switch, which allows you to select the pickups you want to use, is the control that will crackle most often. Volume and tone control knobs can also crackle or cut out. To clean a crackling pickup selector switch or volume and tone knobs, you can use Method 1 below. To locate the pickup selector switch on the inside of the guitar, try to match up the outside location of the switch with the inside location.

If the pickup selector switch and volume and tone knobs are mounted on the pick guard, as is usually the case with Fender Stratocaster guitars, you can clean the controls using Method 2 below.

If the output jack crackles, a wire attached to the jack may be loose. You should consult a repair technician instead of trying to fix the jack yourself. You should also see a repair technician if cleaning does not fix a crackling control.

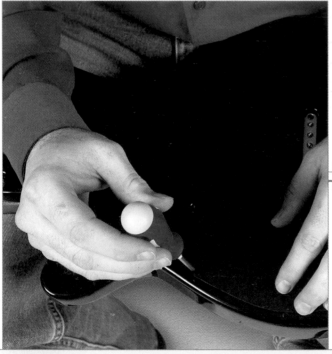
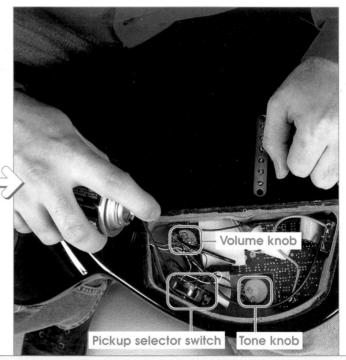

Volume knob

Pickup selector switch   Tone knob

Method 1

1 Obtain an electronic cleaner, sometimes called contact cleaner, that you can use to clean your crackling controls.

2 Take off the back panel on your guitar to access your crackling controls.

3 If your pickup selector switch crackles when you use the switch, spray the inside of the switch with the electronic cleaner.

4 Move the switch to distribute the cleaner throughout the inside of the switch.

5 If a volume or tone knob crackles when you turn it, spray the inside of the knob with the electronic cleaner. Turn the knob on the front of the guitar a few times to distribute the cleaner throughout the inside of the knob.

Tip

I have a hollow body guitar. How do I fix a crackling control?

If you have a hollow body electric guitar, which usually has f-holes like those found on a violin, you cannot use either of the methods shown below to fix a crackling control on your guitar. You should take the guitar to a repair technician to fix any controls that are crackling.

What other maintenance tasks can I perform after removing the pick guard?

After performing Method 2 below to fix a crackling control, you may want to examine and clean the inside of your guitar before replacing the pick guard. You can use a soft cloth to wipe dirt and dust from interior parts. Since all the strings have been removed, you can also take the opportunity to clean the fingerboard. For information on cleaning the fingerboard, see page 240.

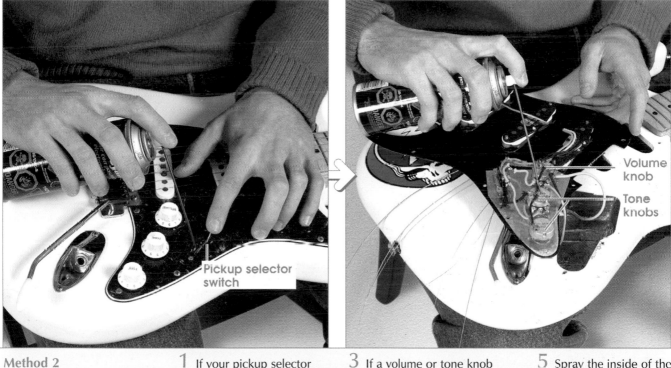

Pickup selector switch

Volume knob

Tone knobs

Method 2

- If the crackling controls are mounted to the pick guard on your guitar, use this method to fix the crackling controls.

1 If your pickup selector switch crackles, spray the electronic cleaner inside the slot of the switch on the top of your guitar.

2 Move the pickup selector switch to distribute the cleaner throughout the inside of the switch.

3 If a volume or tone knob crackles, you first need to remove all the strings from the tuning machines on your guitar, as shown on page 246.

4 Remove the pick guard by loosening all the screws on the pick guard.

5 Spray the inside of the volume or tone knob with the electronic cleaner.

6 Turn the knob a few times to distribute the cleaner throughout the inside of the knob.

fix strap pins

Strap pins are metal posts at each end of the body of an electric guitar that are used for attaching the guitar strap. Over time, strap pins can loosen or fall out of your guitar and require fixing.

To fix a loose strap pin, tighten the screw inside the strap pin. Strap pins may also fall out completely as a result of the wood around the screw wearing away. To quickly fix a strap pin that has fallen out of your guitar, you can insert a flat toothpick into the strap pin hole to

ensure the screw will fit tightly when reinserted into the hole. For a more durable solution, you can take the guitar to a repair professional.

The strap pin, or end pin, on an acoustic guitar is glued into the guitar instead of being screwed in. To reattach an end pin to an acoustic guitar, you can add wood glue to the end pin and reinsert the pin into the guitar's body.

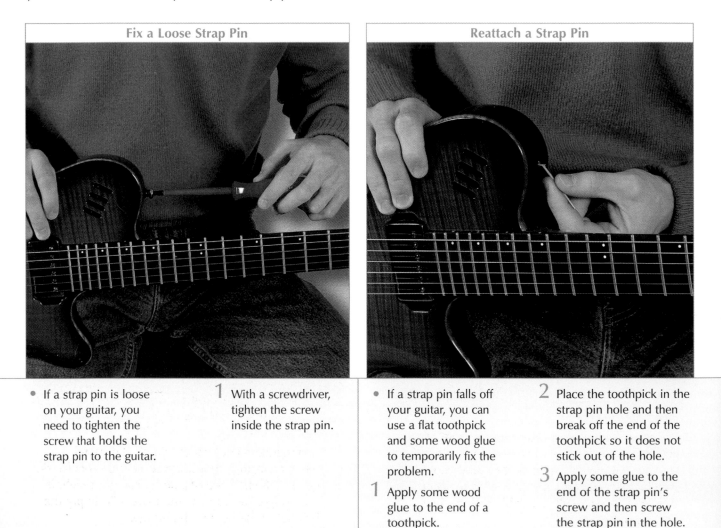

Fix a Loose Strap Pin	Reattach a Strap Pin

- If a strap pin is loose on your guitar, you need to tighten the screw that holds the strap pin to the guitar.

1 With a screwdriver, tighten the screw inside the strap pin.

- If a strap pin falls off your guitar, you can use a flat toothpick and some wood glue to temporarily fix the problem.

1 Apply some wood glue to the end of a toothpick.

2 Place the toothpick in the strap pin hole and then break off the end of the toothpick so it does not stick out of the hole.

3 Apply some glue to the end of the strap pin's screw and then screw the strap pin in the hole.

items to
keep handy

You should keep these guitar accessories handy in case you need them in an emergency.

Amplifier Tubes

You may need to replace the vacuum tubes for your electric guitar's amplifier if the amplifier stops working properly.

Batteries

Many guitar accessories, such as electronic tuners and effect pedals, require batteries. Some electric guitars also have components that use batteries. You should determine the type and number of batteries each device requires so you can have an adequate supply on hand.

If your effect pedals use an AC adapter, you may want to keep an extra adapter with you.

Cables

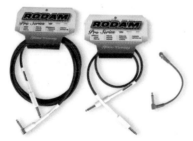

You should keep extra cables for your electric guitar on hand in case the cable you use to connect equipment, such as the guitar and amplifier or the effect pedals, needs replacing. You will need to replace a cable that crackles or does not work.

Picks

Since picks are small and easily lost, you should make sure you always have a good supply of replacements on hand.

Fuses

Electric guitar amplifiers usually contain one or two fuses, which are devices that protect the amplifier from power surges. A new wiring setup in a different location can blow the amplifier's fuse. You will need to replace the fuse before using the amplifier.

Strap

You should ensure you have an extra guitar strap in case the current one breaks. A guitar strap is essential if you plan to stand while playing the guitar.

Strings

It is a good idea to keep an extra full set of strings on hand so you can easily replace a string if one of the guitar strings breaks or if you notice a string sounds dull.

A straightened out paper clip can be useful when changing strings. On some types of electric guitars, the ball end of a string can get caught in the bridge. You can use the paper clip to pry the ball out of the hole in the bridge.

repairs that require a professional

Although you can fix many guitar problems yourself, some repairs require a professional. You can also consult a professional for tasks you are not comfortable performing yourself.

If your guitar is badly damaged, such as if the neck or headstock breaks, a professional may be able to help even if the damage seems irreparable. However, if the repair cost is significant or greater than the value of the guitar, you should consider buying a new guitar.

Fix the Bridge

The bridge is the piece that connects the strings to the body of the guitar. A bridge that is broken, cracked, or lifting off an acoustic guitar should be fixed by a professional.

You will need to fix the bridge on an electric guitar if you experience problems with the tremolo bar, which is a metal bar you attach to the bridge to adjust the pitch of the strings. If the tremolo bar moves too easily when you push it down, or if the bar does not return to its normal position after you push it down and release it, the guitar will go out of tune. If this happens each time you use the tremolo bar, you need to fix the bridge.

Floating bridges can pull up or push down the tremolo bar. These types of bridges require frequent maintenance since they have a lot of moving parts.

Fix or Replace Frets

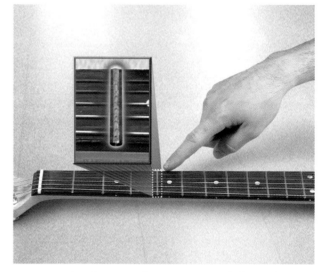

Frets are the thin metal wires situated along the fingerboard, perpendicular to the strings. Frets can sometimes pop out of the fingerboard, especially on electric guitars. If you notice that a note does not change when you hold the string down at a fret, the string is probably hitting a higher fret that is sticking out of the fingerboard. You also need to replace frets that have worn out or are dented from strings being pressed against them.

Adjust the Neck

The neck Is the long, narrow, wooden section between the body and the headstock of the guitar. On most acoustic or electric guitars, the neck has a slight bow, which makes the guitar easier to play and helps prevent the strings from buzzing. If the bow in your guitar neck becomes too deep or too shallow, you need to adjust the neck of the guitar. To adjust the neck, a repair professional must tighten or loosen the tension of the truss rod, which is a steel rod that runs through the neck of the guitar.

To check the bow in the guitar's neck, hold down the 1st string at the first and last frets. Turn the guitar sideways and note the distance between the strings and the frets. There should be a slight dip in the neck at about the mid-point. Repeat this procedure with the 6th string.

The bow in the guitar neck can be affected by age or changes in temperature and humidity, which can cause the neck to swell or shrink. Putting heavier strings on the guitar also places strain on the neck.

You should not attempt to adjust the truss rod yourself, since tightening or loosening too much can permanently damage the guitar.

Fix or Replace the Nut

The nut is the bar at the top end of the fingerboard, between the headstock and neck. The nut on a guitar can break or wear out, requiring replacement or repair.

Fix Output Jack

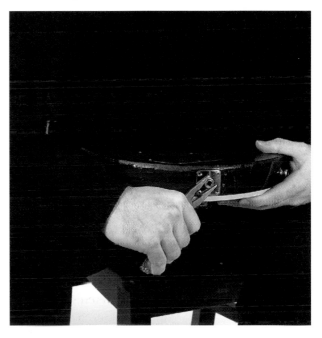

You can plug a cord into the output jack to connect your electric guitar to an amplifier. If the output jack is crackling, you should take the guitar to a repair technician because the jack may have a loose wire. The wires in an output jack can become loose over time from constant use. An output jack may also need replacing if it wears out and stops working completely.

CONTINUED...

repairs that require a professional

Replace Pickups

Pickups are magnets on an electric guitar that sense the vibrations of the strings and convert these vibrations into electrical currents that an amplifier can use to produce sound. If the pickups on your guitar stop working or produce a weaker sound, they need to be replaced by a professional. You can also replace the pickups when you want to change the sound of your guitar. For example, if the pickups do not produce enough distortion, you can replace them with pickups that are designed for special distortion sounds. If you bought a less expensive guitar, you can replace the original pickups with better quality pickups.

Replace Pickup Selector Switch

The pickup selector switch on an electric guitar allows you to select which pickups you want to use. The pickup selector switch can wear out over time and start producing crackling sounds or the sound can cut out. You may need to replace the pickup selector switch if the problem cannot be fixed.

Replace Saddles

Saddles are attached to the bridge and keep each string at the correct height. On acoustic and classical guitars, the saddles are made of plastic or bone and can crack or break easily. You should take a guitar with a cracked or broken saddle to a repair shop to replace the saddle.

On electric guitars, the friction of the steel strings often causes the saddles to grind down and develop burrs. If you notice that strings frequently break at the saddle, you could have a problem with burrs on the saddle. A repair professional may be able to sand down the burrs or the saddle may need replacing.

Replace Tuning Machines

Tuning machines allow you to increase and decrease the tension of each string to change the string's pitch.

The tuning machines on all guitars have gears that can wear out, making the tuning machines less effective. If the tuning machines no longer turn, it is time to replace them. Tuning machines are also prone to broken knobs or bent shafts that will require repair or replacement. You can replace one faulty tuning machine or the entire set. You may want to replace the entire set of tuning machines if you have trouble with more than one of the tuning machines.

Fix Cracks in Wood

On acoustic and classical guitars, cracks in the wood can impair the sound of the guitar. On electric guitars, cracks do not affect the sound produced as much. Wood cracks require the services of a repair professional.

If the lacquer on any type of guitar cracks, this usually indicates the guitar has been handled or stored improperly, exposing it to bumps or unsuitable temperatures and humidity levels. Although cracked lacquer does not usually affect the sound of the guitar, you can have the lacquer repaired.

Fix or Replace Volume and Tone Pots

Tone Volume

On electric guitars, the volume and tone pots (potentiometers) to which the volume and tone knobs are attached, can wear out. You will know a volume or tone pot is worn out if the control crackles, stops working or spins uncontrollably.

Chapter 15

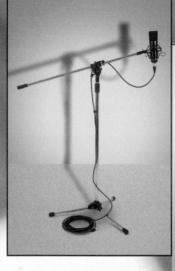

Home recording is an increasingly popular option for musicians, partly as a result of the improvements in home recording equipment that allows people to produce close to professional quality recordings. You can read this chapter to learn how to set up your own home recording studio to ensure the best sound quality for your recordings. You will also learn about specific home recording equipment, such as mixers, microphones and recording devices.

Home Recording

In this Chapter...

Introduction to Home Recording

Recording with Mixers

Recording Devices

Recording with a Microphone

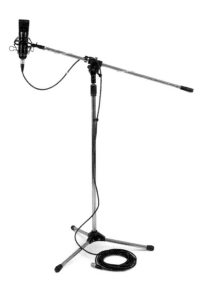

introduction to home recording

Setting up a home recording studio allows you to record music in the convenience of your home. Modern home recording systems generally include all the basic components of professional recording equipment and often produce close to professional-quality recordings.

Before setting up a recording studio, consider whether you can accommodate a permanent studio or a portable studio, what equipment you need and how much you can afford to spend.

Prepare a Room for Recording

There are a number of steps you should take to properly set up your home recording studio. Each room will produce different sound, so you may want to experiment with various rooms to determine which one is best for recording.

Soundproof Room

It is important to make the recording room soundproof so that as little sound as possible passes in or out of the room. To avoid sound coming through the door from outside, pad the top and bottom of the door with soundproofing material.

Dampen Sound

Since sound has a tendency to bounce off hard, flat surfaces, creating an echo, you need to soften the room you plan to use for recording to ensure good audio quality. To dampen the sound, cover the floor, walls and ceilings using rugs, heavy drapes or soundproofing material. Also, remove items, such as extra furniture, that may reflect sound and cause an echo.

Remove Noisy Items

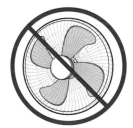

Clear the room of items that make noise, such as a fan or other electronic equipment. Recording equipment also makes noise, so try to keep only essential equipment in the room. It is a good idea to place all your recording equipment in a separate room from the room where you will record the sound. If you cannot remove items from the room, you should cover the items with heavy material. Do not cover up electronic equipment such as a computer or amplifier, however, since the equipment may overheat and malfunction or cause a fire.

recording
with mixers

A mixer is a device that allows you to input live or recorded sounds and then combine and manipulate the sounds.

You can plug input devices, such as a microphone, an electric guitar or an acoustic guitar that has a pickup, into a mixer. The number of channels a mixer has determines the number of input devices you can plug into the mixer. For example, you can obtain a mixer with eight channels that allow you to plug in eight devices.

To work with the mixer, you connect the mixer to a recording device. For information on recording devices, see page 274. You can also connect speakers or headphones to the mixer so you can listen while you are recording sounds or playing back previously recorded sounds.

Tasks You Can Perform With a Mixer

Mix effects

You can use the mixer to incorporate effects, such as reverb, delay or chorus, from effect pedals, a multi-effects unit or rack-mounted effects. For information on effects, see pages 228 to 236.

Adjust EQ

You can adjust the equalization (EQ), which involves boosting or lowering the bass (low) and treble (mid and high) frequencies of the sound from each channel.

Adjust panning

The panning allows you to control which sounds will be sent to the left or the right speaker.

Provide phantom power to microphones

You can use some mixers to provide phantom power to microphones. Condenser microphones often require phantom power. For information on condenser microphones, see page 276.

Adjust fader

You can adjust the fader to change the level of the sound from each channel.

Use preamp

Mixers usually have a built-in preamp that you can use to convert a low-level signal to a high-level signal.

recording devices

A recording device allows you to record sound, such as that from a guitar. Recording devices are either analog or digital. Analog recording devices are no longer commonly used, but digital recording devices are quite popular for home recording. Analog recordings are stored on cassette tapes or reel-to-reel tapes, while digital recordings are stored on CDs, hard disks, MiniDiscs or Flash memory cards. Digital recordings are easier to edit and have a higher sound quality that does not degrade over time. Digital recordings also do not have the background hiss typically heard in analog recordings.

Recording devices record and store each instrument or voice as a separate track. Storing recorded information as individual tracks allows you to later work with each track separately so you can manipulate or add to the recorded information without affecting other tracks.

Multi-Track Recorder

A multi-track recorder is a device that allows you to record one track while playing back another track at the same time. Basic multi-track recorders can record up to 4 separate tracks, while advanced multi-track recorders can record up to 8, 16 or 24 tracks.

You can connect devices, such as headphones, electric guitars and acoustic guitars with a pickup, to a multi-track recorder. You can also connect microphones to a recorder to record acoustic guitars without a pickup or vocals.

4-track and 8-track recorders usually come with built-in mixers. However, 16-track and 24-track recorders often do not have built-in mixers, so you would need to connect an external mixer to the recorder. For information on mixers, see page 273. Many advanced recorders also have built-in effects, such as reverb, delay and chorus, or built-in amplifier modeling, which allows you to imitate the sound of different amplifiers.

Multi-track recorders can store recordings onto cassette tapes, CDs, hard disks, MiniDiscs or Flash memory cards. Digital multi-track recorders allow you to perform limited editing tasks, such as moving or deleting parts of a song. With analog multi-track recorders, the only way to edit a recording is to cut and splice the tape.

MiniDisc Recorder

MiniDisc recorders are becoming increasingly popular. MiniDisc recorders are very small and compact, but they can deliver high-quality recordings. By simply plugging a microphone into a MiniDisc recorder, you can record a live performance or your own music so you can then play the recording back to hear yourself play or share your music with others.

Computer

You can use your computer as a recording device. Your computer must have a sound card that allows you to plug in microphones and other line-level devices, such as electric guitars and acoustic guitars with a pickup. Less expensive sound cards have only one microphone input and one line-level input, but more expensive sound cards can have up to 24 inputs. The sound quality is also better with more expensive sound cards.

You must use recording software to turn your computer into a multi-track recorder. Most recording software includes mixer software that offers most of the same features as an external mixer. Some people, however, use an external mixer to make it easier to send signals into the computer. For example, if you need to connect several devices to a computer with only one input, you can plug all the devices into an external mixer and then connect only the mixer to the computer to avoid having to constantly plug and unplug devices.

Recording software also often has built-in effects, such as reverb, chorus and delay. To share your music with others, recording software allows you to create MP3 or Wave files or burn CDs of your music. Popular recording software for PCs includes Guitar Tracks, SONAR and Cool Edit. For Macs, popular recording software includes Cubase, Logic and Digital Performer.

When using your computer as a recording device, you can record a virtually unlimited number of tracks. You can also perform advanced editing on your tracks, such as looping, or repeating specific bars over and over.

recording with a microphone

Selecting the proper type of microphone is crucial for obtaining the best results in your home recordings. Generally, a higher-quality microphone increases the quality of the sound you are able to record.

Types of Microphones

Microphones come in two basic types—condenser and dynamic. Condenser microphones are generally more expensive and more delicate than dynamic microphones. Condenser microphones also have greater dynamic ranges and better frequency responses compared to dynamic microphones. A greater dynamic range allows a microphone to pick up the quietest or loudest sounds, while a better frequency response allows it to pick up a wider range of low and high frequencies. Condenser microphones require batteries or an external power source to function, while dynamic microphones do not.

Condenser microphones are more commonly used for acoustic guitars, while dynamic microphones are more often used for electric guitars. Since the sounds generated by acoustic guitars are more subtle, you also usually need to use better-quality microphones for acoustic guitars than electric guitars.

Condenser

Dynamic

Microphone Pick Up Patterns

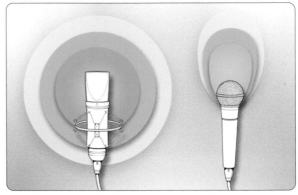
Omnidirectional   Directional

Microphones have two common types of pick up patterns—omnidirectional and directional. Omnidirectional microphones are good for picking up the sound of an entire room, while directional microphones are better for picking up sounds that are directly pointed toward the microphone. Directional microphones are most commonly used for guitars.

Recommended Microphones

Microphones recommended for use with electric guitars include Shure SM57 and Sennheiser MD421. For acoustic guitars, some recommended microphones include AKG 460, AKG 414, Neumann KM184 and Audio-Technica 4033.

Positioning Microphones

There are no set rules for positioning microphones. You should experiment with different microphone positions to achieve the sound you want.

For a more defined sound, place the microphone about an inch from the guitar or speaker. This is known as close miking. If you move the microphone further back, you reduce the amount of bass and sound level, but you get more of the sound of the room. This is known as distant miking.

Acoustic Guitars

Start by positioning the microphone close to the sound hole. If you strum the strings loudly, move the microphone further away from the sound hole. To get less pick noise, position the microphone where the neck joins the body. If fret noise occurs when you move your fingers on the strings, place the microphone closer to the bridge.

Electric Guitars

Start by placing the microphone one inch in front of the center of the speaker. You can also position the microphone behind or to the side of the speaker. Placing the microphone behind the speaker results in a more muffled sound.

Using Multiple Microphones

You can use more than one microphone. For example, you can position one microphone close to the guitar or speaker to get the sound of the guitar and another microphone further away to get the sound of the guitar as well as the room. You can later mix the two sounds together to achieve a grander sound.

Microphone Accessories

You will need a microphone stand to hold a microphone and a microphone cable to connect a microphone to other devices, such as a mixer or recording device. A special adapter is usually required to connect a microphone to a recording device. You may need to buy the stand and cable separately since microphones typically do not come with accessories.

Chapter 16

This chapter is a great resource when you want to access guitar information quickly. Read this chapter to learn where to find and how to interpret guitar information on the Internet. You can use the chord and scale diagrams provided as a quick reference when you want to know how to play a specific chord or scale. There is also a comprehensive glossary of terms you will encounter when learning to play the guitar.

Quick Reference

In this Chapter...

Guitar Information on the Internet

Chord Diagrams

Scale Diagrams

Glossary

guitar information
on the internet

Reading Tablature on the Internet

Many resources on the Internet provide tablature for popular songs you can play on your guitar. Tablature, often called guitar tab, is a notation system that visually depicts the strings on the guitar and indicates the strings you need to press down and at which frets you need to position your fingers.

On the Internet, tablature is written using a standard system of characters and numbers, so any computer will be able to interpret and display the characters and numbers.

Horizontal and Vertical Lines

In tablature on the Internet, the dashed horizontal lines represent the six strings on the guitar. The top line represents the 1st string, and the bottom line represents the 6th string. The vertical lines, called bar lines, help to break down tablature into smaller, more manageable units of time, called bars or measures.

Example of Tablature

```
E  - 3 - - - - - - - - - | - - - - - - |
B  - 3 - - - - - 0 - - - | - - - - - - |
G  - 0 - - - - - 0 - - - | - - - - - 0 - |
D  - 0 - 0 - 2 - - - 2 - | - - - - - - |
A  - 2 - - - - - - - - - | - 0 - 2 - - - |
E  - 3 - - - - - - - - - | - - - - - - |
```

Numbers

The numbers on the lines indicate at which frets you position your fingers. For example, the number 3 indicates you should press the string down just behind the third fret. A zero (0) indicates that you play the string without pressing it down. If there is no number on a line, you should not play that string.

Read the numbers from left to right. When two or more strings have numbers in the same vertical position, you should play the strings at the same time.

Letters and Symbols

Tablature often includes letters or symbols with the numbers to indicate articulation techniques. For information on articulation techniques, see pages 134 to 141. The following is a list of the most frequently used letters and symbols:

Letter or Symbol	Articulation Technique	Example
h	hammer on	5h7 – Press down the string at the 5th fret and then hammer your finger on at the 7th fret.
p	pull off	2p0 – Press down the string at the 2nd fret and then pull your finger off the string.
b	bend string	5b7 – Press down the string at the 5th fret and then bend the note until the pitch is the same as the note at the 7th fret.
/ or \	slide up or slide down	3/5 – Slide your finger along the string from the 3rd fret to the 5th fret.
~	vibrato	7~ – Apply vibrato to the string at the 7th fret.
x	mute	x – Mute the string.

Reading Chord Notation on the Internet

Many Internet sources provide information on the chords you need to play songs, along with partial lyrics for the songs. Chord notations, such as C: X32010, are often given for chords used in a song.

Each character in a chord notation represents one string on the guitar, from the 6th string to the 1st string, moving from left to right. An X indicates you should not play that string and a 0 indicates you play that string without holding it down. A number greater than zero indicates the fret at which you hold down the string.

Example of Chord Notation

O Susanna

```
F            C            G
O Susanna, oh don't you cry for me.

      C                        G    C
I come from Alabama with my banjo on my knee.
```

Chords Used:
C: X32010
F: XX3211
G: 320033

Popular Guitar Web Sites

www.chordfind.com - This site allows you to select a chord to display the fingering for the chord on the neck of a guitar. There is also a left-handed version available for each chord.

www.fender.com - Fender, the makers of the popular Stratocaster and Telecaster electric guitars, maintains this site.

www.gibson.com - This site provides information about Gibson acoustic and electric guitars.

www.harmony-central.com - This site provides product reviews, articles and answers to frequently asked questions about guitars and accessories, and more.

www.jimdunlop.com - The Dunlop Web site is a good place to find guitar accessories, such as picks, straps and capos.

www.lasido.com - Visit this site to find information from the makers of Godin electric guitars and Seagull acoustic guitars.

www.looknohands.com/chordhouse - At this site, you can view and print chord diagrams for specific chords.

www.martinguitar.com - You can find information on the popular Martin acoustic guitars at this site.

www.olga.net - OLGA (On-Line Guitar Archive) offers a huge library of files to help you play songs on your guitar.

www.tabcrawler.com - This online guitar tablature magazine offers tablature and chord notation for thousands of songs.

www.ultimateguitarpage.com/technique - You can find playing exercises, useful tips, information about articulation techniques, and more at this site.

chord diagrams

You can use the following chord chart as a quick reference when you want to know how to play a specific chord. The chords are all shown as chord diagrams.

The horizontal lines on a chord diagram represent the frets and the vertical lines represent the strings. The thick horizontal line at the top of the diagram represents the nut. When a chord is further away from the nut, you will see a number beside the top fret of the chord diagram, specifying the fret where the chord begins. For example, if the chord begins at the seventh fret, 7fr will appear beside the top fret.

The positions of the dots on the lines tell you where to place your fingers. The numbers in the dots tell you which finger to use to hold down each string. You will see the symbols X and ○ above strings that are not held down by any fingers. An ○ indicates that you play the string and an X indicates that you do not play the string. If you see a curved line (⌒) above a chord diagram, you should press down all the strings under the curved line with a single finger, which is known as a barre. For more information on reading chord diagrams, see page 28.

Chord Diagrams

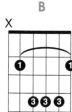
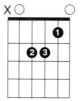

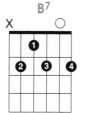
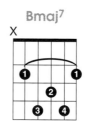
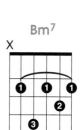
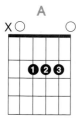
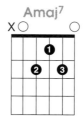
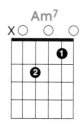
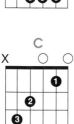
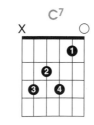
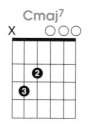
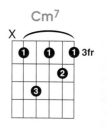

Chord Diagrams (continued)

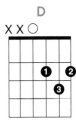
D

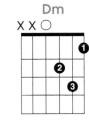
Dm

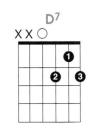
D⁷

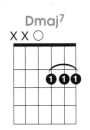
Dmaj⁷

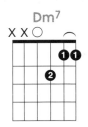
Dm⁷

E

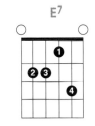
Em

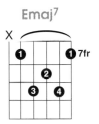
E⁷

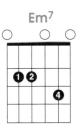
Emaj⁷

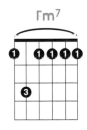
Em⁷

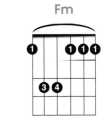
F

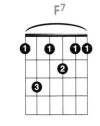
Fm

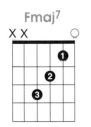
F⁷

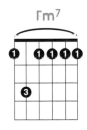
Fmaj⁷

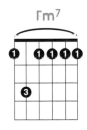
Fm⁷

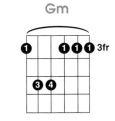
G

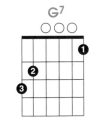
Gm

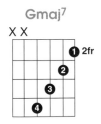
G⁷

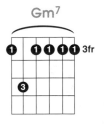
Gmaj⁷

Gm⁷

scale diagrams

You can use the following scale diagrams as a quick reference when you want to know how to play a scale.

The vertical lines in the scale diagrams represent frets and the horizontal lines represent strings, with the 6th string on the bottom and the 1st string on the top. Start to play on the lowest string at the bottom left corner of a diagram and then play one note at a time, moving from left to right. You should play each note on a string before moving up to the next string.

In each scale diagram, the red ovals represent the root notes for the scale you are playing and the black

ovals represent the other notes in the scale. The root note is the note you begin and end the scale on. The positions of the ovals in the diagrams indicate where you press down on each string to play each note.

All the scales shown are movable scales, so you can move the starting, or root, note for a scale to any other fret on the starting string. You can then play the scale in a different key using the same finger pattern. The note played on the starting string at the fret you begin the scale on determines the name of the scale. For more information on playing scales, see page 122.

One Octave Major Scales

Two Octave Major Scales

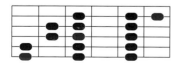 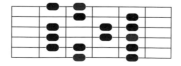 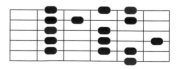

One Octave Minor Scales

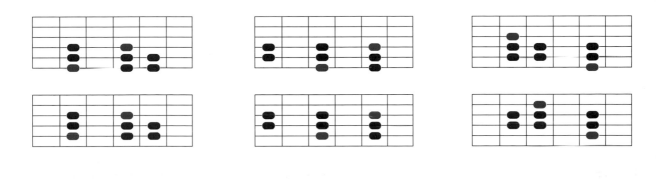

Two Octave Minor Scales

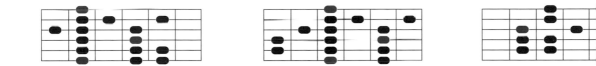

Major Pentatonic Scale

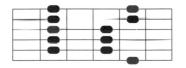

Minor Pentatonic Scale

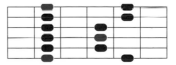

Blues Scale

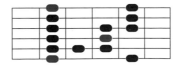

glossary

12-Bar Blues The most common blues rhythm progression, consisting of a group of twelve bars in which a specific sequence of chords is repeated over and over.

A

Accent A symbol (>) that appears above or below a note to indicate you should play the note with more force than you normally would.

Accidental A sharp (♯), flat (♭) or natural (♮) symbol that affects a note.

Acoustic Blues Blues developed in the rural south of the United States and played on an acoustic guitar.

Acoustic Guitar A hollow-bodied guitar that does not require electronic amplification. When you strike strings on an acoustic guitar, the guitar body resonates to produce sound.

Action The height of the strings above the fingerboard.

Add Chord A chord that includes an additional note that is not normally found in the chord.

Alternate Tuning A tuning in which one or more strings on a guitar are tuned to notes other than the standard notes the strings are usually tuned to.

Amplifier An electronic device that connects to an electric guitar to boost its volume and adjust the sound quality.

Amplifier Simulator A device that simulates the sound of many different amplifiers to give you more options.

Arpeggio A technique in which each note of a chord is played separately.

B

Bar A small, manageable unit of time in a song. Also known as a measure.

Barre A technique in which multiple strings are pressed down behind a specific fret with a single finger.

Barre Chord A chord that requires you to use a barre. The finger position for barre chords can be moved to any location on the fingerboard to play a different chord.

Bass Note Strum Style A style that involves picking a bass note and then strumming a chord. Often used in folk and country music.

Bass Strings The three thickest and lowest-sounding strings on a guitar. Also called the 4th, 5th and 6th strings.

Bend An articulation technique that involves pushing or pulling a string across the neck of the guitar to increase the pitch of the note.

Body The largest section of a guitar, which is usually hollow on acoustic guitars and solid on electric guitars.

Bottleneck Guitar *See* Slide Guitar

Bridge The structure that connects the strings to the body of a guitar.

Bridge Pins Pins that fasten the strings in place on the bridge of an acoustic guitar.

C

Capo A device that you can clamp down across the fingerboard at any fret to change the pitch of all the strings.

Carter Style A style named after the Carter Family, which involves playing a melody on the bass (thicker) strings and accompanying chords on the treble (thinner) strings. Typically used in folk and country songs.

Chord Consists of two or more different notes played at the same time.

Chord Diagram A visual representation of the strings and frets on a guitar. The markings on a chord diagram show you how to position your fingers on the fingerboard to play a chord. Also called a chord chart.

Chord Progression The sequence of chords in a piece of music.

Chorus An effect available for electric guitars that makes one guitar sound like many guitars.

Chromatic Scale A 12-note scale that has one half step, or semi-tone, between each note.

Classical Guitar A guitar suitable for playing classical and flamenco music. A classical guitar is similar to an acoustic guitar, except it produces a more mellow sound and has a smaller body, wider neck and nylon, instead of steel, strings. This term can also refer to a style of playing.

Clef A symbol that appears at the beginning of a music staff. A clef determines the pitch of each note on the lines and spaces on the staff. The treble clef (𝄞) is the only clef traditionally used in guitar music.

Common Time The most frequently used time signature, indicated by 4/4 or 𝄴 on the staff. Also referred to as 4/4 time.

Compressor An effect available for electric guitars that boosts the volume of quieter signals and lowers the volume of louder signals to keep the volume level even.

Concert Pitch A standard pitch used for tuning instruments where the A note is tuned to the frequency of 440 Hz (A-440).

Counterpoint A style that involves playing multiple melodies at once. Used mostly in classical music.

D

Cut Time A time signature that is indicated by 2/2 or 𝄵 on the staff. Also referred to as 2/2 time.

Damping *See* Muting

Delay An effect available for electric guitars that repeats the notes you play to create an echo effect. Also called echo.

Distortion An effect available for electric guitars that makes the notes you play sound distorted, producing a harsh, yet bright tone.

Dotted Note A note with a dot beside it, such as ♩. , which indicates you need to add half the value of the regular note to the note you play.

Double-Stop A technique in which you play two notes at a time on a guitar.

Downstroke Refers to striking one or more strings on a guitar toward the floor.

E

Effect Pedal A pedal you place on the floor and step on to turn on or off an effect for an electric guitar. Also known as a stomp box.

Effects Electronic manipulations of the sounds produced by electric guitars.

Eighth Note A note (♪) that you hold for a half beat in the 4/4 time signature. When two or more eighth notes appear in a row, they are joined with a beam (♫).

Electric Blues Blues developed in the northern urban areas of the United States and played on an electric guitar.

Electric Guitar A steel-string guitar that usually has a solid body. An electric guitar has magnetic pickups that convert the strings' vibrations into electrical signals that an amplifier uses to produce the guitar's sound.

glossary

Electronic Tuner The easiest and most accurate device used for tuning an instrument.

End Pin The metal or plastic post at the bottom of a guitar used for attaching one end of a guitar strap. Also known as a strap pin.

EQ (Equalization) Balances the bass (low), middle and treble (high) frequencies of a guitar's sound.

Feedback The piercing sound produced when a microphone or a pickup on an electric guitar picks up its own signal from a speaker.

Fingerboard The flat piece of wood on the neck where you press your fingers down on strings to form notes and chords. Also called the fretboard.

Fingerpick A plastic or metal device you can attach to your finger and use to pick strings.

Fingerpicking A playing technique that involves using your thumb and fingers to pluck or strum guitar strings, instead of using a pick.

First Position A fretting hand position where your index finger plays notes on the first fret, your middle finger plays notes on the second fret, your ring finger plays notes on the third fret and your pinky finger plays notes on the fourth fret.

Flanger An effect available for electric guitars that copies the notes you play and then plays the copies slightly out of sync with the original notes, resulting in an effect that sounds like a jet airplane taking off.

Flat A symbol (♭) indicating that a note should be lowered by one half step.

Flatted Fifth A note that is one fret, or half step, lower than the normal fifth note of a scale. Adding a flatted fifth note to the minor pentatonic scale creates a blues scale.

Flightcase A hard guitar case that offers extra protection for a guitar and is especially useful when traveling.

Free Stroke A technique that involves striking a string with your finger or thumb without letting your finger or thumb rest on the next string. Used mostly in classical guitar.

Fret A thin metal wire embedded in the fingerboard, perpendicular to the strings.

Fret Buzz The sound produced when a string accidentally touches other higher frets while ringing. Fret buzz can also occur when your finger does not press down firmly enough on a string or when your finger presses down on a string too far away from a fret.

Fretboard *See* Fingerboard

Fretting Hand The hand you use to fret, or press down, strings on the fingerboard.

Fuzz An effect available for electric guitars that causes a guitar's signal to sound broken up, producing a bright, almost buzzing tone.

Gig Bag A zippered bag that provides the easiest method of carrying a guitar, but offers the least amount of protection compared to other guitar cases.

Half Note A note (♩) that you hold for two beats in the 4/4 time signature.

Half Step The smallest distance between two notes. On the guitar, the distance from one fret to the next fret on the same string is one half step. Also called a semi-tone.

F

G

H

Hammer-On An articulation technique that involves using a finger of your fretting hand to hit a string on the fingerboard, rather than plucking the string with your picking hand, to play a note.

Headstock The section at the very top of a guitar, where the tuning machines are attached.

I

Intonation Refers to whether all the notes you can play on a guitar are in tune.

K

Key The key of a song determines which chords and scales you can play in the song.

Key Signature Appears just after the clef on a staff. A key signature indicates which notes you must play as sharp or flat and allows you to determine what key a song is played in.

L

Lead Sheet A piece of written music that provides an outline for the melody and harmony of a song, allowing musicians to improvise around the outline.

Ledger Line A short line above or below the staff that indicates a note that is higher or lower than the five lines on the staff.

Lick A short, frequently played sequence of notes. Often found in rock, country and jazz solos.

Locking Nut A device on some electric guitars that clamps the strings into place at the top of the neck. A locking nut allows you to bend strings and use the tremolo bar vigorously without making the strings go out of tune.

Luthier A person who makes guitars.

M

Machine Head *See* Tuning Machine

Major Chord A chord consisting of three different notes, which produces an uplifting, happy sound. A major chord is usually referred to by only its letter name, such as C.

Major Third Note The third note of a major scale. Often added to the blues scale.

Measure *See* Bar

Metronome A device that helps you keep the beat by making a tapping or clicking noise for every beat.

Minor Chord A chord consisting of three different notes, which produces a dark, sad sound. A minor chord is usually written with an "m" beside its letter name, such as Dm.

Mixer A device that allows you to input sounds from a guitar and other instruments to a recording device or sound system.

Movable Chord A chord you can move to any position on the fingerboard, while keeping the same finger shape.

Multi-Effects Unit A programmable device that enables you to use many different effects to manipulate the sound produced by an electric guitar.

Multi-Track Recorder A device that allows you to record sounds on several tracks, with each track usually recording one instrument or voice.

Muting A technique that involves using your hand or fingers to stop or prevent strings on a guitar from ringing. Also known as damping.

N

Natural Symbol A symbol (♮) indicating that you do not need to play a specific instance of a note as sharp or flat.

glossary

Neck The long, narrow section between the body and the headstock of a guitar.

Noise Gate An effect available for electric guitars that cuts out any sound that is below a specified volume level. Useful for preventing the hissing sound produced when you are using effects and momentarily not playing your guitar.

Nut The bar at the top of the fingerboard, between the headstock and neck, which spaces the strings out evenly and keeps the strings at the correct height over the fingerboard.

Nylon Strings Strings made of nylon, which are used on classical guitars. They produce a soft tone and are easier on your fingers than steel strings.

Octave The distance between two notes that have the same letter name and are twelve half steps, or semi-tones, apart.

Octave Divider An effect available for electric guitars that adds notes that are one or two octaves above or below the notes you are playing. Also known as an octaver.

Open String A string you play without holding down, or fretting, the string.

Open Tuning A tuning that allows you to play a chord when you strum all the strings of a guitar without fretting any strings.

Open-Position Chord A chord that is played near the nut and is played by strumming strings without fretting one or more of the strings. Also called a first-position chord.

Overdrive An effect available for electric guitars that causes a guitar's signal to sound distorted, producing a warm, rounded tone.

Pedalboard A unit you can use to organize your effect pedals.

Pentatonic Scale A scale with five different notes. Often used in rock and blues music.

Phase Shifter An effect available for electric guitars that duplicates the notes you play and then plays the copies of the notes slightly out of sync with the original notes, creating a subtle, sweeping sound. Also known as a phaser.

Pick A flat, usually triangular piece of plastic you can use to strike the strings on a guitar. Also called a plectrum.

Pick Guard A plate that protects the top of the guitar from getting scratched when you strum and pick the strings. Also known as a scratchplate.

Picking Refers to striking only one string on a guitar.

Picking Hand The hand you use to pick or strum strings.

Pickup A magnet on electric guitars that converts the strings' vibrations into electrical signals that an amplifier uses to produce the guitar's sound.

Pickup Note A note that appears in an incomplete bar at the beginning of a song.

Pickup Selector Switch A switch that allows you to select which pickups you want to use on an electric guitar.

p-i-m-a Letters used to indicate specific fingers on your picking hand in classical guitar notation. The letter "p" represents your thumb, "i" represents your index finger, "m" represents your middle finger and "a" represents your ring finger.

Pitch Shifter An effect available for electric guitars that creates a note higher or lower in pitch than the note you played and then sounds both notes simultaneously, creating a harmony.

Position A location on the fingerboard where each finger is placed over one of four side-by-side frets. The placement of your index finger determines the name of the position.

Position Markers Dots or decorative markings that help you determine the number of each fret. They are usually found on the top and/or side of the fingerboard. Also called position dots.

Potentiometer (pot) Potentiometers are the volume and tone controls on an electric guitar.

Power Chord A two- or three-note chord in which the second note is five scale notes higher than the root note. Also called "5" chords, such as D5. Popular in hard rock and heavy metal songs.

Pull-Off An articulation technique that involves pulling a finger of your fretting hand off a string on the fingerboard, rather than plucking the string with your picking hand, to play a note.

Quarter Note A note (♩) that you hold for one beat in the 4/4 time signature.

Rack-Mounted Effects Programmable effects that are mounted in a rack cabinet. You can usually control the effects by stepping on a single pedal or a series of pedals.

Relative Tuning Involves tuning the guitar to itself by selecting a string and then tuning each of the other strings relative to that string.

Repeat Markers Symbols that indicate you should repeat specific bars.

Rest A symbol in written music that indicates a period of silence in a song. Each type of rest represents a specific number of beats.

Rest Stroke A technique that involves striking a string with your finger or thumb and allowing your finger or thumb to rest on the next string. Used mostly in classical guitar.

Reverb An effect that makes sound seem as though it is naturally bouncing off walls in a room of a certain size.

Rhythm A pattern of notes based on the length of time each note is held in a piece of music.

Rhythm Slashes Musical shorthand that indicates how to play without using standard musical notation. Some rhythm slashes indicate the exact rhythm to play, while others simply indicate the number of beats you play each chord.

Riff A short, repeated sequence of notes. Usually found in jazz, rock and blues music.

Root Note The first note of a scale, which usually determines the letter name of a scale. The root note also determines the letter name of a chord.

Rotating Speaker Simulator An effect that simulates the sound of a Leslie speaker, producing a swirling effect.

Saddle The item attached to the bridge of a guitar to keep the strings at the correct height.

Scale A series of notes arranged in a specific pattern of steps and half steps. The most common types of scales are major scales and minor scales.

Semi-tone *See* Half Step

glossary

Sharp A symbol (♯) indicating that a note should be raised by one half step.

Shuffle Rhythm A rhythm pattern, common in blues music, in which each beat is divided into three parts, called a triplet. You usually play notes only on the first and third parts of a triplet in a shuffle rhythm.

Sixteenth Note A note (♪) that you hold for a quarter of a beat in the 4/4 time signature. When two or more sixteenth notes appear in a row, they are joined with a double beam (♫).

Slash Chord A chord that is played with a bass note other than the root note of the chord.

Slide An articulation technique that allows you to connect two or more notes by sliding your finger to a different fret on the same string while the string is ringing. The term can also refer to a bar or tube that you slide along the strings.

Slide Guitar A style of playing that involves sliding a bar or tube, known as a slide, along the strings on the fingerboard. Commonly used in blues guitar.

Slur A curved line connecting two or more different notes on the staff, indicating that the transition between the notes should be smooth.

Sound Hole A hole that releases the sound from the body of an acoustic guitar.

Soundboard The top, or face, of an acoustic guitar. When you strum the strings, the soundboard vibrates, producing the guitar's sound.

Staccato A dot above or below a note on the staff that indicates the note should be played short and detached from the adjacent notes.

Staff Five horizontal lines on which music is written, with each line and space between the lines corresponding to a letter name for a note.

Steel Strings Strings made of metal, which are used on electric and acoustic guitars. These strings sound louder and brighter than nylon strings, but are tougher on your fingers.

Step The equivalent of two half steps. On a guitar, a step is the distance between two frets on the same string. Also called a tone.

Strap Attaches to a guitar and fits over your shoulder to secure the guitar in front of you so you can easily play the guitar while standing.

Strap Pin A post on the body of a guitar that is used for attaching one end of a guitar strap. The strap pin at the bottom of a guitar is also called an end pin.

String Bending *See* Bend

String Retainer A device found on the headstock of some electric guitars that pulls some or all of the strings closer to the headstock to improve the tone and sustain of the strings.

String Winder A device that allows you to quickly turn a tuning machine to loosen or tighten a string, which is useful when changing strings. Also called a peg winder.

Strings The thin metal or nylon wires, numbered 1 through 6, which create notes when strummed or picked.

Strumming Refers to striking two or more strings.

Suspended Chord A chord in which the middle note is replaced with a different note to change the tone of the chord. Also called a sus chord.

T

Sustain Refers to how long a note plays before fading away.

Tablature A notation system that indicates which strings you need to press down and which frets you need to position your fingers behind.

Tempo Refers to the pace of a song. Often specified by an Italian term or by a specific number of beats per minute, such as ♩ = 80.

Thumbpick A plastic or metal device you can attach to your thumb and use to strike strings.

Tie A curved line that joins two notes that have the same pitch, indicating that you hold the first note for the combined value of the two notes.

Time Signature A symbol, found at the beginning of a music staff, that is made up of two numbers, one on top of the other. The top number indicates the number of beats in each bar and the bottom number indicates the type of note that counts as one beat.

Tone *See* Step

Tonic *See* Root Note

Travis Picking A style named after country guitarist Merle Travis, which involves using your thumb to continually alternate between playing two bass notes on the bass strings, as your index, middle and sometimes ring finger play the melody on the treble strings.

Treble Strings The three thinnest and highest-sounding strings on the guitar. Also called the 1st, 2nd and 3rd strings.

Tremolo An effect available for electric guitars that rapidly changes the volume of the notes you play to produce a wavering sound.

Tremolo Bar A metal bar that connects to the bridge of an electric guitar. You can use a tremolo bar to change the angle of the bridge to adjust the pitch of the strings. Also called a whammy bar, vibrato bar and tremolo arm.

Triplet A single beat divided into three parts, indicated by a group of three notes joined by a beam or curved line with "3" marked above.

Truss Rod A steel rod found inside the neck of a guitar, which helps ensure the neck will not bend or warp from the tension of the strings.

Tuning Machine A device used to adjust the tension of a string to tune, or change the pitch of, the string. Also called a machine head, tuning peg, tuning key and tuner.

Turnaround A series of notes you play between repetitions of a 12-bar blues progression.

U

Upstroke Refers to striking one or more strings on a guitar toward the ceiling.

V

Vibrato An articulation technique that involves producing a steady fluctuation in a note's pitch by repeatedly bending and releasing the string.

Volume Pedal An effect available for electric guitars that allows you to control the volume level of your guitar's sound.

W

Wah-Wah An effect available for electric guitars that allows you to vary the bass (low) and treble (high) frequencies in a guitar's sound, producing a sound like a person saying "wah."

Waist The curved area in the middle of a guitar's body.

Whammy Bar *See* Tremolo Bar

Whole Note A note that you hold for four beats in the 4/4 time signature.

index

index

index

index

index

Did you like this book? MARAN ILLUSTRATED™ also offers books on the most popular computer topics, using the same easy-to-use format of this book. We always say that if you like one of our books, you'll love the rest of our books too!

Here's a list of some of our best-selling computer titles:

Guided Tour Series - 240 pages, Full Color

MARAN ILLUSTRATED's Guided Tour series features a friendly disk character that walks you through each task step by step. The full-color screen shots are larger than in any of our other series and are accompanied by clear, concise instructions.

	ISBN	Price
MARAN ILLUSTRATED™ Computers Guided Tour	1-59200-880-1	$24.99 US/$34.95 CDN
MARAN ILLUSTRATED™ Windows XP Guided Tour	1-59200-886-0	$24.99 US/$34.95 CDN

MARAN ILLUSTRATED™ Series - 320 pages, Full Color

This series covers 30% more content than our Guided Tour series. Learn new software fast using our step-by-step approach and easy-to-understand text. Learning programs has never been this easy!

	ISBN	Price
MARAN ILLUSTRATED™ Windows XP	1-59200-870-4	$24.99 US/$34.95 CDN
MARAN ILLUSTRATED™ Office 2003	1-59200-890-9	$29.99 US/$41.95 CDN
MARAN ILLUSTRATED™ Excel 2003	1-59200-876-3	$24.99 US/$34.95 CDN
MARAN ILLUSTRATED™ Access 2003	1-59200-872-0	$24.99 US/$34.95 CDN

101 Hot Tips Series - 240 pages, Full Color

Progress beyond the basics with MARAN ILLUSTRATED's 101 Hot Tips series. This series features 101 of the coolest shortcuts, tricks and tips that will help you work faster and easier.

	ISBN	Price
MARAN ILLUSTRATED™ Windows XP 101 Hot Tips	1-59200-882-8	$19.99 US/$27.95 CDN

MARAN ILLUSTRATED™ **Piano** is an information-packed resource for people who want to learn to play the piano, as well as current musicians looking to hone their skills. Combining full-color photographs and easy-to-follow instructions, this guide covers everything from the basics of piano playing to more advanced techniques. Not only does MARAN ILLUSTRATED™ Piano show you how to read music, play scales and chords and improvise while playing with other musicians, it also provides you with helpful information for purchasing and caring for your piano.

ISBN: 1-59200-864-X

Price: $24.99 US; $34.95 CDN

Page count: 304

MARAN ILLUSTRATED™ **Dog Training** is an excellent guide for both current dog owners and people considering making a dog part of their family. Using clear, step-by-step instructions accompanied by over 400 full-color photographs, MARAN ILLUSTRATED™ Dog Training is perfect for any visual learner who prefers seeing what to do rather than reading lengthy explanations.

Beginning with insights into popular dog breeds and puppy development, this book emphasizes positive training methods to guide you through socializing, housetraining and teaching your dog many commands. You will also learn how to work with problem behaviors, such as destructive chewing.

ISBN: 1-59200-858-5

Price: $19.99 US; $27.95 CDN

Page count: 256

MARAN ILLUSTRATED™ Knitting & Crocheting contains a wealth of information about these two increasingly popular crafts. Whether you are just starting out or you are an experienced knitter or crocheter interested in picking up new tips and techniques, this information-packed resource will take you from the basics, such as how to hold the knitting needles or crochet hook, to more advanced skills, such as how to add decorative touches to your projects. The easy-to-follow information is communicated through clear, step-by-step instructions and accompanied by over 600 full-color photographs—perfect for any visual learner.

ISBN: 1-59200-862-3

Price: $24.99 US; $34.95 CDN

Page count: 304

maran illustrated YOGA

MARAN ILLUSTRATED™ Yoga provides a wealth of simplified, easy-to-follow information about the increasingly popular practice of Yoga. This easy-to-use guide is a must for visual learners who prefer to see and do without having to read lengthy explanations.

Using clear, step-by-step instructions accompanied by over 500 full-color photographs, this book includes all the information you need to get started with yoga or to enhance your technique if you have already made yoga a part of your life. MARAN ILLUSTRATED™ Yoga shows you how to safely and effectively perform a variety of yoga poses at various skill levels, how to breathe more efficiently and much more.

ISBN: 1-59200-868-2

Price: $24.99 US; $34.95 CDN

Page count: 320

MARAN ILLUSTRATED™ **Weight Training** is an information-packed guide that covers all the basics of weight training, as well as more advanced techniques and exercises.

MARAN ILLUSTRATED™ Weight Training contains more than 500 full-color photographs of exercises for every major muscle group, along with clear, step-by-step instructions for performing the exercises. Useful tips provide additional information and advice to help enhance your weight training experience.

MARAN ILLUSTRATED™ Weight Training provides all the information you need to start weight training or to refresh your technique if you have been weight training for some time.

ISBN: 1-59200-866-6
Price: $24.99 US; $34.95 CDN
Page count: 320

MARAN ILLUSTRATED™ **Guitar** is an excellent resource for people who want to learn to play the guitar, as well as for current musicians who want to fine tune their technique. This full-color guide includes over 500 photographs, accompanied by step-by-step instructions that teach you the basics of playing the guitar and reading music, as well as advanced guitar techniques. You will also learn what to look for when purchasing a guitar or accessories, how to maintain and repair your guitar, and much more.

Whether you want to learn to strum your favorite tunes or play professionally, MARAN ILLUSTRATED™ Guitar provides all the information you need to become a proficient guitarist.

BOOK BONUS!

Visit www.maran.com/guitar to download MP3 files you can listen to and play along with for all the chords, scales, exercises and practice pieces in the book.

ISBN: 1-59200-860-7

Price: $24.99 US; $34.95 CDN

Page count: 320